# JOOMLA!™ 1.5 & Virtuemart™ Websites for Small Business

# CorporationGURU Books

## Other great books from CorporationGURU and Michelle M. Griffin, PhD (abd)

The Joomla books are part of the "Elephants Can't Change" series in order to assist corporations and business to become agile instead of participating in the "invent it here syndrome"

### Business Books
Elephant's Can't Change but Leopards Can!!!
Strategic Organization Development Roadmap (2008)
Employ!!! Performance (2008)

### Computer/Web Design Books
Joomla! 1.5 & Virtuemart: The Power is at your Fingertips
Joomla! 1.5 & Virtuemart Websites for Sports and Clubs
Joomla! 1.5 & Virtuemart Websites for Small Business
Create a Website in an Hour with Joomla 1.5 (2008)
Joomla! 1.5 & Virtuemart Websites for Not for Profits (2008)
Joomla! 1.5 & Community Builder Websites for Schools & Churches (2008)
Joomla! 1.5 & Virtuemart for Restaurants (2008)
Joomla!1.5 & Community Builder for Doctors & Health Care (2008)
Joomla! 1.5 & Community Builder (2008)
Creating Bilingual Sites with Joomla! 1.5 (2008)

### Fiction Books
Mafia: Dead Bosses are Back for Revenge! (2008)

## Available on Amazon

# Joomla! 1.5™ & Virtuemart™ Websites for Small Business

## Michelle M. Griffin, PhD (abd)

Corporation Guru Inc.
www.corporationguru.com
Delaware * Chicago * Orlando

BookSurge Publishing
North Charleston, South Carolina

Library of Congress Cataloging Control Number -2008908434
Griffin PhD, Michelle
Joomla! 1.5 & Virtuemart Websites for Small Business by Michelle M. Griffin, PhD
Includes bibliographical references.
p. cm.
ISBN: 1-4392-1053-5
1. Griffin PhD, Michelle 1963- .
2. Management – United States.
3. Computers
4. Internet
5: Web Design
I. Title

Copyright © 2008 by CorporationGuru Inc.. All rights reserved. Printed in the United States of America. Except as permitted under the United States Copyright Act of 1976, no part of this publication may be reproduced or distributed in any form or by any means, or stored in a data base or retrieval system, without the prior written permission of the publisher. Except in the case where quotations embodied in critical research articles or reviews.

Joomla! is the trademark of Open Source Matters a not for profit corporation.
Virtuemart is the trademark of Virtuemart a not for profit corporation in Germany.

CorporationGuru or Michelle M. Griffin are not in any way affiliated with Open Source Matters or the Joomla! project or Virtuemart. We are also not associated with any extensions or modules discussed in this book.

CorporationGuru books are available at special quantity discounts to use as premiums and sales promotions or for use in corporate training programs. For more information, please visit the www.corporationguru.com.

The author and publisher specifically disclaim any liability that is incurred from the application of the contents of this book.

The editor for this book was Christine L. Banerjee
It was set by CorporationGRAPHIC, www.corporationgraphic.com and all sites are hosted by www.spiderweby.com.

ISBN:1-4392-1053-5
Library of Congress Control Number: 2008908434
Visit www.booksurge.com or www.corporationguru.com to order additional copies.
Published by BookSurge Publishing North Charleston, South Carolina
co-Published by CorporationGuru, Chicago, Illinois.
First Edition, September, 2008

# Dedication

To all the Open Source Developers who are changing and shaping the future of this world. With this I am donating 5% of profits from this book, each month to an Open Source Not for Profit organization.

If you find you use Joomla or Virtuemart or any other Open Source component. Please donate to these organizations, for the continued development of the Open Source platform.

# TABLE OF CONTENTS

| | |
|---|---|
| Introduction | 25 |
| Finding a Webhoster | 29 |
| JOOMLA! Hosting Requirements | 35 |
| Subscribing to a Hosting Service | 37 |
| Using the Cpanel | 39 |
| Installing Joomla! | 49 |
| Joomla Administration | 57 |
| Module Manager | 63 |
| Module Manager- Changing | 67 |
| Global Checkin | 73 |
| File Manager | 75 |
| Updating Global Configuration | 81 |
| Templates | 85 |
| Articles | 97 |
| Edit an Article | 101 |
| Loading an Editor Component | 105 |
| Article Section Manager | 115 |
| Article Category Manager | 117 |
| Article Trash | 119 |
| Editing a Front Page Article | 121 |
| Polls | 125 |
| Menu Manager Overview | 127 |
| Modify Main Menu | 131 |

Table of Contents

| | |
|---|---|
| Weblinks | 137 |
| Wrappers | 141 |
| Updating the Logo | 145 |
| Media Manager | 151 |
| Banner Manager | 155 |
| Search | 165 |
| User Manager | 169 |
| Upgrading | 177 |
| Overview | 179 |
| Virtuemart Installing | 189 |
| Virtuemart Modules | 201 |
| Virtuemart Configuration | 213 |
| Virtuemart Store | 229 |
| Virtuemart Payment Methods | 231 |
| Virtuemart Tax Rate | 235 |
| Virtuemart Categories | 237 |
| Virtuemart Manufacturer | 241 |
| Virtuemart Products | 243 |
| Virtuemart Configuration Update | 255 |
| Virtuemart Product Layout | 259 |
| Virtuemart Browse Page Layouts | 263 |
| Virtuemart Order Process | 269 |
| Virtuemart Order Status | 285 |
| Virtuemart Orders | 287 |
| Virtuemart Inventory | 291 |

| | |
|---|---|
| Virtuemart Report | 293 |
| Virtuemart Account Maintenance | 295 |
| Extensions Overview | 297 |
| Image Slide Show | 301 |
| Attachments | 307 |
| View Source | 315 |
| Silent No Right Click | 317 |
| Editor Switch | 321 |
| Employment Opportunities | 323 |
| Speeding up your Website | 327 |
| Search Engine Optimization | 329 |
| Site Security | 335 |
| Joomla Pack Backup | 337 |
| Index | 343 |
| Biography | 351 |
| Coupons | 353 |

# FIGURES

| | |
|---|---|
| Figure 1: Cpanel Display | 30 |
| Figure 2: Name Servers | 38 |
| Figure 3: Cpanel | 39 |
| Figure 4: Add Email Account | 40 |
| Figure 5: Configure Email Account | 41 |
| Figure 6: Outlook Configuration after you click Yes | 42 |
| Figure 7: Add Email Account | 43 |
| Figure 8: Check Pop3 and Next | 44 |
| Figure 9: Enter Email | 44 |
| Figure 10: Email completion | 45 |
| Figure 11: Email Naming | 46 |
| Figure 12: Outgoing Server (SMTP) | 47 |
| Figure 13: Click Next - Email Setup | 48 |
| Figure 14: Click Finish | 48 |
| Figure 15: CPanel | 49 |
| Figure 16: Website blank | 50 |
| Figure 17: Fantastico Screen Shot | 50 |
| Figure 18: Begin Joomla Installation | 51 |
| Figure 19: Install Joomla | 52 |
| Figure 20: Joomla Install Finish | 53 |
| Figure 21: Joomla Administration Information | 54 |
| Figure 22: Your Website | 55 |
| Figure 23: Joomla administrator screen | 57 |

Figures

Figure 24: Joomla Dashboard ................................................ 58
Figure 25: Joomla Screen Right Toolbar .............................. 59
Figure 26: Module Manager ................................................. 59
Figure 27: Administrator Module Manager ........................... 60
Figure 28: Administrator disable ........................................... 61
Figure 29: Module Manager ................................................. 63
Figure 30: Your website ........................................................ 64
Figure 31: Popular Disable ................................................... 64
Figure 32: Popular Module gone .......................................... 65
Figure 33: Module Manager Columns .................................. 67
Figure 34: Module Manager – Login Form ........................... 70
Figure 35: Module Form ....................................................... 71
Figure 36: Login Form Module moved to Right Side ............ 72
Figure 37: Global Check-in .................................................. 73
Figure 38: Cpanel ................................................................. 75
Figure 39: File Manager Selection ....................................... 76
Figure 40: File Manager View .............................................. 76
Figure 41: File permissions .................................................. 77
Figure 42: htaccess file change ........................................... 79
Figure 43: Change Permission screen ................................. 80
Figure 44: Configuration.php file .......................................... 81
Figure 45: Global configuration Dashboard ......................... 82
Figure 46: Global Configuration ........................................... 83
Figure 47: Permissions ........................................................ 84
Figure 48: Template Manager .............................................. 85

Figure 49: Beez Template — 86
Figure 50: JA Purity — 86
Figure 51: JA Purity Template Configuration — 87
Figure 52: Params.ini file location — 88
Figure 53: Change Permissions Params.ini — 89
Figure 54: JA Purity PureWhite Background — 90
Figure 55: Rhuk_Milkway — 90
Figure 56: Window Explorer IPOD as Extra Drive — 92
Figure 57: Install Template — 93
Figure 58: Template Success — 94
Figure 59: New Template Example — 95
Figure 60: Modules Position for Rocket Theme Template — 96
Figure 61: Article Manager — 97
Figure 62: Article Parameters — 99
Figure 63: Welcome to Joomla — 101
Figure 64: Welcome to Joomla Article — 102
Figure 65: JCE Reviews — 105
Figure 66: JCE Download — 106
Figure 67: JCE download for Joomla! 1.5: — 108
Figure 68: Saving a file — 108
Figure 69: Download JCE — 109
Figure 70: JCE Main Screen — 110
Figure 71: JCE Editor Mambot/Plugin — 110
Figure 72: Install JCE — 111

## Figures

Figure 73: JCE Install Success .......... 112
Figure 74: Global Configuration .......... 112
Figure 75: User Manager .......... 113
Figure 76: User Detail .......... 113
Figure 77: JCE Editor Format .......... 114
Figure 78: Section Manager .......... 115
Figure 79: Section Detail .......... 116
Figure 80: Section Manager Updated .......... 116
Figure 81: Category Manager .......... 117
Figure 82: Category Detail .......... 118
Figure 83: Category Manager Changed .......... 118
Figure 84: Article Trash .......... 119
Figure 85: Permanently delete .......... 120
Figure 86: Joomla News .......... 121
Figure 87: Adding an article image .......... 122
Figure 89: Website .......... 123
Figure 90: Poll Manager .......... 125
Figure 91: Poll Detail .......... 125
Figure 92: Poll changed .......... 126
Figure 93: Menu Manager .......... 127
Figure 94: Main Menu .......... 128
Figure 95: Home Menu Parameters .......... 129
Figure 96: Website changed to JoomlaEase .......... 130
Figure 97: Website .......... 131
Figure 98: Main Menu .......... 131

Figure 99: New Menu Item 132
Figure 100: Menu Item Detail 134
Figure 101: Sub Menu Detail 135
Figure 102: Website 135
Figure 103: Weblinks 137
Figure 104: Web Link Categories 138
Figure 105: Web Link Change Category 138
Figure 106: Weblinks JoomlaEase 139
Figure 107: Website 139
Figure 108: Resource Menu 141
Figure 109: Change Type 142
Figure 110: Menu Item Detail Screen 142
Figure 111: Wrapper 143
Figure 112: Website Wrapper 143
Figure 113: Website with top menu changed 144
Figure 114: Image Folder 146
Figure 115: Upload 147
Figure 116: Replace File 147
Figure 117: Upload Complete 148
Figure 118: Website with new Logo 149
Figure 119: Media Manager 151
Figure 120: Banner Media Manager 151
Figure 121: Banner Image enlarge 152
Figure 122: Media Manager/Stories 152

Figure 123: Media Manager Upload 153
Figure 124: Website Banners 155
Figure 125: Banner Manager 156
Figure 126: Banner Categories 157
Figure 127: Banner Client Manager 157
Figure 128: Client Manager Detail 158
Figure 129: Banner Manager 158
Figure 130: Banner Detail 159
Figure 131: Banner Detail Page 160
Figure 132: Banner Module 161
Figure 133: Advertisement Module 162
Figure 134: JoomlaEASE Website 164
Figure 135: Search Parameters 165
Figure 136: Website Search 165
Figure 137: Search Results 166
Figure 138: Search Recording 167
Figure 139: User Manager 169
Figure 140: User Manager Detail 169
Figure 141: User Login 170
Figure 142: Registration 171
Figure 143: User Manager with new registration 172
Figure 144: Email notification of user registration 172
Figure 145: Email Notification to New User 173
Figure 146: New User Activation 173
Figure 147: User Manager Enabled 174

Figure 148: User authorization levels 174
Figure 149: Default WYSIWYG Editor: 176
Figure 150: Fantastico upgrade 177
Figure 151: Continue Joomla Upgrade 178
Figure 152: JoomlaEase Website 180
Figure 153: Install RokMiniNews 181
Figure 154: Rokmininews Parameters 182
Figure 155: Rokmininews View 183
Figure 156: ROKNews Rotator 184
Figure 157: User Manager 185
Figure: 158: Media Manager 185
Figure 159: Article 186
Figure 160: Sample with Rotator News 187
Figure 161: Virtuemart Website 189
Figure 162: Virtuemart Download 190
Figure 163: Complete Package for Joomla 1.5 download 190
Figure 164: Virtuemart Save 191
Figure 165: Windows Explorer Virtuemart Folder 192
Figure 166: Virtuemart Unzipped 193
Figure 167: Install Virtuemart 194
Figure 168: Virtuemart installed 194
Figure 169: Virtuemart Store 195
Figure 170: Virtuemart Download 195
Figure 171: Virtuemart Patch Download 196

Figure 172: Virtuemart Patch Save 196
Figure 173: Virtuemart Check for Updates 197
Figure 174: Upload a Patch. 197
Figure 175: Virtuemart Patch Upgrade 198
Figure 176: Virtuemart Patch upgrade Finished 199
Figure 177: Modules 201
Figure 178: Install 203
Figure 179: Module Manager 204
Figure 180: Virtuemart Cart Detail 204
Figure 181: Website Cart 205
Figure 182: Login Module 206
Figure 183: Product Categories 206
Figure 184: Tree 207
Figure 185: Revised Website 208
Figure 186: All In One 209
Figure 187: Product Scroller 210
Figure 188: Website Revised 211
Figure 189: Virtuemart Admin 213
Figure 190: Extended Layout 214
Figure 191: Virtuemart Configuration 215
Figure 192: Virtuemart Global Custom Settings 219
Figure 193: Virtuemart Security 220
Figure 194: Virtuemart Site 220
Figure 195: Virtuemart Site 222
Figure 196: Virtuemart Site Configuration Button 223

| | |
|---|---|
| Figure 197: Theme Settings | 223 |
| Figure 198: Virtuemart Shipping Config | 224 |
| Figure 199: Virtuemart Checkout Config | 225 |
| Figure 200: Virtuemart Download Config | 225 |
| Figure 201: Virtuemart Feeds Config | 226 |
| Figure 202: Virtuemart Control Panel | 227 |
| Figure 203: Statistics | 227 |
| Figure 204: Store Navigation | 229 |
| Figure 205: Store Summary | 229 |
| Figure 206: Store Information | 230 |
| Figure 207: Virtuemart Control Panel | 231 |
| Figure 208: Payment Methods | 232 |
| Figure 209: Check Detail | 232 |
| Figure 210: Check Configuration | 233 |
| Figure 211: PayPal Configuration | 233 |
| Figure 212: Paypal Test Mode | 234 |
| Figure 213: Tax Rate | 235 |
| Figure 214: Tax Rate Detail | 235 |
| Figure 215: Product Categories | 237 |
| Figure 216: Category Detail | 238 |
| Figure 217: Category Image | 239 |
| Figure 218: Image update | 239 |
| Figure 219: Category Tree | 240 |
| Figure 220: Category Parent | 240 |
| Figure 221: Manufacturer list | 241 |

Figure 222: Manufacturer Details 241
Figure 223: Control Panel 243
Figure 224: Product Listing 244
Figure 225: Product Folders 244
Figure 226: Product Listing Category 245
Figure 227: Product Details 245
Figure 228: Display Values 247
Figure 229: Product Status 248
Figure 230: Product Attributes setup 249
Figure 231: Website Products and Attributes 250
Figure 232: Sample Invoice with Attributes 250
Figure 233: Product Status Date 251
Figure 234: Product Dimensions 251
Figure 235: Product Image 252
Figure 236: Related Products 252
Figure 237: Product Overview 253
Figure 238: Product View 254
Figure 239: Global Configuration update 255
Figure 240: Virtuemart Configuration 256
Figure 241: Virtuemart Configuration updated 256
Figure 242: Joomla Global Configuration 257
Figure 243: Website 259
Figure 244: Website 3 across 259
Figure 245: Category Tree 260
Figure 246: Category Detail 260

Figure 247: Website Products 2 across 261
Figure 248: Category Detail 263
Figure 249: Browse_3 264
Figure 250: Managed 264
Figure 251: Browse_1 265
Figure 252: Browse_2 266
Figure 253: Browse_4 266
Figure 254: Browse_5 267
Figure 255: Browse_lite_pdf 267
Figure 256: Home Website 269
Figure 257: Products Category 269
Figure 258: Add Items to Cart 270
Figure 259: Update Cart 270
Figure 260: Update Quantity 271
Figure 261: Delete Item from Cart 271
Figure 262: Registration 272
Figure 263: User Registration Form 273
Figure 264: Manage User Fields 274
Figure 265: Checkout Step 1 275
Figure 266: User Registration to Customer 276
Figure 267: User Registration to Administrator 276
Figure 268: Create Shipper 276
Figure 269: Shipper Rate 277
Figure 270: Shipping Module List 277
Figure 271: Flex Shipping 278

Figure 272: Configure Shipping    278
Figure 273: Step 2 - Select Shipper    279
Figure 274: Step 3    279
Figure 275: Step 4    280
Figure 276: Pay by Purchase Order    281
Figure 277: Pay by Paypal    281
Figure 278: Customer Order Confirmation    282
Figure 279: Website Download    283
Figure 280: Download Area    283
Figure 281: List Order Status Types    285
Figure 282: Order Status Detail    286
Figure 283: Order List    287
Figure 284: Order Detail    288
Figure 285: Order History    288
Figure 286: Order Status Confirmed Email    289
Figure 287: Customer Views Order    290
Figure 288: View Inventory    291
Figure 289: Product Detail Screen    291
Figure 290: Configuration    292
Figure 291: Report Screen    293
Figure 292: Report by Product    294
Figure 293: Website login    295
Figure 294: Account Maintenance    295
Figure 295: Account Information    296
Figure 296: Joomla Website    297

Figure 297: Extension Page 298
Figure 298: Extensions Printout 299
Figure 299: Images Extensions 301
Figure 300: Image Slideshow Extension 301
Figure 301: Image Slideshow detail page 302
Figure 302: Download Image Slideshow 302
Figure 303: Extension Manager 303
Figure 304: Module Manager 303
Figure 305: Image Slideshow Detail 304
Figure 306: Website Slideshow 304
Figure 307: Media Manager in Stories Folder 305
Figure 308: File Upload 305
Figure 309: Slideshow detail 306
Figure 310: Attachment Extension 307
Figure 311: Attachment Download 307
Figure 312: Download page 308
Figure 313: Success install 308
Figure 314: Plugin Manager 309
Figure 315: Attachment Parameters 309
Figure 316: Article 310
Figure 317: Upload Attachment 310
Figure 318: 500 Error 311
Figure 319: File Manager 311
Figure 320: 500 Error Index.html 312

Figure 321: File Manager Copy index.html 312
Figure 322: Attachment folder with Index.html 313
Figure 323: Attachment Manager 313
Figure 324: Website Attachment 314
Figure 325: Sample Website 315
Figure 326: View Source 316
Figure 327: Find Module 316
Figure 328: Silent No Right Click 317
Figure 329: Download 318
Figure 330: No Right Click Module 318
Figure 331: ND Editor Switch 321
Figure 332: Installed Editor Switch 322
Figure 333: Employment Listing 323
Figure 334: Employment Menu 324
Figure 335: Companies 324
Figure 336: Categories 325
Figure 337: Contacts 325
Figure 338: Websites 326
Figure 339: Configuration Cache 327
Figure 340: Cache Manager 328
Figure 341: Module Manager 328
Figure 342: Google Verify 330
Figure 343: Verify Meta tag Selection 330
Figure 344: Google Verify 331
Figure 345: Plugin Manager 331

| | |
|---|---|
| Figure 346: Plugin Key | 332 |
| Figure 347: Verified | 332 |
| Figure 348: Googlebot stats | 333 |
| Figure 349: Index Stats | 333 |
| Figure 350: Joomla Pack | 337 |
| Figure 351: JoomlaPack Website | 338 |
| Figure 352: Download JoomlaPack | 338 |
| Figure 353: JoomlaPack Control Panel | 339 |
| Figure 354: Backup Now | 340 |
| Figure 355: Backup Site | 340 |
| Figure 356: Backup Complete | 341 |
| Figure 357: Manage Backup Files | 341 |
| Figure 358: Download Files | 342 |
| Figure 359: Release Locks | 342 |

# Introduction

This book is written for small businesses who seem to pay more than large corporations to get things done. Don't waste money on having a website built, have you or your staff build it and control the contents and updates. This book walks you through step by step on building a Joomla! 1.5 and Virtuemart powered website in just a few hours.

### What is a content management system?

A content management system is a package of Internet software applications, which allow you to take full control over your website without any knowledge of html, UNIX or PHP. Whether you are a large corporation, a not for profit, entrepreneur or a sport team, open source content management puts the power at your finger tips to be as simple or complex as you can imagine.

The content management system is database driven, using an SQL database you can now have people register online, send newsletters to your customer database and email your customers, all through your website. No more separate databases maintaining customer records. If you are a small company and have not ventured into the large ERP software packages like SAP or Oracle, you can conduct all your business through a content management system. We will describe a package called Virtuemart an ecommerce tool to track inventory and sales.

The most fantastic thing about content management systems you can use forms on your website, you can add, edit, delete and manage data and content; build a community, have a picture gallery, latest news, post careers, create and manage the design and structure of your site and its navigation system; include images the abilities of a content management system are endless and it is right there at your finger tips.

Joomla and other products we describe in this book are not for profit companies. They need your support. If you are a sports team and you would have spent money to build a site; please donate to Open Source companies like Joomla and Virtuemart.

When you are through with this book, you will have a fantastic website which is as simple or complicated as you want and spend virtually no money.

With this book, you will have a working website up within less than an hour with full ecommerce functionality if you desire. This book is a step by step process to achieve a beautiful looking website without spending a lot of money.

So how much does it cost to build a website, basically only whatever you pay your webhoster per month and the person you have maintaining your website. Webhosting ranges from $5.95 to $40 a month for shared hosting to full dedicated servers running $500 a month for large corporations.

Don't fret, we will walk you through the process from beginning to end and it will be fun while you are doing it. We are also assuming you have used the internet before and you are familiar with going to Google or Yahoo and searching for an item.

One note for you to keep in mind. I am not a fan of hacking the code. I was a consultant for 20 years on SAP, Oracle and Baan large scale Enterprise software for corporations. Customizing code only leads to problems with upgrading and patching. I have been using Joomla and Virtuemart for almost 4 years and have never needed something so bad that I hacked the code. This book is written for the non-programmer and developer.

Once you learn about Joomla; you may develop the bug to hack, I advise against this. If you have to have a feature then work with the developers to add new features. They are always looking for input, since they are very proud of their software. Also don't forget to donate. The more you donate, the more weight you carry on feature requests being implemented.

So let's get started, we are going to start with the basics, so if you are a little more advance then skip to the chapter you have not completed.

Special note, since all major components called use the term control panel. I will use the word Dashboard interchangeably for the Joomla Control Panel to try and distinguish it from all the other control panels. Therefore when you see Dashboard it means Joomla Control Panel.

# Website (Domain) Name

The first thing you need to do is buy a domain name. Now there are a ton of domain names out there. But you may not be able to buy the first name you want because it may already be taken. Be creative and come up with a number of different names. I actually go out to www.Dotster.com and type in domain names until I find one I like.

There are a few keys to creating a domain name:
• Keep it memorable – your customers need something they can spell and remember.

• Keep it short as possible, the longer it is the easier to misspell as they are trying to find your site. When a website is spelled wrong it either drops out to a Ask.com – which is irritating, because you can't go back. Ask locks you in the site or it drops you out to a company which slams you with viruses because you typed something close to the name of a famous company. Either way try to make it easy on your customers to find you.

• Be descriptive, many times I will use parts of words to make up the site name. For instance, the name of the holding corporation for Spiderweby is Center for Economies of Change Corporation. I found that CEO.com was taken, CEOC.com was taken therefore I purchased www.centereoc.com, economiesochange.com and ceochange.com. I purchased all three, because I wanted flexibility in what name I was going to use, since I was undecided in the beginning. Now I just use www.centereoc.com with economiesofchange.com and ceochange.com as redirects to www.centereoc.com.

Do you see how I took the name and developed different

variations which are still descriptive of the name?

When you do a test search for your domain name, you will see all kind of extensions. These different extensions exist in order to make the internet more organized. These domain extensions are known as top level domain name (TLDN). Pages from a website then are represented after the domain name; for instance, www.centereoc.com/index or www.centeroc.com/customer. Below are the current domain extensions, just to name a few:

- .com – are commercial enterprises from small businesses to large corporations
- .edu – are educational institutions
- .gov – are government organizations
- .mil – are military organizations
- .net – are network and webhosting organizations
- .org – are non profit organizations
- .info – are for informational sites
- .mobi – are mobile device websites
- .biz – are for commercial organizations also but the .com is still the most common selection for commercial use.
- .us – are United States websites
- .tv – are news stations and video sites
- .name- are intended for use for people's real names
- .jobs – this is restricted to employment related sites.
- .travel – classifies travel related sites.

There are also country domain names which you will run across the more you use the internet. A few common country domain name extensions, found regularly on the internet:

- .ca – Canda
- .cn – China
- .de – Germany
- .dk – Denmark
- .es – Spain

- .fi – Finland
- .fr – France
- .gb or .uk – United Kingdom
- .hk – Hong Kong
- .it – Italy
- .in – India
- .jp – Japan
- .mx – Mexico
- .ru – Russia
- .se – Sweden

Once you settle on a name and you find it available you have to register the name. All domain names are registered through ICANN (Internet Corporation for Assigned Names and Numbers). But you can't purchase directly from ICANN, you have to go through a registrar. There are hundreds of registrars. If you would like to look one up, you can go to www.internic.net which is the register for all domain resellers. Again, I just use Dotster, since I have been using them for years and have had zero issues with them.

To register your domain, you need to buy it. This requires you to use your credit card and sign up online or over the phone. It is a pretty straight forward process. Just watch that you are paying for the time frame you want the domain name, meaning 1 year, 2 years or 3 years. Some companies force you to the 3 year but you need to change it to the length you want. Just realize, if you sign up for only a year, next year you have to renew the domain name. If you forget, because you don't use the email address any longer you signed up with, you will lose your name. It is awful to lose a name which you have built a relationship on it.

Also remember nothing is truly free. There are a lot of

companies which will give you a free domain name with a one year webhosting. Once you leave this webhoster they have locked your name and you either have to stay with them to keep it or change your domain name all together. It is better to pay regular price for your domain and not be locked in. A normal domain name costs $10 to $20 dollars with no restrictions.

Once you lost your domain name, the bulk domain buyers buy it up and you then sometimes have to pay hundreds of dollars to get it back. This is very important to remember, your domain name is critical don't allow yourself to lose it by not paying attention to the expiration.

Also, many domain registrars will try to add additional services like web hosting or who is privacy to your domain name registration. You can delete these; you do not have to buy all the services. Just ensure it shows the domain name and anything else you want to purchase.

Once you have purchase your domain, your registrar should send you an email with the registration and how to log in and change the Nameservers. The nameservers are critical these are what tells the internet where your website can be found. The nameserver is usually tied to your webhosters IP address unless you contracted for your own IP address.

You receive your nameserver names from your webhoster. There are typically two nameservers they are for instance: ns1.centereoc.net and ns2.centereoc.net.

At the back of this book, I have included a coupon for 3 months free webhosting, in order for you to learn how to build your website and then decide your future. I have tried to remove the stress of learning something new, without having to navigate through all the webhosters, trying to figure out which one is best.

If you decide to use the 3 month coupon the nameservers are:
ns1.centereoc.net
ns2.centereoc.net.

Therefore go to the next chapter to begin to see how to sign up for a webhoster.

**Special note**: Now, in order to rank better in SEO (Search Engine Optimization) it is better to have your own IP address tied to your name servers. This way you are seen as a separate entity away from your webhoster. The dedicated IP address is extra money, but it is worth it. The IP address can run from $5 to $50 dollars a year depending on who are hosting with. Do this down the road, don't do it right this minute. With the new features in Joomla 1.5 many sites do not need dedicated IP address as they did in the past.

# Finding a Webhoster

People, who are looking for webhosting for the first time, will find it overwhelming. So let's start from the beginning.

## Web Hosting Types

The first question to think about is what type of site you are going to be maintaining. Most first timers start with a shared webhoster service. This runs around $6.95 a month to $20.00 a month based on what you are looking for. Given the competition between hosting companies you can find a good webhoster at $6.95 a month. Spiderweby (www.spiderweby.com) tries to stay cost competitive with other webhosters. Remember we offer a coupon for 3 month of free webhosting.

The most basic web hosting is called Shared Web hosting: What this means is a company has a server (web host) and they rent you space on their server. On one web server there could be 1000's of sites; all sharing the same resources like RAM, bandwidth and operating systems. Don't be scared, servers can host all these websites with no problems and there are administrators in the background ensuring that no one website steals too much space from the other.

Your webhoster needs to have the following in order for you to have control of your website:

• It must have CPANEL; this is your command center for your website. By having cpanel you are able to setup email accounts, redirect domains, park domains and maintain your sql servers as well as access the root (system files) area of your website. Many webhosters include it free and some charge for the use of it. Try to find one which includes it. Figure 1, shows what a CPANEL looks like.

**Figure 1: Cpanel Display**

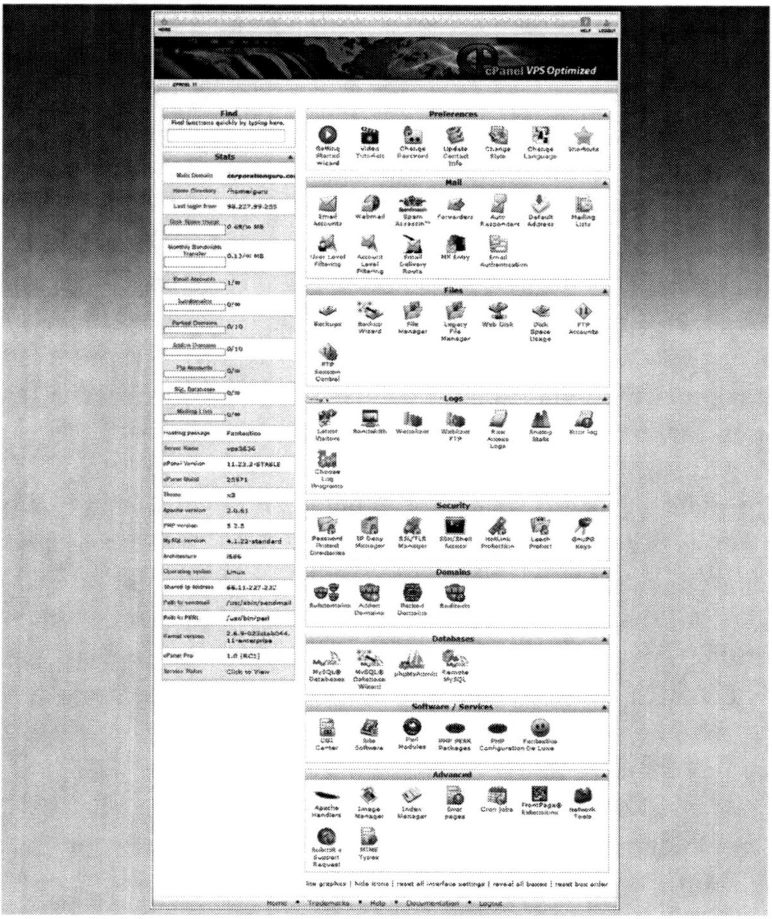

- Storage: You also need a webhoster who gives you at minimum 1,500 gig storage but preferably unlimited storage.

- Data Transfer Rate: Industry standard is 15,000 gigs data transfer per month (this should serve just about anyone's needs who do not require their own virtual private server).

- Database: In order to install Joomla, you need SQL database ability. Preferably they give you unlimited databases. Even though most people only use a few.

- Emails: 50 to unlimited emails addresses are pretty standard with most services.

- FANTASTICO, this is critical. You do not want to maintain and install Joomla the manual way. FANTASTICO keeps up to date on the latest versions of Joomla. The process of installation is extremely easy, with FANTASTICO. Some webhosters give it free and some charge for it.

- You need to be able to FTP files to your servers. This allows you to change images and change logos.

Those are the most critical things you need with a webhoster in order to easily build your site. One last thing, you need which is nice to have, is root access to your file manager. If you go back to Figure 1: cpanel, you notice there is a file manager. You need to be able to make the configuration file writable in order to update it this is critical to SEO (Search Engine Optimization), which we will discuss in another chapter.

Special note: Check how long it takes once you subscribe to the webhosting service to setup your account. It can take from 1 hour to 10 days, depending on the webhoster. If you are like me, patience is not a virtue and I want it done fast.

For beginners, they fall into the trap of the cheapest, but then get nickel and dimed to death. You want a Webhoster with a low per month cost, which includes cpanel, good disk space, sql databases, with adequate bandwidth and fantastico.

Your main concern is availability and how quickly can the technical team recover you from an error. Be forewarned, though many hosting companies will charge through the nose for rebuilding your site for you. If you follow the guidelines throughout the book, you will be fine. It is when you learn a little and you begin experimenting that your site crashes or takes a long time to load.

There are other types of hosting, which we will explain high level, you will need to be a more advanced user to utilized these options. Once you venture down these paths, I have found very few webhosters willing to help you through the learning curve. Therefore I recommend you stay with shared services, until you get your feet wet.

The other services are a VPS (Virtual Private Server) or a Dedicated Server. The VPS runs roughly ($40 dollars a month to $100 a month).

A VPS is a server (computer) which is partitioned into multiple servers. Each segment appearance and capabilities simulate that of a stand alone server. Each VPS is considered independent and can be rebooted. The nice thing about VPS is that you have root access to control your files. But, there is a lot more responsibilities to maintaining a VPS. With a VPS everything is extra Cpanel and Plesk (server administration). There is a much longer learning curve. My recommendation if you are going to use VPS then get it with CPANEL, because it is much easier to maintain individual sites with it. Then use the Plesk for server maintenance and backups. If you are a demanding web user, many webhosters many force you to a VPS, since you take up to much server space, server bandwidth or server resources. Be forewarned running a VPS is very demanding.

Another option is the DEDICATED SERVER, this is where you lease an entire server not shared with anyone. The most powerful web hosting service is this method, which costs roughly $75-$500 a month. This option is similar to being your own Information Technology department, you find in corporations. This requires someone who understands Apache Servers, PHP, SQL and how to maintain a server.

My last recommendation, is whatever webhoster you choose, sign up for a month of service, if you like them then continue to pay by the month or by the year. If you don't then switch, now that is a pain if you spent a lot of time building your website, but in the end it is better to find a webhoster which fits your needs. I would actually by the com, .net and .org versions of the domain names. Then if one webhoster turned out to be no good, I would sign up with another webhoster, rebuild the site with the .net domain name then when done, redirect and park the .com website to the .net. This way the site was never down until I found the right fit.

I have used a lot of web services, and could not find one that gave me everything I need. Therefore this is how Spiderweby started, in order to ensure our servers had the requirements we were looking for. My groups are very demanding, and this is also why when customers subscribe with us, we give many of the same functionality we require to the customers.

# JOOMLA! Hosting Requirements

This book is written for Joomla! 1.5. The following are the settings required of your webhoster in order for Joomla to work:
- PHP 4.2.x or above
- MySQL 3.23.x or above
- Apache 1.3.x or above
- XML Must be enabled through your PHP installation
- Zlib must be enabled through your PHP installation
- You need root access to modify your .htaccess file, your folders when adding custom files and configuration file.
- Must be able to execute PHP scripts.
- Mod_Rewrite module within PHP

# Subscribing to a Hosting Service

This is relatively straight forward. Typically you fill out an online form or have to call a number. You will need to give a credit card to pay either by the month or the year. This credit card stays on file with the webhoster for them to bill monthly or yearly they will send you a notice for you to go online and repay.

Some hosting companies offer free domain names with one year of service. Other companies have you pay for your domain names. Domain names range in price from Free to $15.00 with renewal every year. Even though it says free, you need to check the portability of the name if you leave that webhoster. You also need to be able to ensure you can change the nameserver if you leave the webhoster also. Some domain name providers make it very difficult to leave or change if you are hosting with them. I myself use Dotster. They are reliable and you have full access to modify your domain name servers. I prefer to keep my webhosting and domains separate.

Once you subscribe to a service, it usually takes anywhere from 1 hour to 7 days for your webhosting company to set up your server.

Note once you sign up with a webhoster, you need the name server address then you have to go back to your Domain registrar log into your account and change the name server.

This is what it looks like on Dotster, since this is where I host my domains. Note the section which states name servers, you have to click the link Update Name Servers. Then enter your nameservers, click add and then enter the second name server press add then enter your email address. Name servers always begin with ns1.webhosteruniquename.net or com and ns1.webhosteruniquename.net or com. For example, the nameservers for Spiderweby are ns1.centereoc.net and ns2.centereoc.net

**Figure 2: Name Servers**

# Using the Cpanel

While you are waiting on the nameserver to resolve, this takes anywhere from 24 hours to 2 days; you can begin building your website. Your webhoster will send you directions on how to enter your Cpanel.

The first time you enter the Cpanel the "Getting Started wizard" appears. Play it the first time, it gives a general overview of the Cpanel.

Next look down the side of the Cpanel there is a listing of your Disk Space Usage, Monthly Bandwidth, Number of E-mail accounts, SQL databases, Email addresses, etc…

**Figure 3: Cpanel**

The first to do is create an email address. Find the Mail section of your cpanel. We need to create a few email address based on your needs. I create one with my name at my domain. The others are usually a customer service account and sales account.

**Figure 4: Add Email Account**

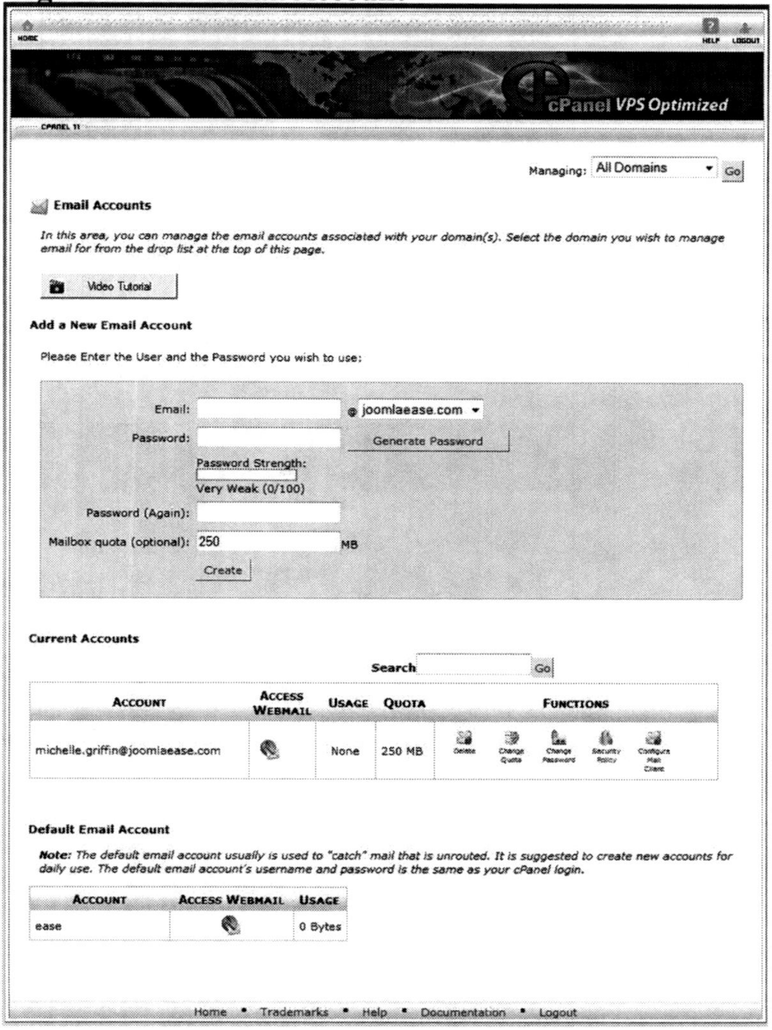

Click on the email account button. Enter your email address and password. Click Create.

But you have to watch using a generic customer service or sales because it will be considered junk email in some email systems. Therefore I always come up with something that looks like a name. Instead of using customerservice@centereoc.com, I will use customer.service@centereoc.com. But really this is a personal preference how you want to label your e-mail.

Once the email is created it will ask you, "Do you wish to configure the account to work with an outlook client". Click YES.

**Figure 5: Configure Email Account**

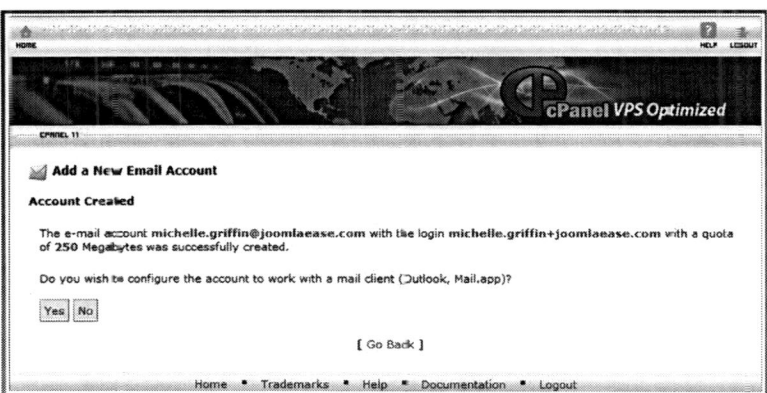

You can either configure Outlook to receive your email or you can read your email on line. This section is for business with out an IT department. If you have an IT department then skip over this section, contact your IT group to set up the email.

48    Joomla!™ 1.5

**Figure 6: Outlook Configuration after you click Yes**

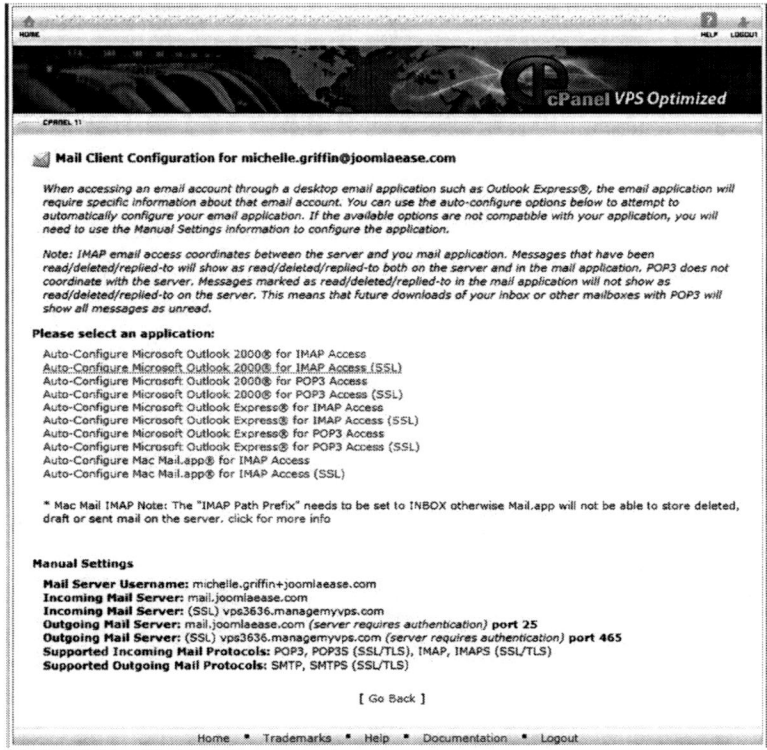

Next, go out your email program. We are going to show you how to configure Microsoft Outlook. If you have another email program it will be close to the same.

Open Outlook

Go to  Select Tools/Email Accounts.

Select Add new Account and click next.

Using the CPanel 49

## Figure 7: Add Email Account

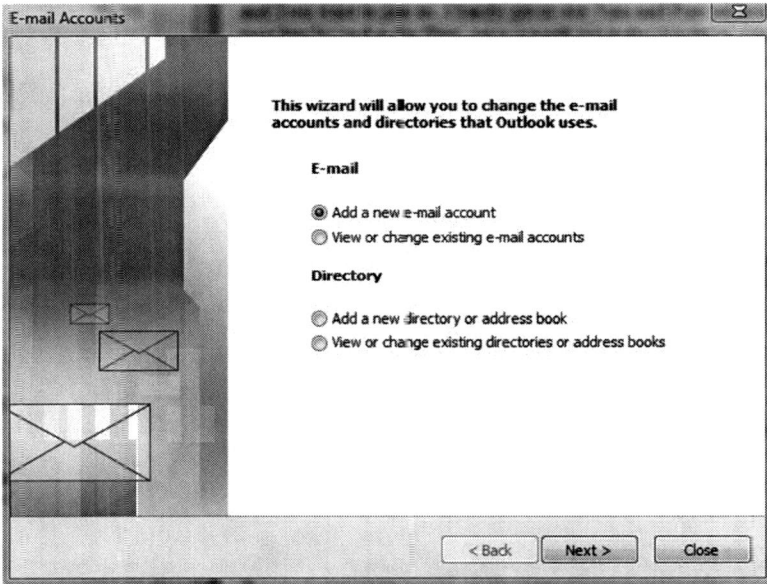

The next screen, select Pop3 and click next.

A screen similar to figure 9 will pop up.

Enter your Name

Email Address

Enter the Username created in Figure 4

Enter Password

Incoming Pop3 - this information is found in Figure 6

Outgoing SMTP - this information is found in Figure 6

50    Joomla!™ 1.5

## Figure 8: Check Pop3 and Next

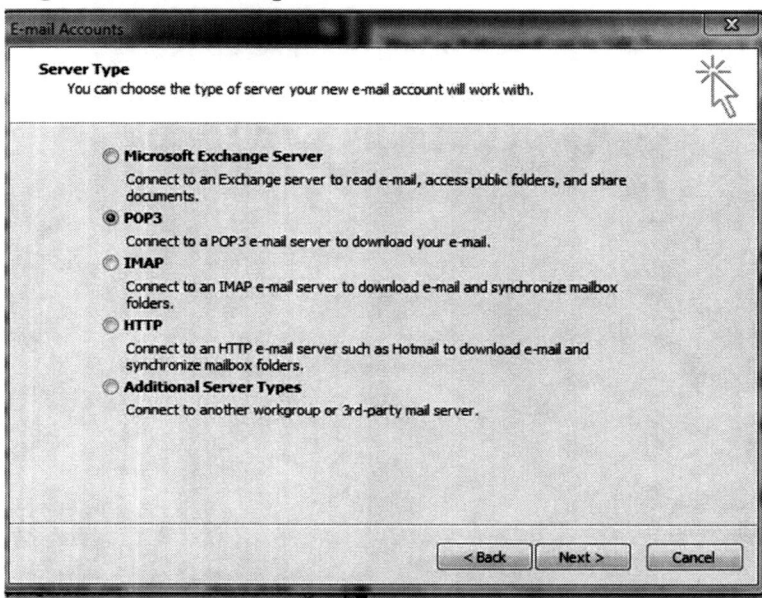

## Figure 9: Enter Email

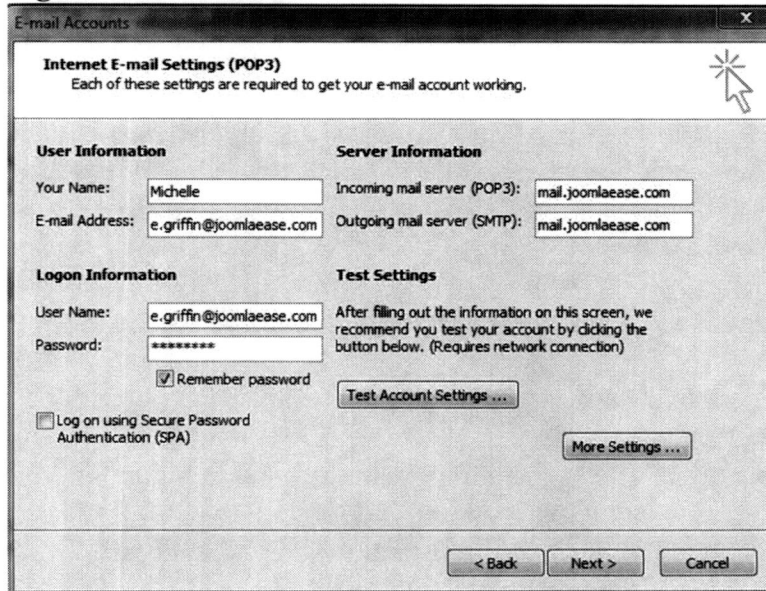

Using the CPanel 51

Click Test Account Settings, if everything is correct the Status will show completed.

**Figure 10: Email completion**

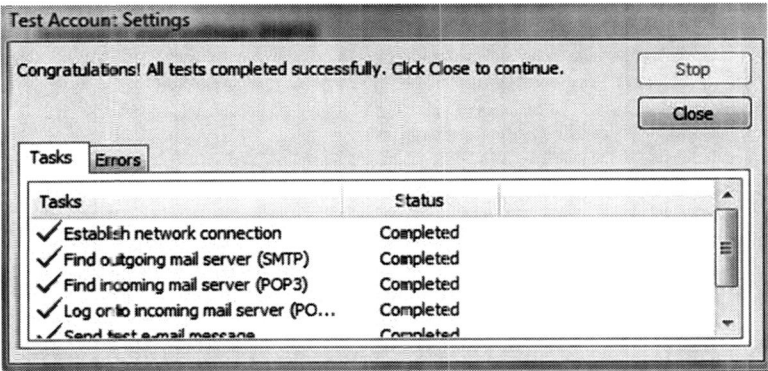

If an error comes back then something was missed spelled, go back and review the previous screen. If you find everything is spelled correctly then go back to the Cpanel and reconfigure for Outlook, described in the beginning of this section.

If the Pop3 (incoming mail) shows completed, this means you are receiving your email.

If the SMTP (outgoing mail) fails, this is your local internet provider requires a username and password. Go to the next step below to enter your username and password.

### Figure 11: Email Naming

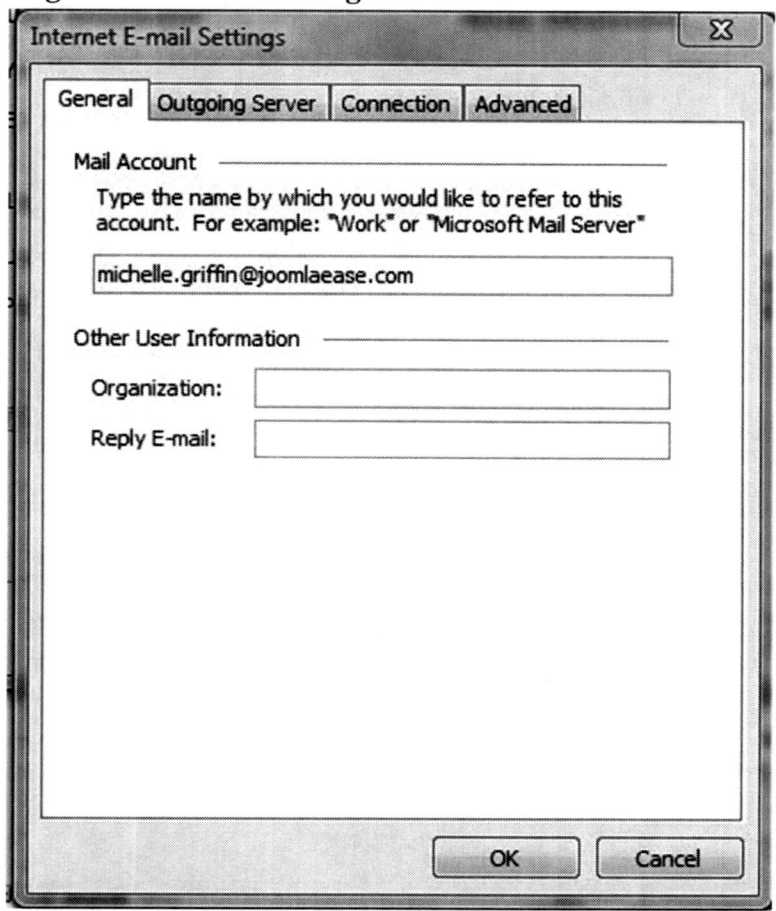

If you don't know it, then contact your internet provider for this information. Once it all shows completed press the close button. Press the "More Settings" button. You need to give your email account a name. Now, some of you may be using a telephone company as your internet provider. Some of these require Outgoing Server authentication (SMTP). Which is the 2nd tab, you may need to enter your username and password.

Using the CPanel 53

**Figure 12: Outgoing Server (SMTP)**

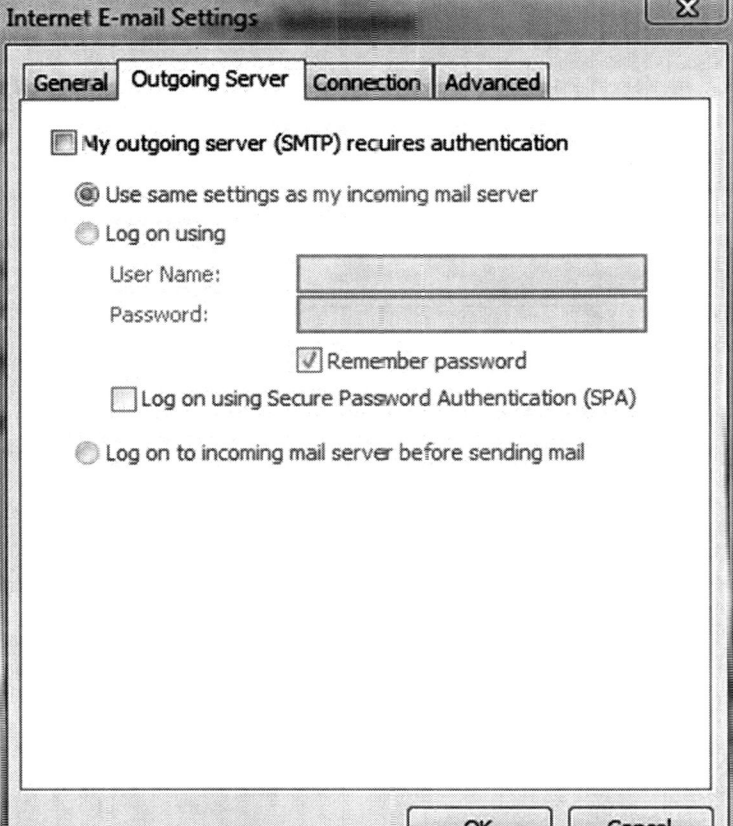

If the outgoing server fails when testing, contact your Internet provider to ask them how to setup the SMTP in Outlook.

When done click ok, you are now back to the add email screen, click next and click finished your email account is setup.

54    Joomla!™ 1.5

### Figure 13: Click Next - Email Setup

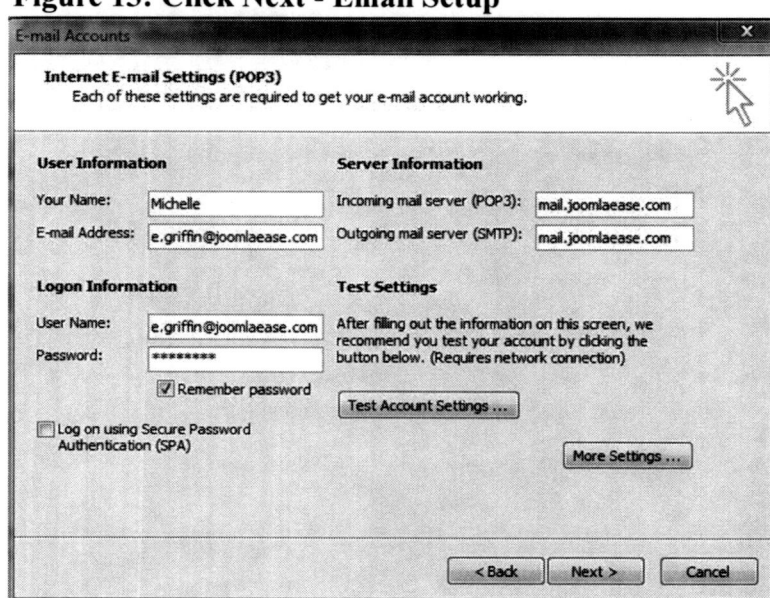

### Figure 14: Click Finish

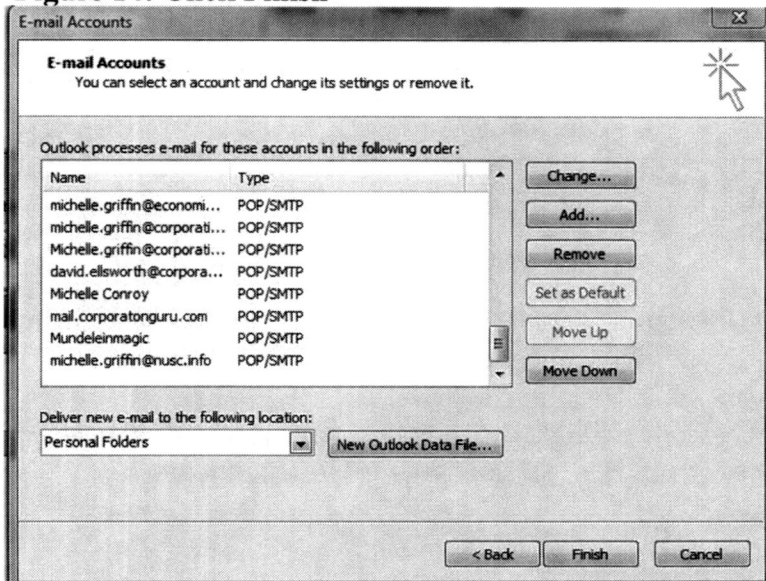

# Installing Joomla!

Now, go back to your Cpanel, hopefully you left it open.

**Figure 15: CPanel**

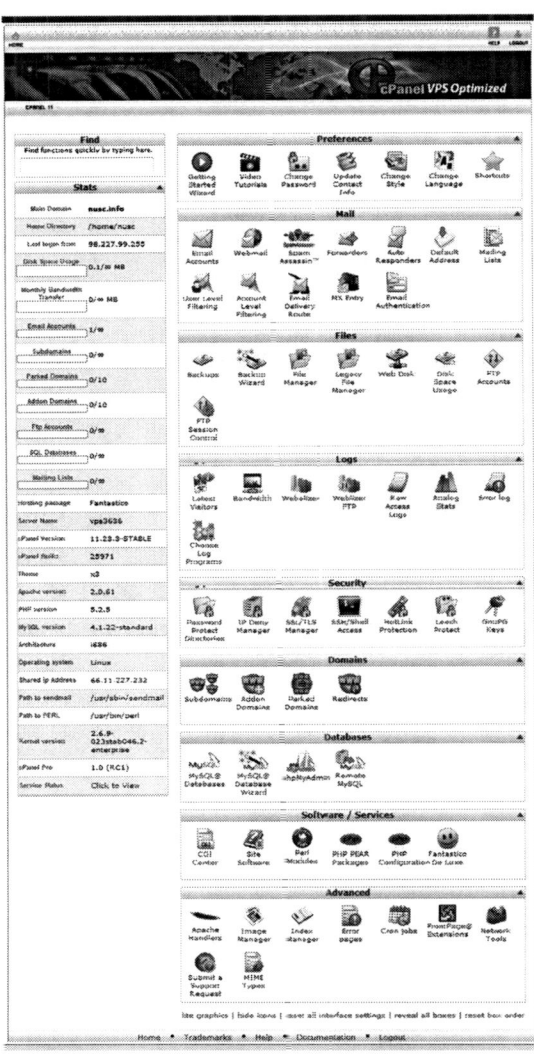

If not log back in. Scroll down the screen until you find Fantastico, it is located under the Software/Services section.

Open another internet screen and type in your website address. Your screen should look like this.

**Figure 16: Website blank**

Now the fun part! Go back to your Cpanel, and if you have not click the Fantastico button do it now.

Do not get carried away, you can't install everything on this page. Your are trying to build a professional website, overtime you will learn what the other features are. I will explain briefly. Your screen should look like this.

**Figure 17: Fantastico Screen Shot**

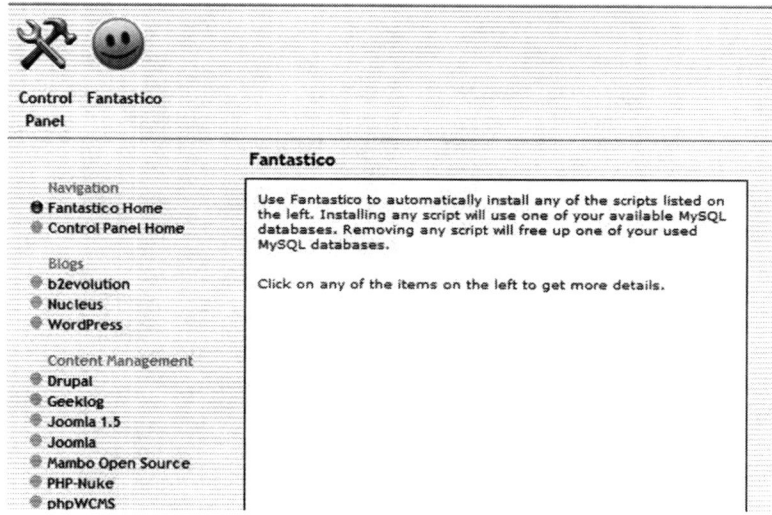

Installing Joomla! 57

Fantastico is cool, since it installs PHP scripts for you. Now some of this stuff works together others do not. Please don't get carried away installing scripts. The section we are focused on is the Content Management.

**Figure 18: Begin Joomla Installation**

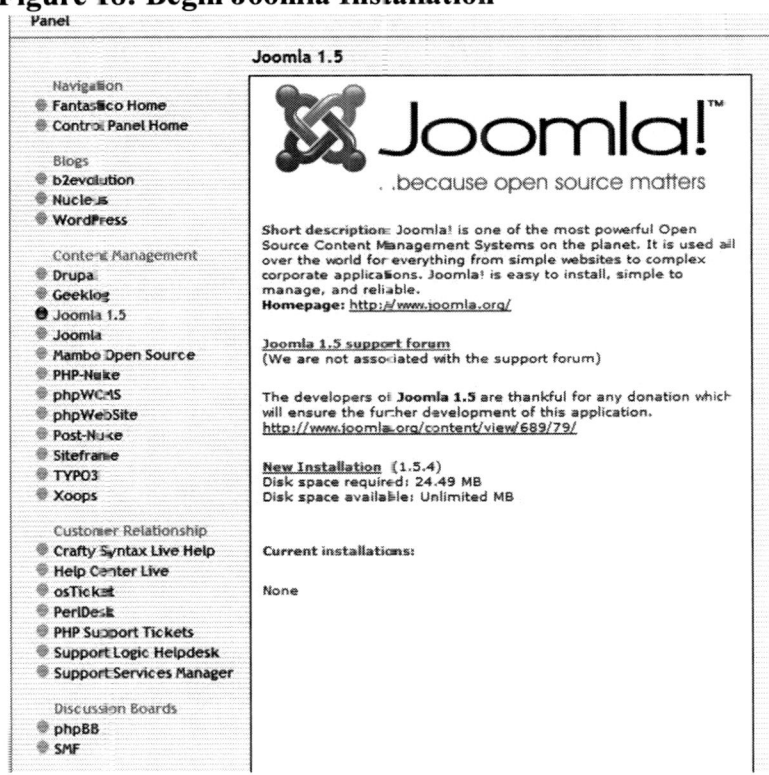

You see Drupal, Mambo, Joomla 1.5 and others. These are all what is called content management software. It is all Open Source; some are easier to use then others. Drupal and Joomla are the industry leaders at the moment in Open Source. Drupal requires a little more IT knowledge then Joomla. Drupal and Joomla can be compared to the Apple and Microsoft companies of the world.

58    Joomla!™ 1.5

This book is focused on Joomla! 1.5 therefore this is what we are going to install. Now, here it comes press the button Joomla! 1.5. The following screen appears.

Click New Installation, the following screen appears:

**Figure 19: Install Joomla**

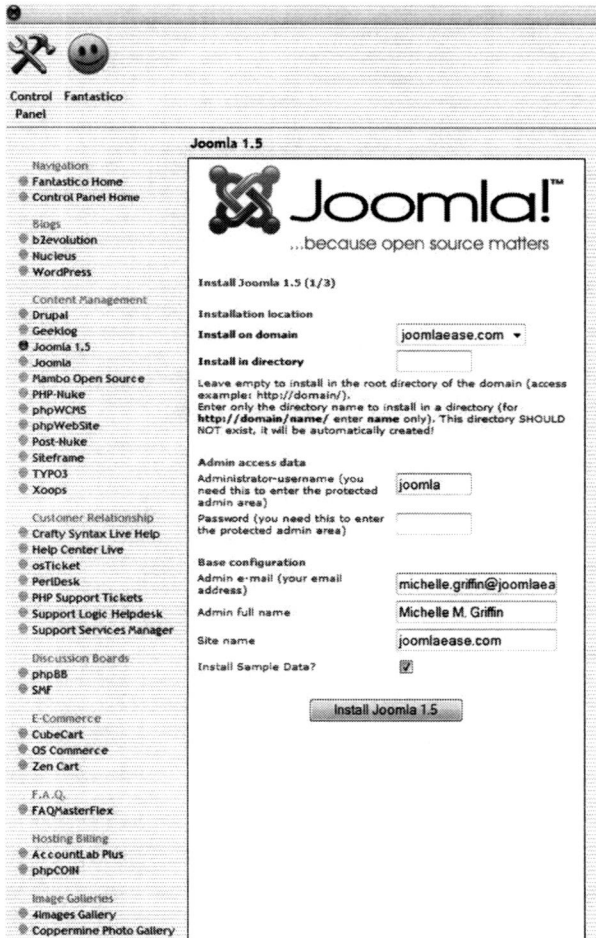

Installing Joomla! 59

Enter in your administration username and password. This is username and password you will use to enter the Joomla dashboard. Enter something you will remember.

Make sure your email address you created is in the admin email. Verify the site name. Press Install Joomla! 1.5

The following screen appears, now it will create your SQL database and install Joomla. Click Finish Installation.

**Figure 20: Joomla Install Finish**

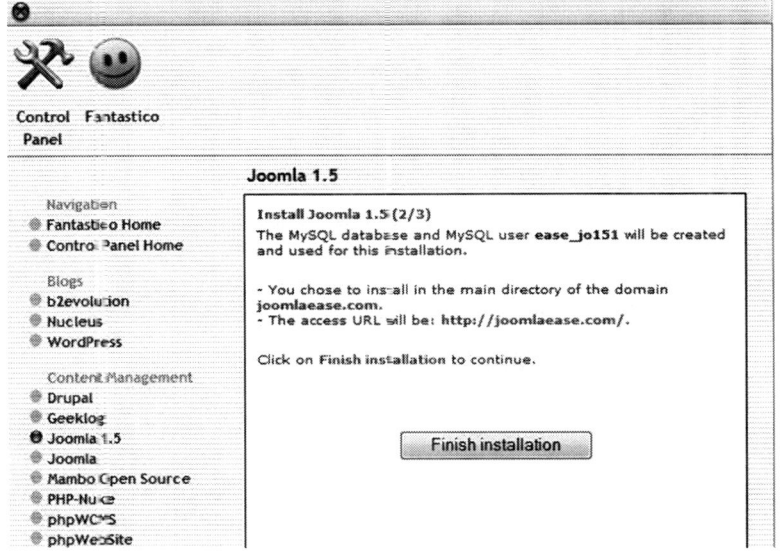

Once the installation finishes the following screen appears:

This is information is very important, write it down or print it out and do not lose. Your access to the Joomla Dashboard is www.yourdomainname.com/administrator.

Your username and password is shown. When finished reviewing click back to Joomla! 1.5 overview.

## Figure 21: Joomla Administration Information

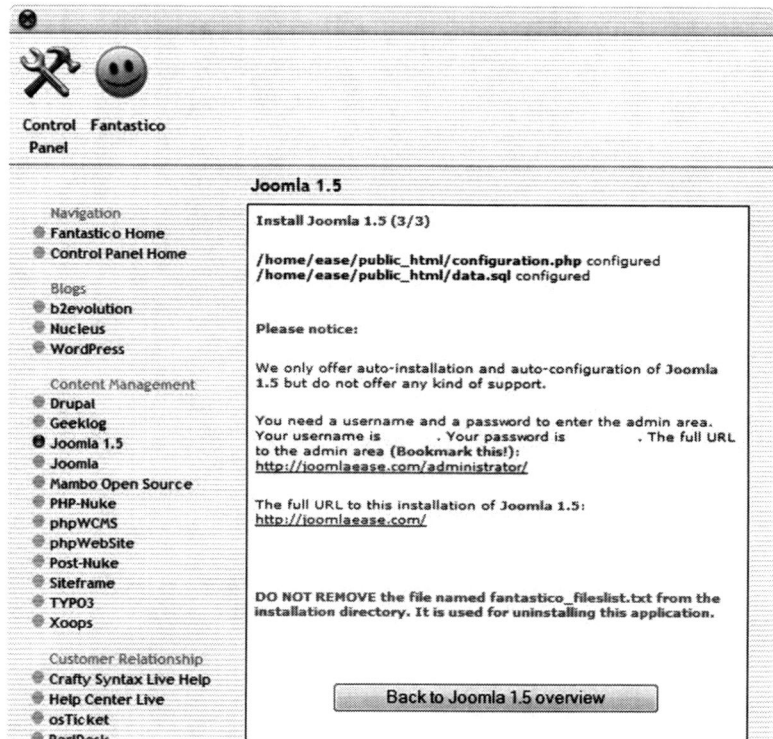

Hurray you have done it, you created your first website, all within less than 30 minutes if you were fast.

Go back to the other internet screen and retype your domain name.

Your screen has gone from being just a folder to having an actual website on it. It should look like this.

Installing Joomla! 61

**Figure 22: Your Website**

We are done with the Cpanel for now; you can close out of it. Congratulations for getting this far. Do you see how easy that was? You have conquered the first challenge, now for the fun!

# Joomla Administration

Let's open a new internet session. You are going to want two internet screens open, one will be your website and the other will be the Joomla dashboard (administrator).

Go to the Joomla administrator log in screen. Enter your Username and password press login.

Note: The Joomla administrator has an automatic log out after 15 minutes. Security feature, for all your corporations, which require automatic logout.

**Figure 23: Joomla administrator screen**

You are now entering the Joomla dashboard. Do you see the blurbage on the right hand side, read it carefully! I will show you how to remove it, but don't remove it until you are comfortable with what it says.

Security is a huge issue. Therefore when we open files and make them writable, you must remember to make them unwritable right afterwards.

**Figure 24: Joomla Dashboard**

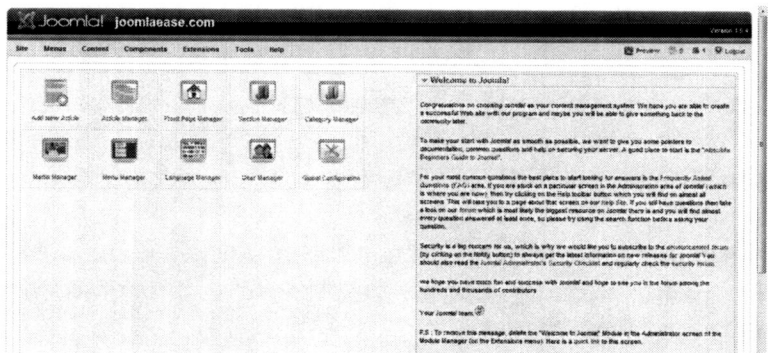

Definitely sign up for the security alerts from Joomla.

This is your site, long after you finish with this book, you have to follow Joomla on developments and security warnings. Joining and participating in the forums are also good for you to go from a beginner to an advance user.

From this point forward, I will show you how to do things, in Joomla.

Try it or don't try it from this point forward it is your decision. Do you see the little green arrow next to the Welcome to Joomla, scroll down to Logged in users and click the little green arrow next to it.

It closes the other window and opens Logged in users. Below that are popular and recent added articles. Click each of the green arrows to see what information they provide.

Joomla! Administration 65

**Figure 25: Joomla Screen Right Toolbar**

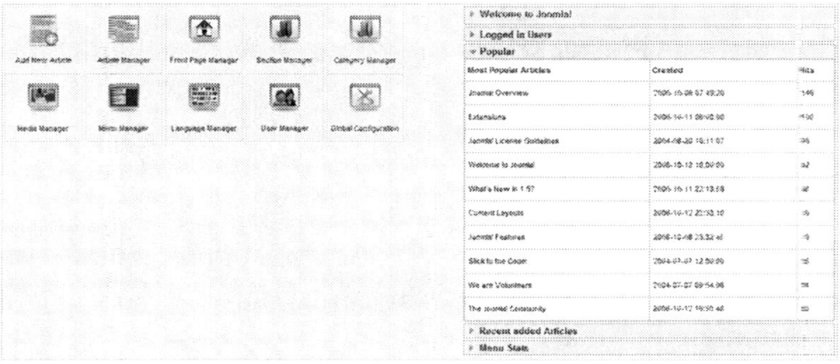

The first thing we are going to show you is how to customize your administration area.

After you have read the Welcome to Joomla, I like to turn it off.

To turn it off we go to the top toolbar and highlight Extensions/ Module Manager.

**Figure 26: Module Manager**

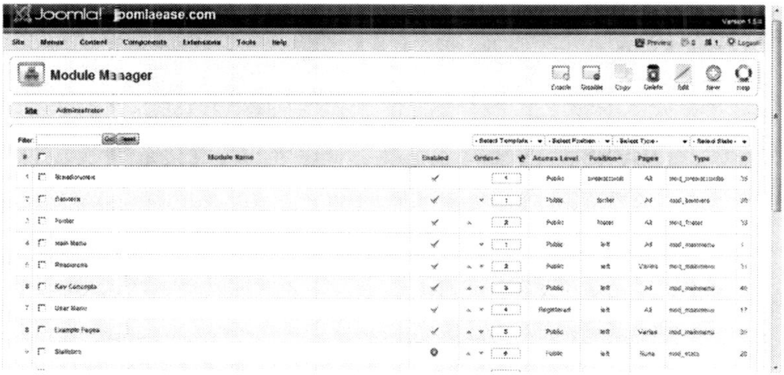

The menu manager pops up.

Do you see the checkmark under the enabled column, check marks mean enabled and red circles with an x through it means disabled. If you look just below the Module Manager name it says site or administrator.

Site means the website and Administrator means your dashboard. We are going to modify the dashboard first, click on the Administrator link.

**Figure 27: Administrator Module Manager**

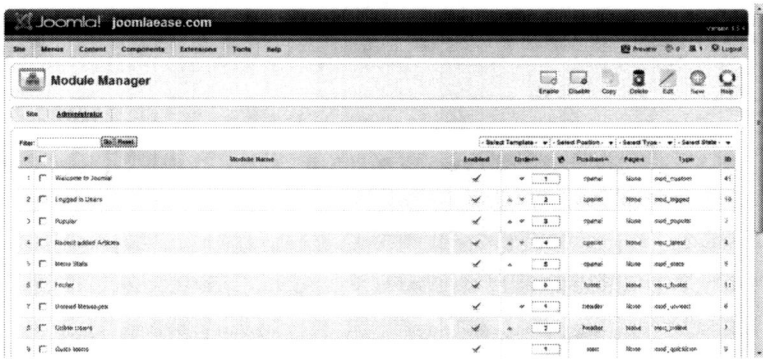

Do you see the first line shows a module named, "Welcome to Joomla" and it shows Enabled with a check mark; we are going to disable this module.

In front of the "Welcome to Joomla" put a check in the box. On the same line as the words, Module Manager on the right there are icons. Press the disable icon. Your screen now looks like this. Now go Site on the top toolbar and click Control panel. Look on the right and the Welcome to Joomla is gone. Now, we

Joomla! Administration 67

have not deleted anything, all we did is disable it and it can be re-enabled at anytime.

So Joomla is this simple, it is just turning on and off modules and moving things around to create a unique look.

**Figure 28: Administrator disable**

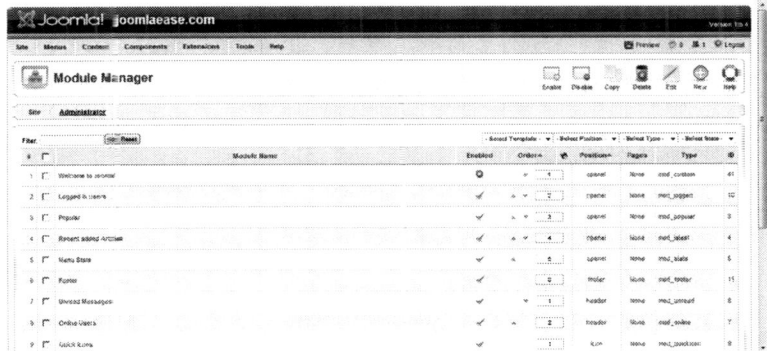

Now that we did a simple administrator change, let's change a module on our website.

Go back to the Module manager, do you remember how? Extensions/Module Manager

# Module Manager

Module Manager turns parts of your website on and off. At least one module is required in Joomla. This is very flexible so we will start with the basics and become more advanced toward the end of the book.

You should be at the module manager screen:

**Figure 29: Module Manager**

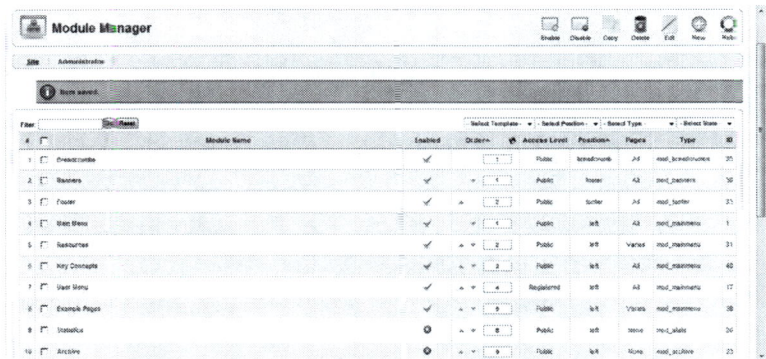

Now, click on your other internet screen and look at your website. Yours should look like this the next screen shot.

Do you see the module popular on your website?

We are going to disable this module.

70   Joomla!™ 1.5

**Figure 30: Your website**

Toggle back to the Module manager in your dashboard.

Find popular module and disable it.

If you have noticed it is not on the first page. You need to scroll to the bottom of the page and click next.

Now check the box in front of popular and click the disable button.

**Figure 31: Popular Disable**

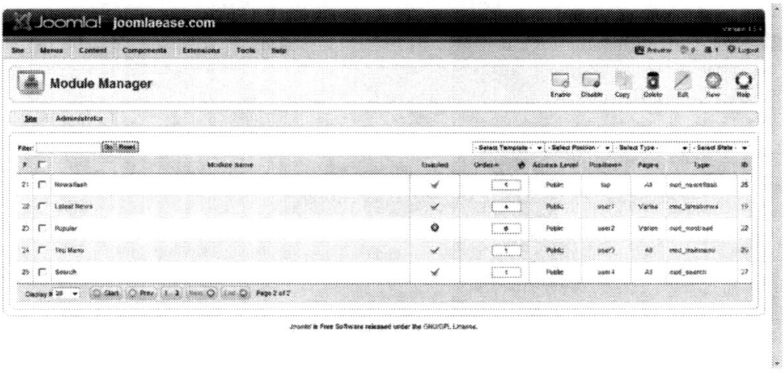

Module Manager 71

Now go back to your website and refresh the screen, if you see two blue arrows heading in opposite direction this is refresh.

Did your popular module disappear? Now go back and re-enable it, refresh and relook at your website.

Try turning other modules on and off to see what happens. Don't forget to go back and forth to the first page and second page.

**Figure 32: Popular Module gone**

# Module Manager- Changing

Now let's move module around a little bit. Let's go back to the module manager. Remember it is located under extensions/module manager. Now looking across the module manager there are a number of columns.

Figure 33: Module Manager Columns

The columns are:
- # a number automatically assigned by Joomla

- Checkbox – Check this box to select an item and then click a command icon for instance disables or enable. There is a global checkbox on the column heading bar. If you check this box it selects everything on page. Go ahead and select the global check box and click disable. Now go back to your website, many of the modules have disappeared. Now go back and re-select the global and click enable go back to your website, the modules showed back up again.
- Module name – This is the name of the module. You can click on the name to open the module for editing. (You can also rename the modules when editing).

- Enabled – A green checkmark or a red circle with an X showing whether the module is enabled or disabled. Click the checkmark or red circle to enable or disable directly on the line. Go ahead and try it.

- Order – The order to display the modules. This means module 1 will be in the first position. Look at the position column; find the position labeled 'left'. This means that all modules with position left are located in the left column of your webpage. Look and see what module is number 1. It is "Main Menu" now go to your website and look at where Main menu is, it is in the first position in the left column. When you have multiple modules in the same position, you can order which comes first and which comes last.

- Access Level: Each module has security built around it, you can have modules which are Public and everyone can see them. You can have modules Registered, where only customers who are registered can view them. There is also, special these are users who have rights to change the website from the webpage. These are authors or editors of content for your website. Notice on your module screen the User Menu is registered, meaning only registered users will see this.

- Position: The position is where the module is displayed. We briefly covered in discussing the Order column. Positions are defined in template for the page.

- Pages: You can dedicate which modules show up on what pages based on the menu items.

# Module Manager- Changing 75

- The type and Id are system identification and for this book, we will not be touching this area.

Now go to the bottom of the module page, there is a display button, showing 20. This means that 20 modules can be displayed at once. If you drop down the box, you see you can change it to any number of views. When you change the display let's say to 50, it stays as long as your current session is active. Once you log out it goes back to 20. I personally do not change this very often.

Back at the top of the module page there is a toolbar with icons, here are the descriptions:

- Enable – turns modules on. This button influences the Enable column

- Disable – turns modules off. This button influences the Disable column.

At this point, the rest of the icons we will not using until latter. Therefore we will discuss then.

Let's move the modules around a little bit. Find the "Login Form" module. We will place with this one. If you toggle to your website, you find the Login Form is on the left side in the 4th position. But when you look at the Module Manager it is labeled 8th position.

Let's look at the screen in detail.

76    Joomla!™ 1.5

**Figure 34: Module Manager – Login Form**

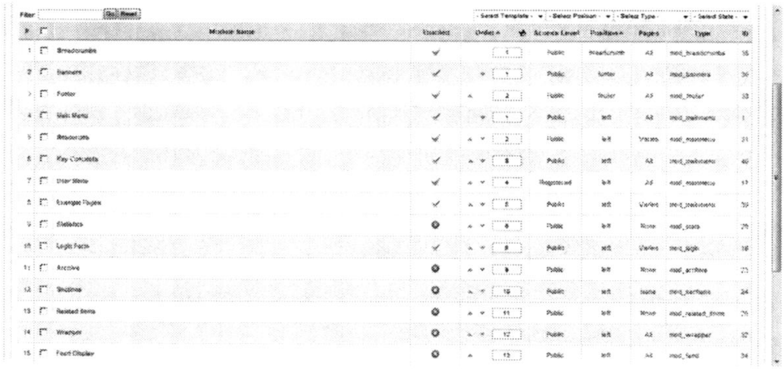

Notice on the left column Main Menu is 1st, Resources is 2nd, Key Concepts is 3rd, User Menu is registered therefore does not count, Example Pages is 5th but really 4th on the website, Statistics is disable therefore does not count, and Login Form is 8th position but has moved to the 5th position on the website. But, wait a second. When you look at the website Login Form is in the 4th position.

Which one is missing?

Do you see that Example Pages is linked to Key Concepts? So now we want to move Login form to the 1st position. In order to edit a module we have to click on the module name for that module. Click on the underlined module name of Login Form.

Before we move the module positions, let's go through this form.
•Title: You can change this field to fit your needs. I like to rename it to whatever type of website I am building. For instance,

let say it is a Baseball site for a team called the Bandits. Then I would call it Bandits Login. This personalizes the website to your needs.

**Figure 35: Module Form**

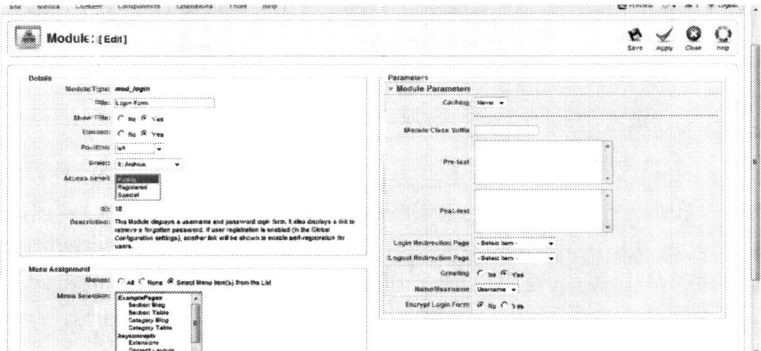

- Show Title: This hides the title or shows it. On module's I show my custom titles but on Articles, I many times hide them. It is all personal preferences.
- Enabled: Enables or Disables the module.
- Position: This is all the positions the module can be placed in on your website. The positions are based on the template. The template defines the placement of modules on the page.
- Order: This is what order the module will be placed based on the position. This was discussed in the Module Manager section.
- Access level: This was discussed in the Module Manager section
- Menus: All you to select what page the module will fall on. If you select "All" it is all pages in the website. If you select Menu Item from list, then based on the Menu Selection box, the pages will only show up in that place. Go back and look at Example Pages in the Module Manager. Notice how the menu

only shows up on certain pages and on the front page it shows up under Key Concepts.

We will cover Parameters later in this book.

Now, let's go back and change the Login Module position to the right side, and put it in the first or second position after polls. Change the Position box to Right and the Order to 0:Main Menu.

Another word of advice, when in Joomla do not hit back space, always save and exit the screens through the icons. If you backspace you end up locking up modules and we have conduct a Global Check-in which we will discuss next. Notice the Login Form has moved. You can play around and move modules around your website.

**Figure 36: Login Form Module moved to Right Side**

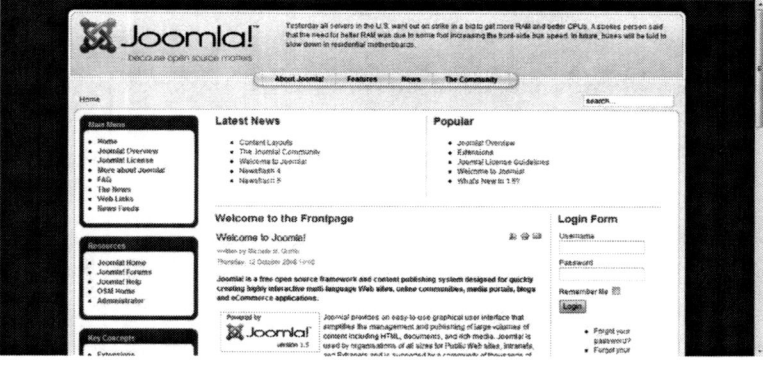

# Global Checkin

This is important to know and understand. When you exit a screen in Joomla it is best to Save or Cancel; pressing the back button causes some session to lock up. To test a session locking up do the following.

Go back into the Login Form we just discussed in the previous Chapter. Instead of hitting save or cancel, click the back button in Internet Explorer . This will cause the module manager to lock up. To unlock you can do one of two things. Go back into the module and exit it properly using Save or Cancel. Or use the Global Check-in.

The global check-in is found under on the toolbar under Tools/ Global Check-in. Do you see in the figure below, I have two sessions locked. They are showing with a checkmark. Just entering the session re-checks all sessions back in. Pretty simple and straight forward, but can be a nuisance if you work fast and a session locks on you. Therefore handy to know.

Figure 37: Global Check-in

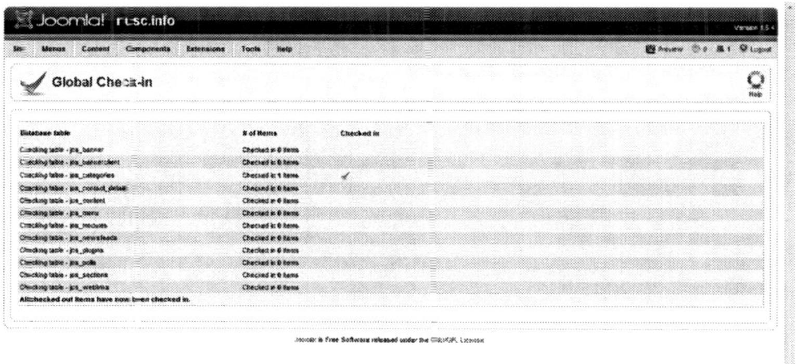

# File Manager

Before we get into the aesthetics and the articles of your website, we need to learn about files and permissions.

In order to access the file manager you will need to open your Cpanel again.

Go back to the Cpanel section to review how to log in.

**Figure 38: Cpanel**

Under Files this is an icon labeled File Manager. Double click on this icon.

The following box opens up. Select Web Root and check the box for hidden files then press GO.

82    Joomla!™ 1.5

**Figure 39: File Manager Selection**

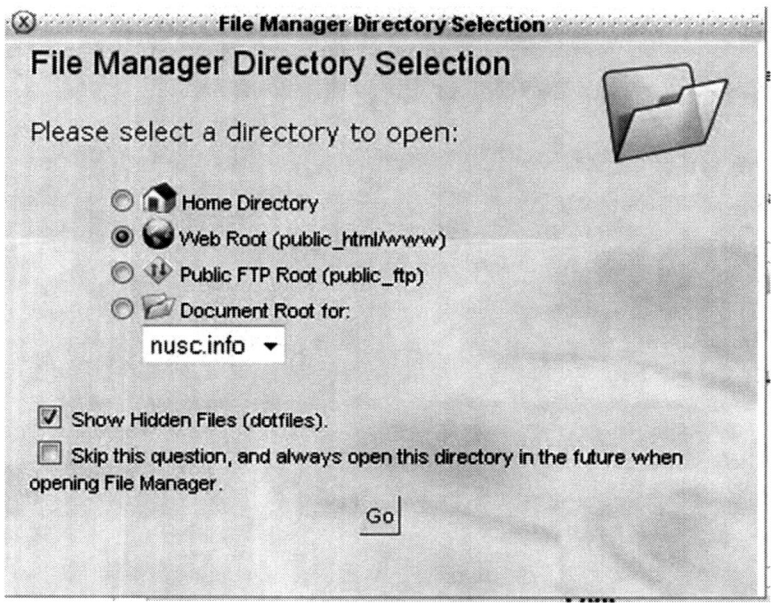

The view below show be what you see once you press GO.
**Figure 40: File Manager View**

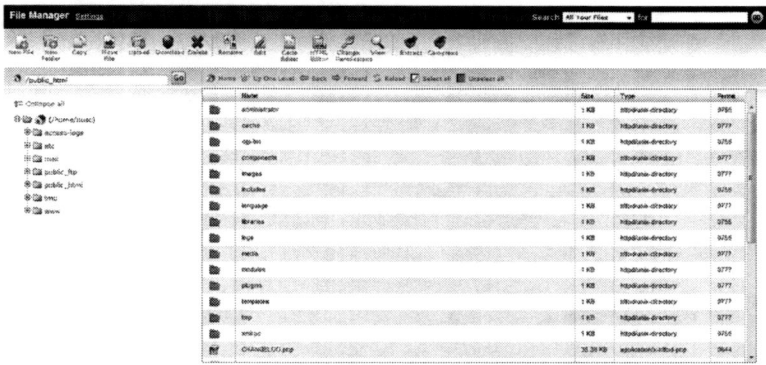

Before we change anything, you need to learn about permissions.  When you look to the far right column on the

File Manager Permissions 83

diagram on the previous page, you see numbers 777, 755, 644 these are permissions on the file. These numbers are critical to security of your site. You do not want people to screw up your website, because you left permissions open where anyone can access your files.

The first number means Owner permissions

The second number means Group permissions

The third number stands for World permissions (basically anyone anywhere)

**Figure 41: File permissions**

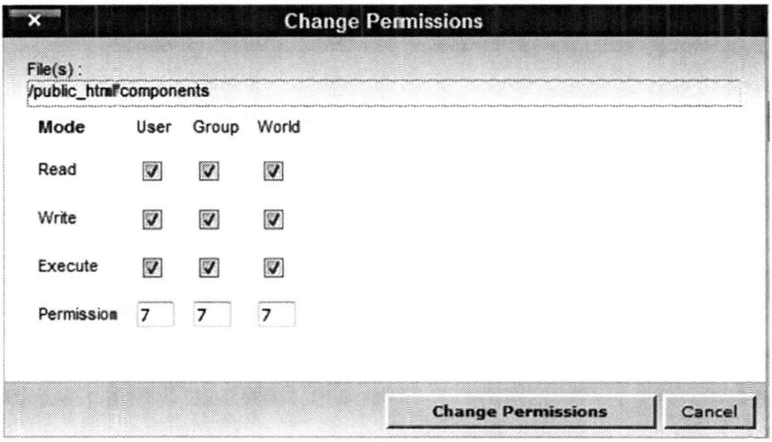

Within each number there are different numbers based on read, write or execute access. Permissions is defined in UNIX as:
- r- Read permission - is either a 4 or -
- w– Write permission – is either a 2 or -
- x- Execute permission – is either a 1 or –

For example if a permission is set at 777, this means the following:

Owner   Group   World
rwx     rwx     rwx
421     421     421

Now, let's say the permissions are 755, this means the owner can do everything but group and world can read or write:

Owner   Group   World
rwx     rwx     rwx
421     4-1     4-1

Another example, is 644, this is typically used for system files or folders:

Owner   Group   World
rwx     rwx     rwx
42-     4--     4--

So now that you know about permissions, we need to modify a few file permissions and then once we are done with the files we need to change them back.

The first thing we have to do is rename the .htaccess file. If you notice it is only 0 bytes. This is a dummy file. We need to replace it with the htaccess.txt file which is the file the bots search for from the search engines. Without this file in place the search engines cannot find your website. This is the 1st step in any SEO optimization process.

We need to do is rename the .htaccess file to htaccess1.txt. You must remove the period in front of the htaccess file and then rename it. This file is renamed by clicking on the name in the file manager and click okay.

File Manager Permissions  85

Second, we need to rename htaccess.txt to .htaccess. You must add the period in front of the htaccess and remove the .txt.
Your directly should look like this now.

**Figure 42: htaccess file change**

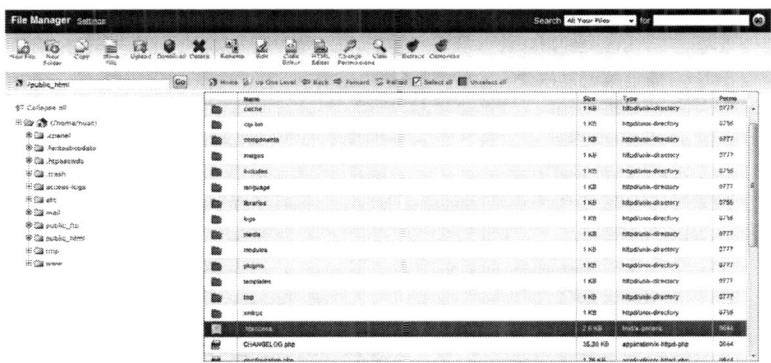

The item we need to change is the configuration.php file. This file controls the backend of Joomla and also allows your website to begin to increase its rankings when searched for on search engines. Notice this file is 644 permissions; we need to change it to 777. Make our changes in Joomla and then change it back to 644. This file is very critical; to security therefore do not forget to change it back.

Highlight the line for configuration.php. Now if you click to much there will be other lines highlighted. This is annoying. You will need to click off the other lines, make sure only the configuration.php line is highlighted. Then go to the tool bar on top and click on the change permission icon.

This pops up the following screen:

**Figure 43: Change Permission screen**

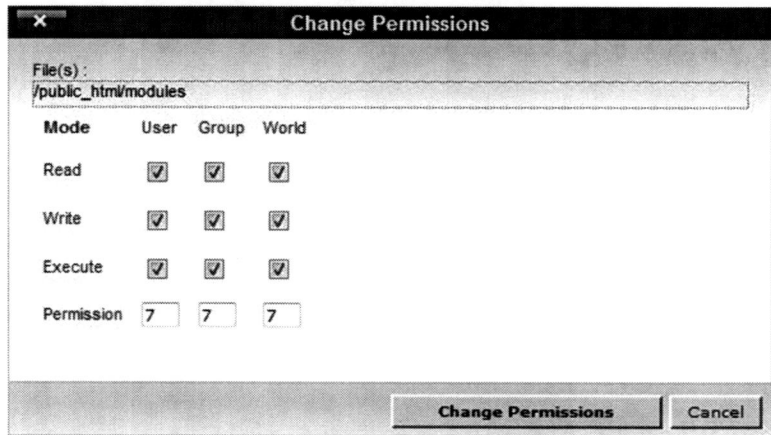

Change it to 777 by checking all the boxes. Click change permissions.

Okay, now let's go back into the Joomla dashboard; leave the cpanel open and the file manager. We will be coming right back to it. You will probably have to log back in.

# Updating Global Configuration

When you are back at the main dashboard, go to the toolbar. The first selection on the toolbar is site. If you place your mouse over this a drop down menu appears and you need to select GLOBAL CONFIGURATION.

**Figure 44: Configuration.php file**

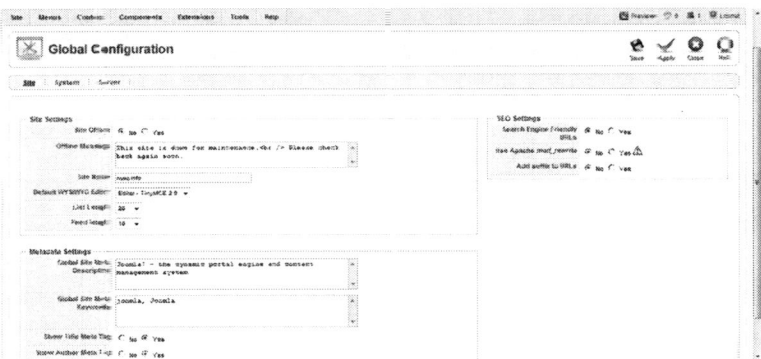

The first thing we are going to do is reset the SEO settings. In order to increase your site rankings you have to have friendly names and you must have .html show up as suffixes on your URL's (site address). This area is critical to your site rankings.

To do this right, you must follow these directions.

First under SEO Settings change the Search Engine Friendly URL's to YES then click the save icon. (DO NOT CHANGE ANYTHING ELSE).

This sends you back to the main dashboard. There should be a Blue line, which states the global configuration file was updated.

### Figure 45: Global configuration Dashboard

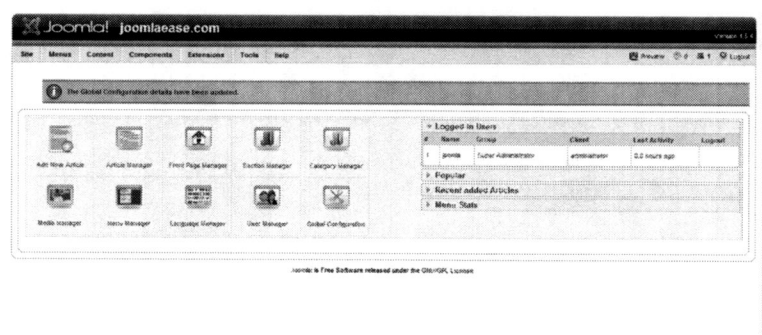

Go back into the Global Configuration file. Again it is under Site/ Global Configuration.

Now, we need to update the SEO Setting for Add Suffix to URL's. Change this to YES and click Save again.

Finally, go back into the Global Configuration again. Under SEO Setting change Apache Mod_rewrite to YES and click Save.

Now, the SEO section is done for now.

We want to go back into the Global Configuration file and we will update the meta data. Meta data is what search engine's use to show your site when a key word is used.

Under Global Site Meta Description, delete the text which is there and enter a description as to what your site does.

Then under Global Site Meta Keywords enter all the keywords someone would search for your site in the search engines. The words are separated by a comma. Do not use sentence only keywords. Below is how your configuration file should look. Do not change anything else at this time.

**Figure 46: Global Configuration**

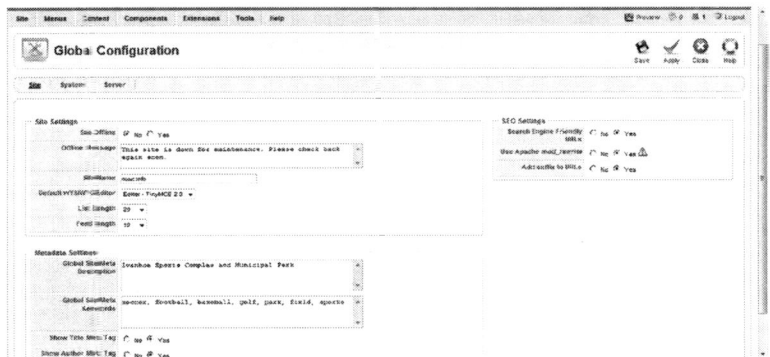

Now we need to go back and reset the permissions to 644 from 777.

Go back to your Cpanel screen File Manager.

You will need to refresh the screen or the Change Permission icon will not work.

Highlight the configuration.php file and click the change permissions icon on the toolbar.

Change the boxes to the following:

**Figure 47: Permissions**

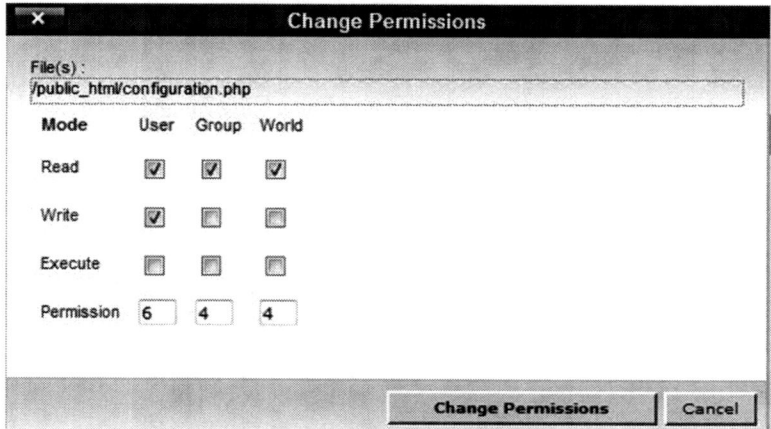

# Templates

Now that we fixed the Global configuration file, we will modify the template. In order to modify the standard template, we have to change the permissions of the file which manages the template.

First, lets go into the Joomla dashboard and look at the templates; on the dashboard toolbar go to Extensions/Template Manager. Joomla! 1.5 comes with 2 templates. But, you can subscribe to services where additional templates can be purchased. I subscribe to Rocket Themes. They have versatile templates and have never found an error in them. Plus they are always coming up with new stuff.

**Figure 48: Template Manager**

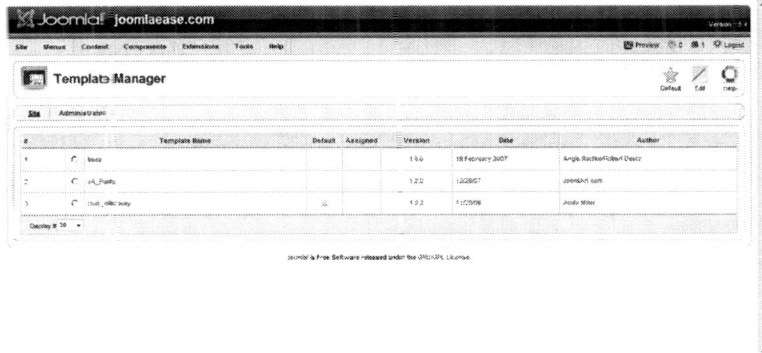

If you notice there are two templates pre-installed. Let's change the default template from rhuk_milkay to beez. You do this by clicking the circle in front of the template name and then clicking the default icon. Now go back to your website and refresh the page. You should not see the page has changed to the new template as shown in the figure.

### Figure 49: Beez Template

Let's go back and change the default to the JA Purity template. Then refresh your website.

### Figure 50: JA Purity

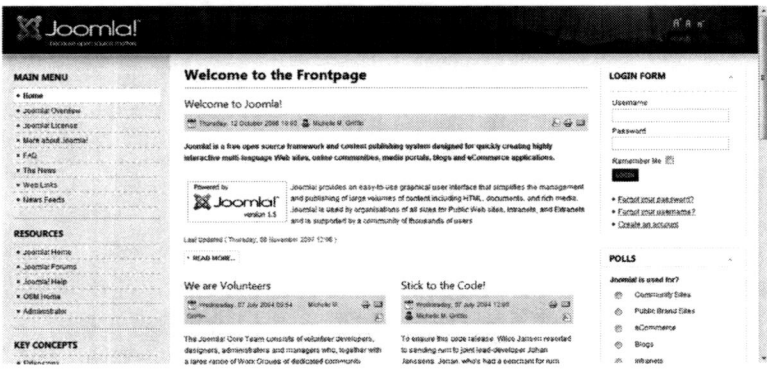

This template is a really nice default template. Until you have your Logo designed you can add your organizations name within the template. There are also quite a few variations. Let's keep this as our main template and tweak it to fit your needs for your site.

Go back to your Joomla Dashboard and reset your template to the original template. Click on the circle in front of the template name and click Default. Refresh your website; it is back to the original look. Now let's begin to tweak the template. Click on the template name and it takes you to the configuration screen.

**Figure 51: JA Purity Template Configuration**

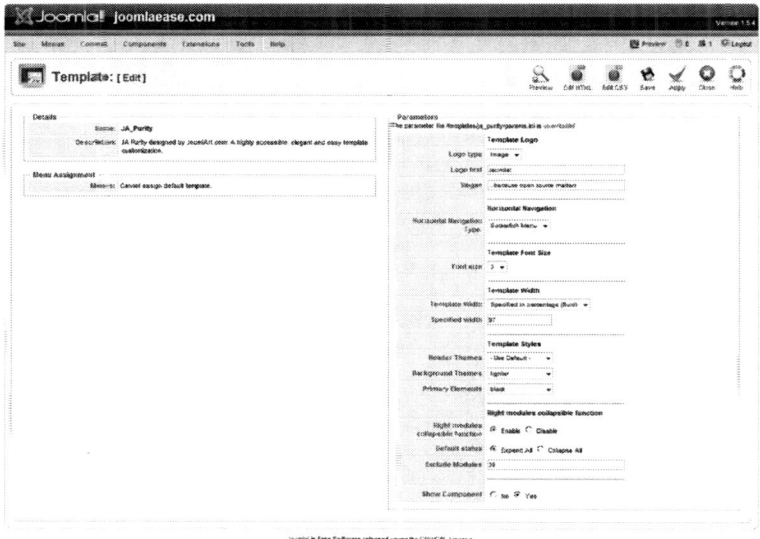

Now there are a few modifications you can do with this for instance changing the Joomla logo at the top of your site. Type in the Logo text you would like to have appear then click save. Then refresh your website.

If you noticed nothing changed. The reason why is because the file is unwritable. Go back to the Joomla Dashboard and back to the Template Manager.

Click on the Template name for JA Purity; notice the right hand side above the template logo it says the params.ini file is unwritable; to change anything on the template we need to change the permissions of the params.ini file.

Go to the Cpanel File Manager (remember we did this in the last chapter).

The params.ini file is located in the Template folder, in the name of the template we are using which is JA Purity. (Double click Templates then double click JA Purity).

**Figure 52: Params.ini file location**

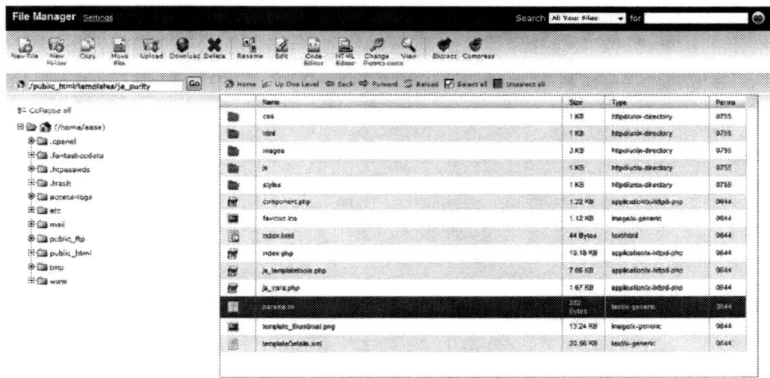

Open up the template folder and highlight the params.ini and change the permissions to 777. The changing of permissions was discussed in the previous chapter, if you forgot how to do this.

Once you change the permissions, leave the File Manager open, because we will need to change the permissions back to 644.

## Figure 53: Change Permissions Params.ini

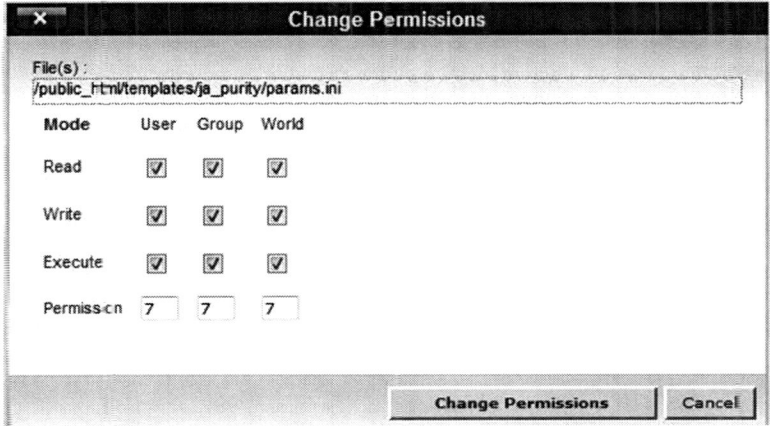

Go back to the Joomla Dashboard to the Template Manager (Extensions). Change the following:
1. Logo Type to Text
2. Logo Text - Enter your Company name
3. Slogan - Enter your Phone Number
4. Refresh your website

This is a simple logo, but will suffice until you are right to upload your logo image in a few chapters.

Let's change some of the other settings within this template.

Since we are playing, change a setting and refresh your website, see what it changed. If you like it keep it otherwise change your site until you like what see.

The next change I made is Background Themes to PureWhite and the primary elements to Red.

### Figure 54: JA Purity PureWhite Background

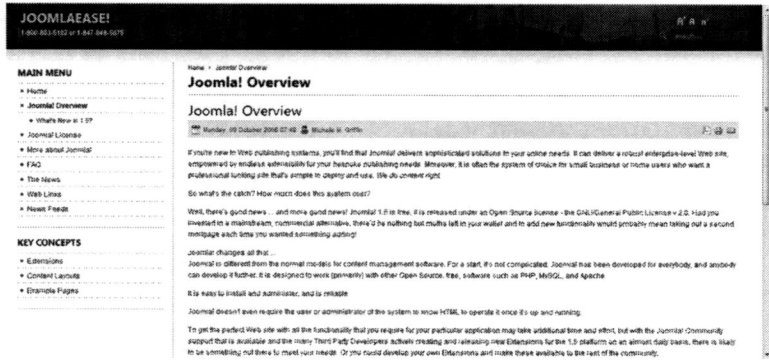

Now that we have looked at the JA Purity template, do not forget to go back and change the permissions in the CPanel File Managers /params.ini file.

While you are there go into rhuk_milkway and change it params.ini file so you can look at the different variations for this template.

### Figure 55: Rhuk_Milkway

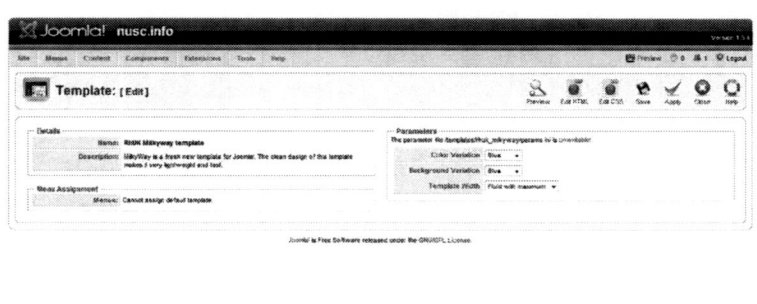

If you look on the right hand side there is a Color Variation and Background Variation buttons.

Just change the color and click save. Then go back to your website and refresh the screen to see the effect. Given this book is black and white, I can not show you the color changes.

Templates add a flavor to your website; it makes it personal and unique. There are many companies on the internet who have free templates or templates you pay for. Some of the sites with free templates are:
- www.joomla24.com
- www.rockettheme.com
- www.joomlashack.com
- www.spiderweby.com

Many webhosters give you free templates access when you subscribe to their hosting service for a year. There are a 1000's of templates to choose from which are free or you pay a minimal amount. At www.spiderweby.com they offer you full support with access to many templates. Just remember you are looking for Joomla 1.5 templates.

A sidenote: There are 1000's of Joomla modules and templates you can download and use on your site. In order to keep them organized, I recommend keeping a Joomla folder or a download folder in your documents folder where all your modules and templates are stored on your computer.

**Figure 56: Window Explorer IPOD as Extra Drive**

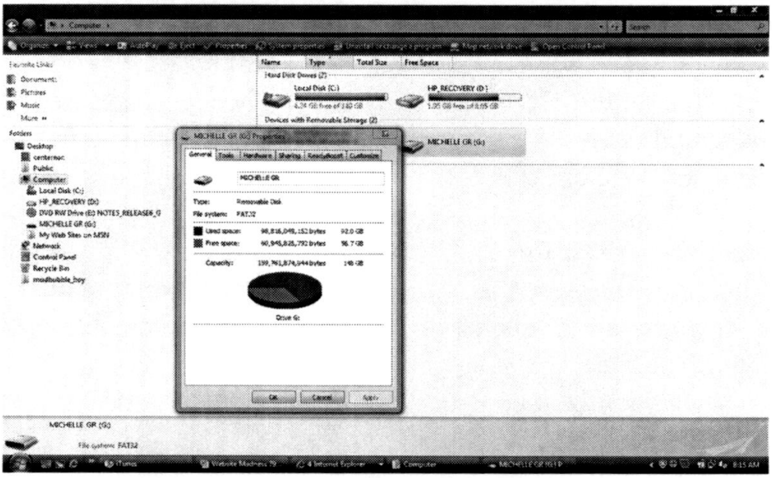

If you have a hard drive which is pretty full, many people don't know their IPOD by Apple is an extra hard drive.

I have a 160 GB IPOD hook to my computer all the time and store all my files on it, versus my laptop.

If you want to see how the IPOD works go to Windows Explorer or My computer, you will notice your IPOD as the G: drive.

I actually keep all my files on my IPOD then when I travel to a customer site, I can hook up to any computer if I don't want to pull out my laptop. I will show you how to download modules in the next chapter.

Side Note: This book is based on the latest version of Joomla 1.5. Do not load Joomla 1.0 Legacy, even though it says compatible I have found issues. Once you are experienced then you can decide if you want to turn on Legacy, which I will tell you how to do at the end of the book.

Templates 99

Let's show you how to install a template. I am going to use a template from www.rockettheme.com. Why did I choose Rocket Theme, because I like all the modules positions they provide versus many templates which only have the basic positions.

To install Templates you go to Extensions on the toolbar in your Joomla Dashboard; select Install/Uninstall.

Note, you go to the same place to install new templates, modules, and components all are straight forward.

**Figure 57: Install Template**

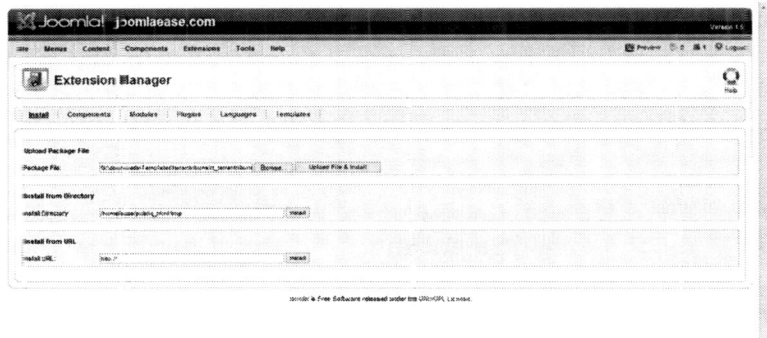

Browse for your template file. It will have the extension .tgz extension (this is a Unix file).

If the template or modules installed correctly the following screen will appear.

### Figure 58: Template Success

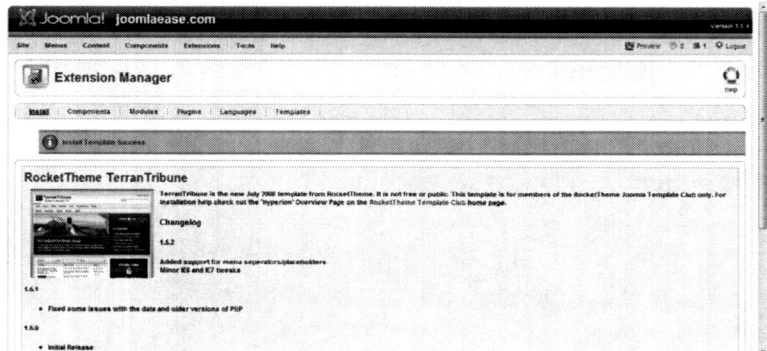

In order to change the template we have to go back to the Template Manager, under Extensions/Template Manager.

We then are going to change the template to Default. We learned this at the beginning of this chapter.

The next screen shot shows how a template can change the look of your website dramatically.

With this template it comes with 22 modules positions. See the flexibility by having extra module position allows.

For the next few chapters, I am going to use the JA Purity template. Therefore I will go back into Extensions/Template Manager and set it as my default.

## Figure 59: New Template Example

**Figure 60: Modules Position for Rocket Theme Template**

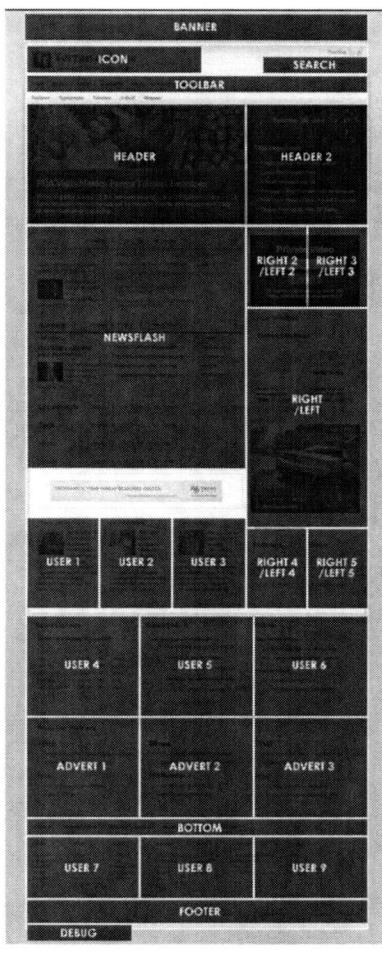

# Articles

We are now going to begin customizing the website with our own content. To change and add article content is located on the toolbar under Content/Article Manager.

**Figure 61: Article Manager**

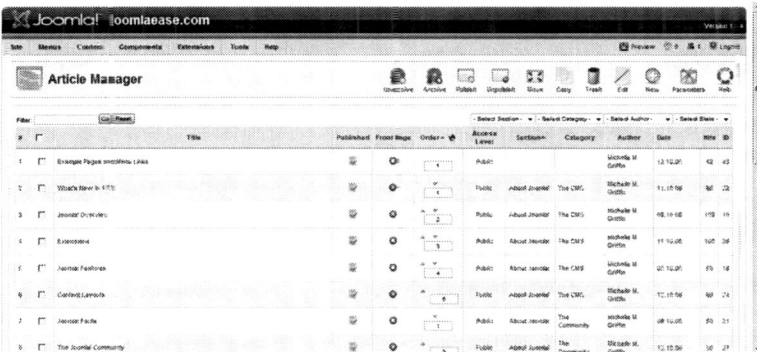

The functionality is pretty cool. There is a lot of functionality here so we will start with the basics, many of the columns functionality are the same as the Module Manager which we covered in a previous chapter.

• Checkbox- is used to activate an icon on the top of the screen, let's say publish or unpublish.

• Title- is the name of the article.

• Published- has a checkmark if published or a red circle with an x if not published.

• Front page – This is content which appears on the front page. If this is unchecked it will not appear on the front page of your website.

- Order – is the position of the article compared to other articles, which come at the top of the website.

- Access Level – is public or registered. Registered means they must have an account and be logged in.

- Section – These are defined by you. Each article must belong to a Section and Category. Security can also be applied to this, where let's say you are hosting a sports page and you have different editors. You can authorize users based on Sections to edit.

- Category – goes along with sections. There can be multiple categories within a section.

- Author – Who created and edited the article.

- Date- The date last edited

- Hits – How many people read the article.

ICONS

- Unarchive – put a file archived back into production

- Archive – place file in archive mode (when Archived the article is still there just grayed out, must be unarchived before it can be edited again.

- Publish – Show article on website

- Unpublish – Hide article from website

- Move – Select new Category for article

Articles 105

- Copy – Select article and copies existing article, marks it unpublished. Need to Change name and republish.

- Trash – sends articles to trash (does not really delete them until you go to Trash and finally delete them.

- Edit – Edit article, you can also click on the title to Edit.
- New – Create new article.

- Parameters- change global article settings.

**Figure 62: Article Parameters**

The parameters I changed are the following; it is personal preference if you change them.
- Author Name – Hide
- Created Date and Time - Hide
- Modified Date and Time – Hide

You can play around with the parameters as you build your site, to determine what you want on or off.

# Edit an Article

Since the sample Joomla data was loaded there are a load of articles to edit or we can create new. If you look at your website the main article is Welcome to Joomla, do you see it in the middle of the screen shot below. This article we need to find in the article manager. It is located on the second page with a section of NEWS.

If you don't want to search through the documents, if you knew the section was news you can filter the articles by looking up only Sections. Just below the icons there are filters. If you drop down the Select Section box, and pick NEWS it will show you only that section. Just remember once you turn on a filter the filter stays on until you log out.

**Figure 63: Welcome to Joomla**

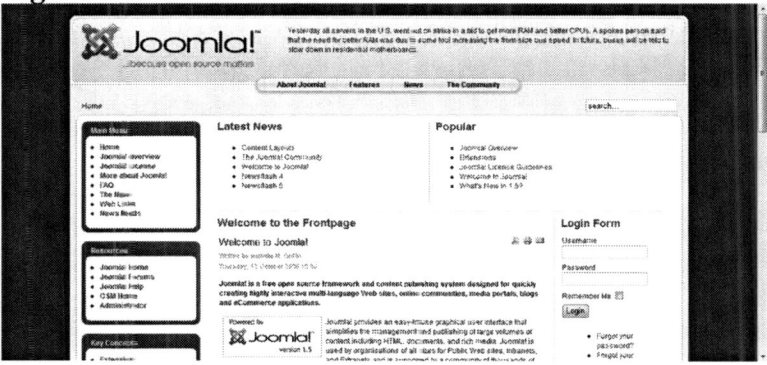

Also notice on the website front page, do you see the Author name and edit time, depending on the site, I am creating I hide this in the parameters screen as discussed above.

Let's click on the Welcome to Joomla article and look at the edit page.

This page, you notice has an image, as well as different bolded text. We need to add our own personal text in there. But first let's look at the editor.

**Figure 64: Welcome to Joomla Article**

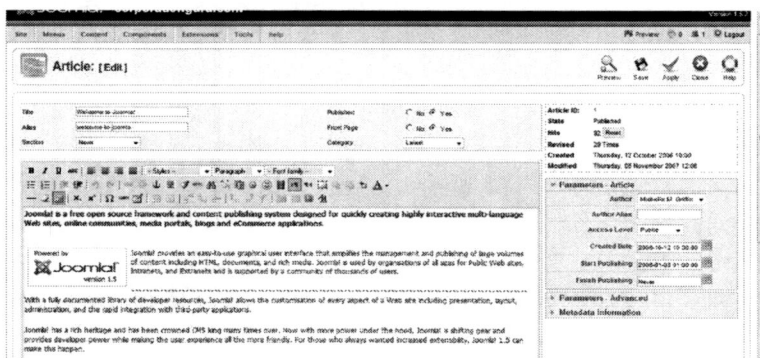

I myself prefer an enhanced editor. The TinyMCE editor can be enhanced by the JCE editor. This is the standard editor many people who use Joomla use. The differences are this

• if you drop down the Paragraph selector it shows Heading 1, Heading 2, Heading 3 but does not show you what it looks like.

• Under font family, it just list the fonts in plain text with the JCE Editor it enhances it showing what the fonts look like. There are also additional plugins which make the editor feel like a traditional word processor.

This is just a few differences, so I will walk you through the fields on this page. But then we will edit the article in the next chapter, after we install the JCE editor component.

# Edit an Article 109

The important features of the article screen are the following:
- Title – name of article, this will appear on the website.

- Alias – This needs to be a single word or multiple words tied together with a dash or underscore. This is used by the search engines to index your page. Therefore try to keep it simple but descriptive.

- Section – is the area this article belongs to. Every article must have a section and category

- Category – which category within the section does it belong.

- Published – Yes or No

- Front Page – Yes or No

Over on the Right there is Article Parameters, these are only changed if you want to. Otherwise they will use the global settings discussed earlier in this chapter.

The most important thing is the Meta Description and Meta Keywords. Remember we did it for the Global Configuration.

This is important to fill out; this will be found by the search engine robots. The more key information the higher you website will appear.

Just realize no matter what you do it takes 3 to 6 months for your website to move up the ranks. The more it is searched the better. If you made changes then save or if you have not then exit. Let's learn how to install the JCE editor

# Loading an Editor Component

If you are like me, you like to have an editor which is "What you see is What you get" (WYSIWYG).

There is an editor which comes with Joomla, it is called Tiny MCE is a WYSIWYG, but I change it to JCE Editor. You can use the Tiny editor or I will walk you through on how to install the JCE editor.
**Step 1**: Go to www.joomla.com (A good idea to register on this site, so you can look at the forums). Check out the Extensions Overview Chapter in order to see how to find Extensions on the Joomla Website
**Step 2:** On the toolbar on the Joomla website click Extensions (Now, don't get to excited there are 3,000 extensions, some are Non-Commercial (free) and some you pay for Commercial. You will learn how to download, and then you can experiment me on your site, after it is built. Just try to stay with Native 1.5 modules.

**Figure 65: JCE Reviews**

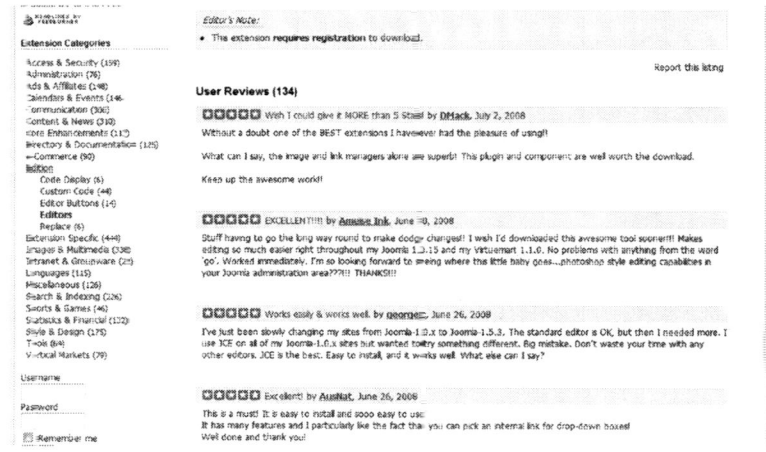

112    Joomla!™ 1.5

Step 3: You can search on this site for editors or scroll down to Edition/Editors and click on this link.

Step 4: Look for JCE – Note: when ever looking for a new module or component, look at the reviews. I have downloaded a few modules which break the site. I try to stay with stable versions which others have written about. Click on the Reviews link to see the reviews.

Scroll up the page, and press download. This will open a new screen. Which is the JCE homepage, some sites if you are downloading would like you to register.

**Figure 66: JCE Download**

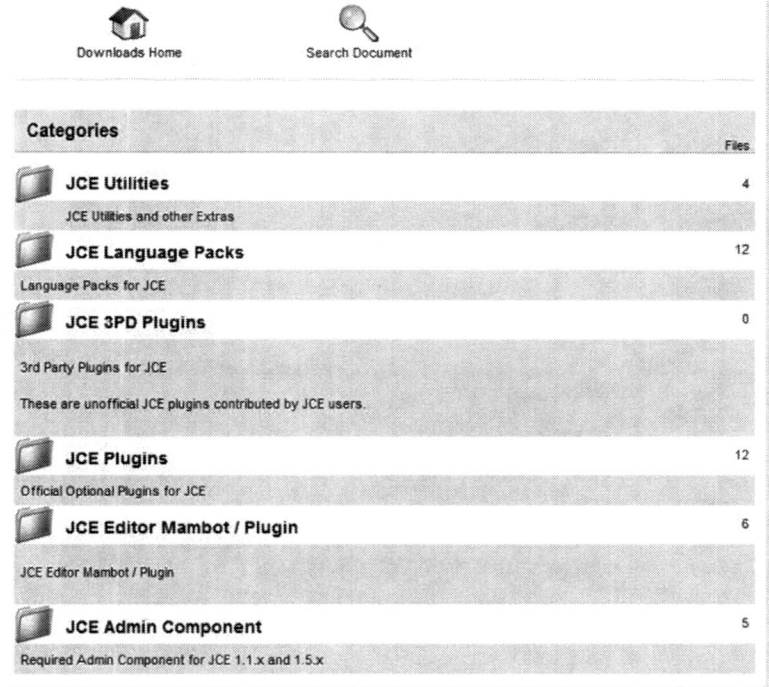

Loading an Editor Component  113

Side Note: There are different versions of modules and components. My recommendation is only use RC1 or above on your website. This is an officially released version. The releases follow the following:

• Beta 1 – Major revision or new module or component – Not PRODUCTION ready

• Beta 2 – Better than Beta 1 – NOT PRODUCTION READY

• Beta 3 & 4 – some modules may not go through this stage. This means still NOT PRODUCTION READY

• RC1 - Release Candidate 1 – means initial Production Ready (this means it can be used in production site, but there may be bugs.)

• RC2-RC4 – Enhanced released candidates- usually minor stuff being fixed. Usually when it passes RC2 – I will use it knowing it could break something or have bugs.

• Production – Is officially Production Ready – and ready for mass public use. Of course, there could still be bugs, which are never found until a lot of people are using it.

Now that you are on the JCE page, we are looking for the JCE Admin Component. Click on the link. It brings us to the download page.

We need the JCE Admin Component for Joomla 1.5. Click on this link it brings you to the download page.

114    Joomla!™ 1.5

**Figure 67: JCE download for Joomla! 1.5:**

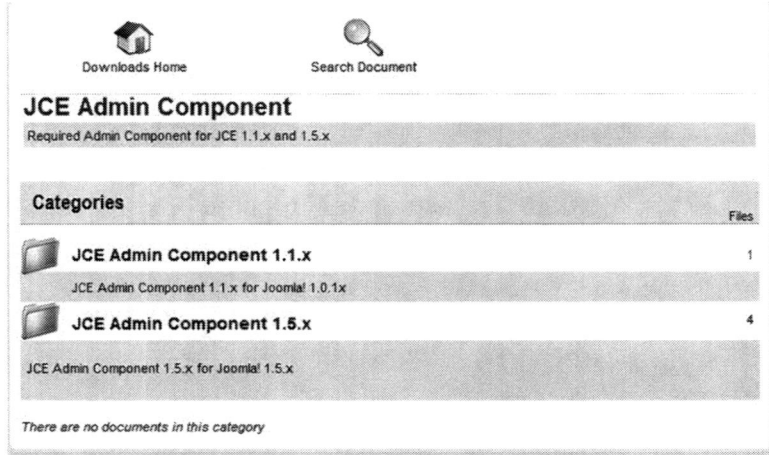

Click on JCE Administration component 1.5.0 the link has a yellow open box in front of it, see Figure 45.

**Figure 68: Saving a file**

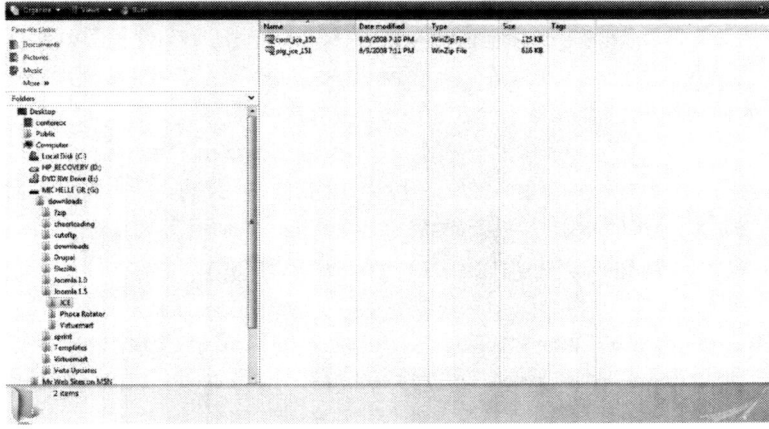

Loading an Editor Component  115

This pops up a box to run or save. You need to save it on your computer in the folder you created for Joomla files.

I recommend you create a subfolder for it also.

When the screen shows to save file, on the right side search for your folder where you are saving your Joomla files. Click new folder, name it the name of the download (JCE) and save the file to this folder.

**Figure 69: Download JCE**

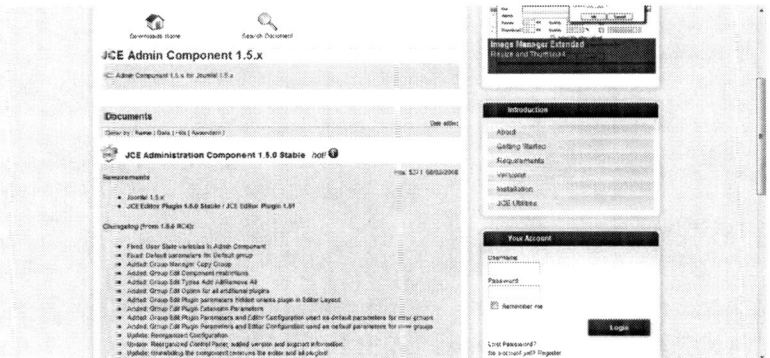

Before we leave we also need the Editor plug-in, which is required. Therefore use the back button on your Internet Explorer to go back a few screens. We want to be back on the following page.

### Figure 70: JCE Main Screen

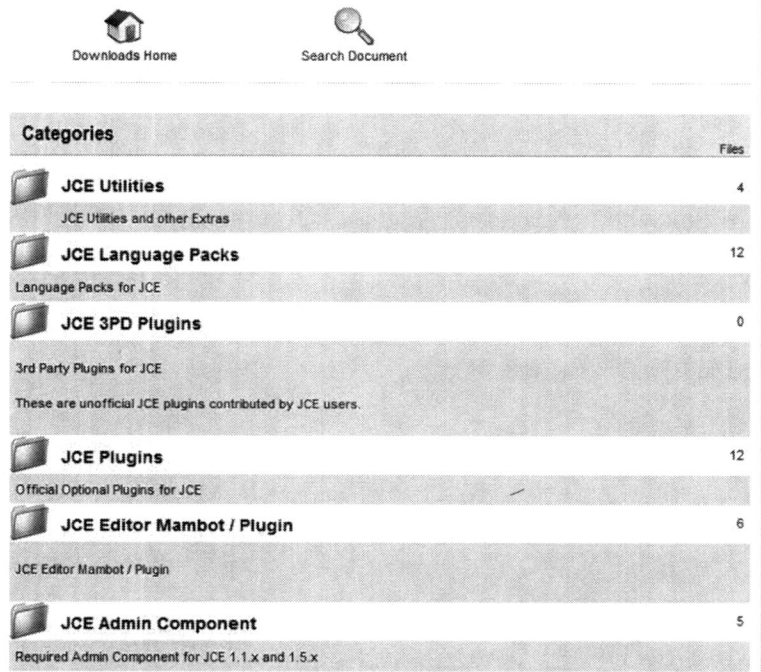

Click on the JCE Editor Mambot/Plugin hyperlink on the next screen click on JCE Editor Plugin for Joomla! 1.5.

### Figure 71: JCE Editor Mambot/Plugin

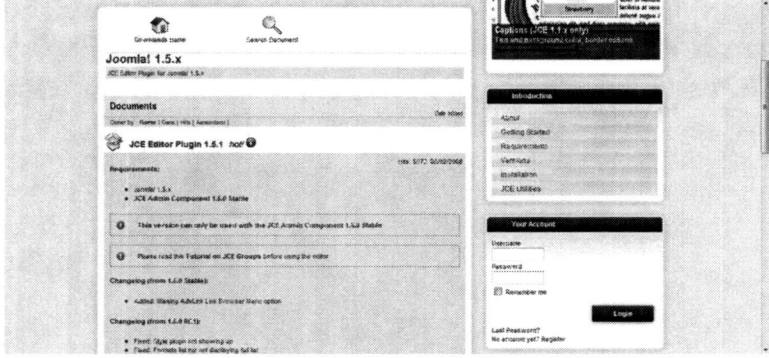

Loading an Editor Component 117

Download the JCE Editor Plugin the hyperlink with the yellow box next to it. Save it in the same folder as you saved the JCE Admin component.

Now, we close out of the Joomla website and JCE. Let's install the editor. Go back into your Joomla Dashboard; you may need to log in. Now we are going to install the JCE component. To do this, it is the same way install Templates. Go to Extensions Install/Uninstall.

Put your cursor in the Package Name field and browse for the file on your computer. Then click upload and install.

**Figure 72: Install JCE**

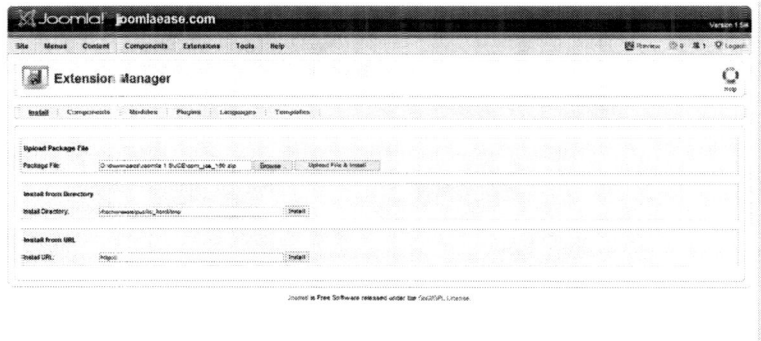

Scroll to the bottom of the install page, once the JCE Admin component successfully installs and browse for the JCE Editor plug-in. Click Upload file and install.

### Figure 73: JCE Install Success

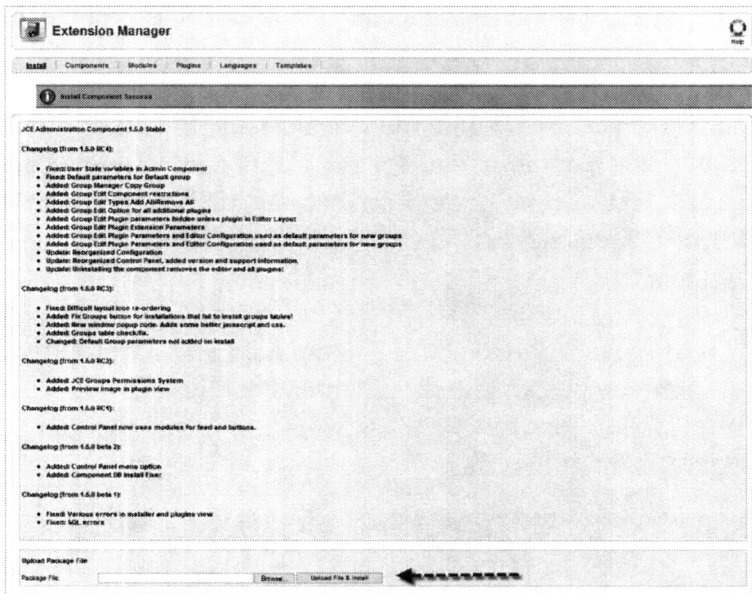

Now that we have changed the editor, we now need to update the editor in the User Manager or Global configuration.

### Figure 74: Global Configuration

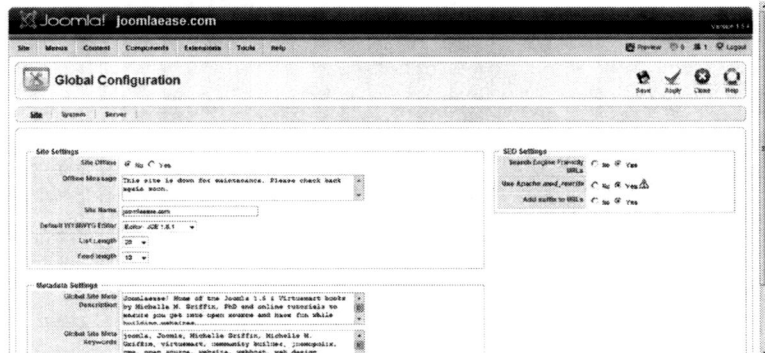

## Loading an Editor Component 119

If you want to update in the Global Configuration then refer back to the Global Configuration chapter. You will need to go in and change the permissions in File Manager for the configuration.php file to 777. Then go to Joomla and update the file. Don't forget to go back and reset the permissions to 644, when you are through.

To update in the User Manager, go to Site/User Manager. Click on your name. On the User Manager Detail sheet, change the User Editor to JCE.

**Figure 75: User Manager**

**Figure 76: User Detail**

While you are changing any users which were previously setup to JCE for the Editor also change the Time zone to your time zone.

Why do you want the JCE Editor, because it adds additional features to the editor to make similar to what we use today for word processing.

Let's go back into the article manager and edit the Welcome to Joomla article.

Open the article up by clicking on the article title. Then drop down the box for Format. If you remember under the other editor, it just said, paragraph, header1, header 2.

Now with JCE installed, it shows what each will look like, if you selected header 1, header 2, etc... If you look under Font, it now shows you what the fonts and font size will look like.

There are additional features, and you can also go out to the JCE website and download additional tool bars for additional WYSIWYG functionality.

**Figure 77: JCE Editor Format**

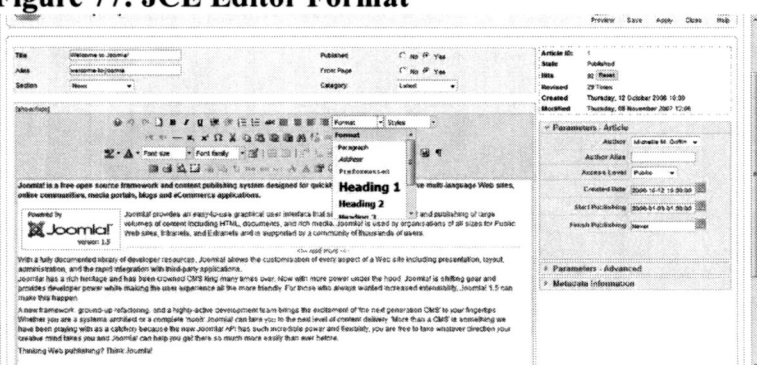

# Article Section Manager

Now that we have discussed the Article Manager and modified articles; we need to ensure that we have Sections setup in order for us to control where articles are published and on what page.

The Section Manager is located in the Joomla Dashboard under Content/Section Manager on the top navigational bar.

Sections are top level folders, where as Categories are sub-folders within the top level Folder.

Let's go in and change the Section names which are the defaults installed with Joomla.

**Figure 78: Section Manager**

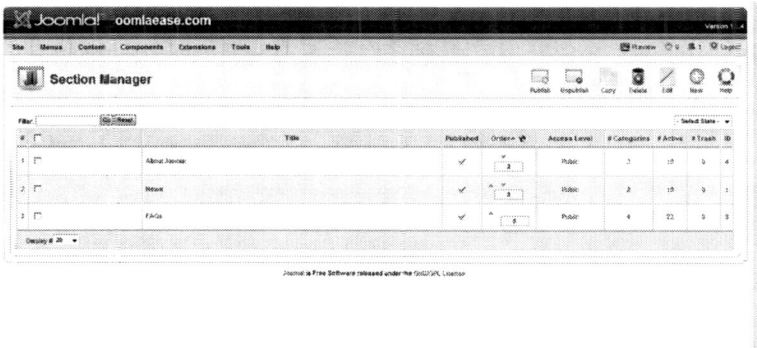

As you can see there are 3 default sections. Given I am creating a soccer website, I am going to name them Soccer Corner, Soccer News and Soccer FAQs. You can change yours to whatever you want to fit your site.

We can either modify the existing section which are there or delete them and create new ones. I am just going to modify them. To do this, just click the Title and it brings you to the Section Detail page, where I am going to change the Title and add a description. When finished click Save.

**Figure 79: Section Detail**

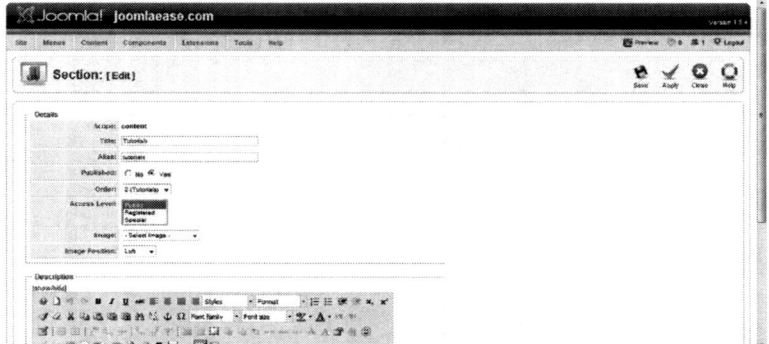

Go ahead and add all the sections you need.

**Figure 80: Section Manager Updated**

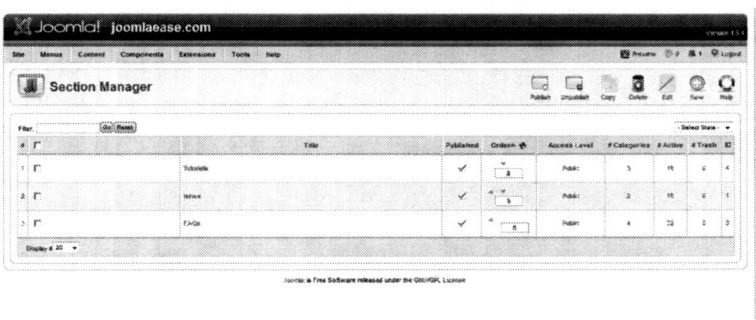

# Article Category Manager

A Category is a sub-item of a Section. There can be multiple categories within a section.

The category manager is accessed via Content/Category Manager.

**Figure 81: Category Manager**

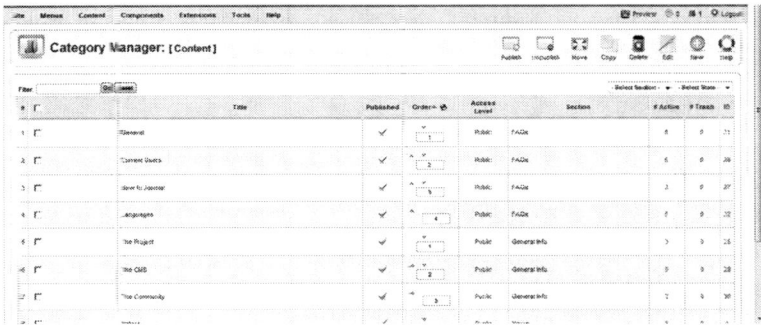

As with the section manager, you can either modify the default categories or delete them. If you look under Section you can see what section the category is tied to.

Go ahead and make changes to the Categories.

Note, it will not let you delete a category or a section if there is content still attached, meaning there is an article. You will need to go into the Article Manager and change the Section and Category if you want to delete them.

Let's edit the categories.

### Figure 82: Category Detail

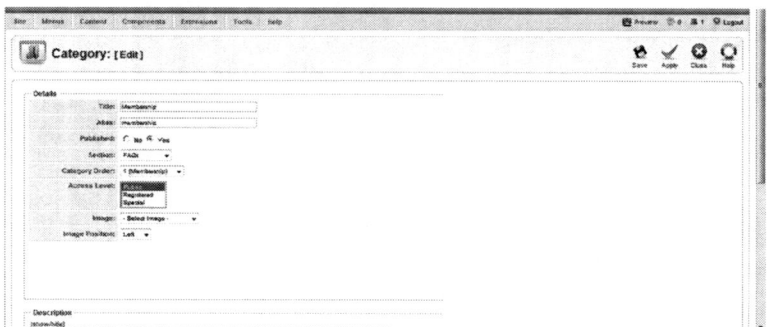

I am changing all of them to fit the soccer theme, I have created. Change yours to fit your site.

### Figure 83: Category Manager Changed

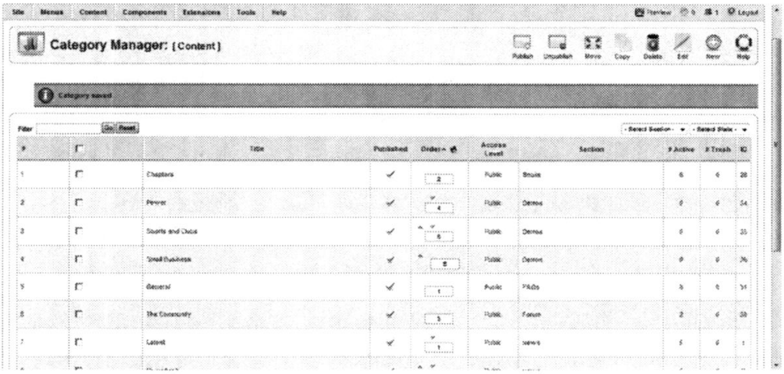

# Article Trash

In order to delete a Section or Category, there cannot be any article tied to it.

Even articles that have been deleted in the Article Manager are not really deleted. They are sent to the Article Trash.

Therefore you must go to the Article Trash to cleanup the deleted articles. The article trash is located in Contents/Article Trash. I have deleted a number of excess articles, in which we modified back in the article section.

**Figure 84: Article Trash**

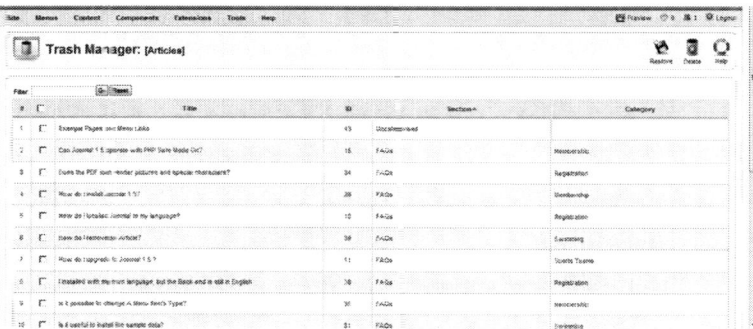

In my case, I am not going to be using the category Fees, which I created in the last chapter. Therefore I am going to delete it. But first I am going to delete all the articles in the trash, since they are generic to Joomla and I will not be using them.

Special note: You should read many of the articles, because it adds additional help on how to do certain topics in Joomla, which I may have missed in this book.

First check all the articles tied to the category or section you will be deleting. A category must be deleted before a section. Then once all categories are deleted then the actual section can be deleted.

Also, if you accidently deleted a document from the Article Manager, you can check the box in front of the document and click the Restore icon at the top of the screen.

**Figure 85: Permanently delete**

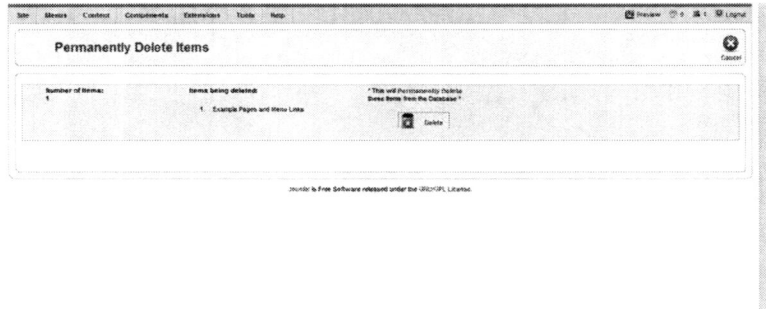

Select the documents you want to delete and press the Delete Icon. Then the permanently delete screen appears press the Delete button.

Now go back to your Category Manager, and check the category you wish to delete. Press delete. If it does not delete, it means there are still articles tied to it. You will need to go back to the Article Manager and Trash to find out what is tied to the category.

# Editing a Front Page Article

Let's go out and officially edit the Welcome to Joomla Front Page article. I am going to build a Business website focused on Joomla as part of the initial tutorial. You can build the same or create whatever site you would like. Remember it is easy to change, once you go through the tutorial the first time and then go back and re-create your site your way.

Open up the Welcome to Joomla Front Page article.
Step 1: Change the title to Welcome
Step 2: Change alias to welcome
Step 3: Leave Category and Section for now.
Step 4: Delete the Joomla Text
Step 5: You can write your content in word processor and paste it into the document or you can type your paragraph. Let's save and go out to or website and see how it looks.

**Figure 86: Joomla News**

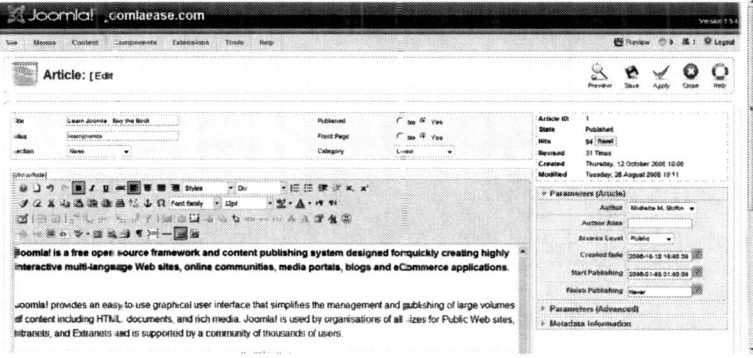

Now that you have changed this article, let's add a picture to it. Go out the internet and find a picture you would like to upload. It needs to be a jpg, gif or png file. I am going to add an image of my book.

128  Joomla!™ 1.5

Once you find an image you like you need to save it to your computer. To save to your computer, right click the image and click save as. Browse to the folder you save your Joomla files then save.

Let's add your image to your article, we created in this section. At the bottom of your article there is an image button. Before you click it, put your cursor where you would like the image added. I am going to add mine to the first line of the article in the center.

Therefore I am going to hit enter at the first line to add a line above the first line. Then click the center button.

   Then you go to the bottom of the article and click image. This pops up an image box. Browse for your file and click start upload. Now sometimes, the image does not load on the first time. I assume this is a minor bug, which isn't fixed at the time of this writing. If it does not appear with the other icons, just click browse again, find your file and click start upload. It should be there now.

**Figure 87: Adding an article image**

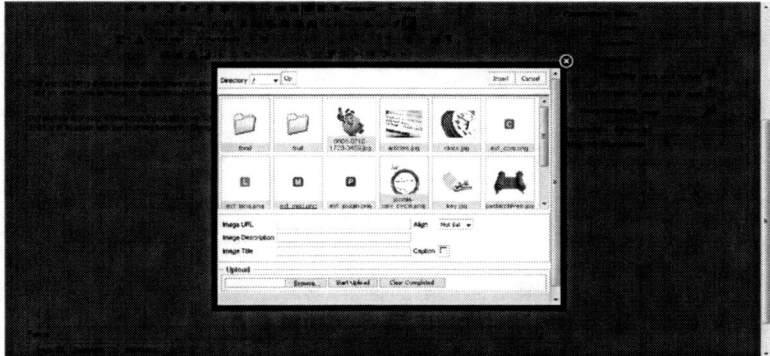

**Figure 88**: Article Detail

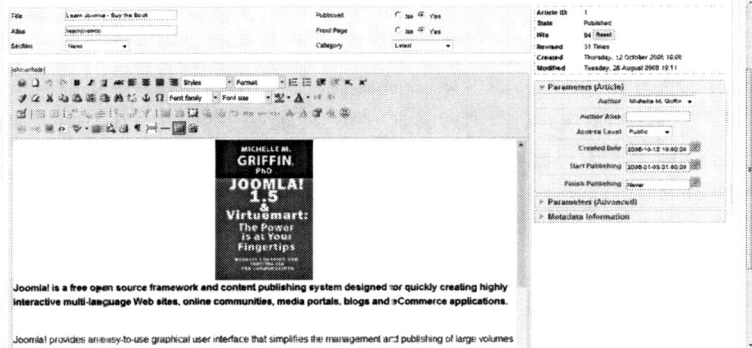

I have never had to upload an image more than twice. Once the image appears, click on it then click Insert. Your image should be in your article, now click save. Refresh your website and look at your new article.

**Figure 89**: Website

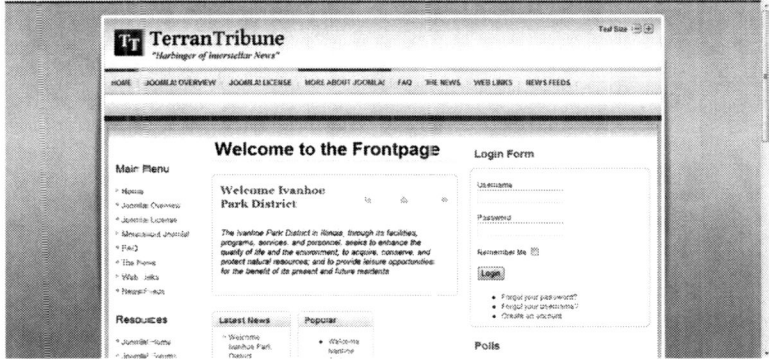

Now that you know how to change articles, any articles with the section NEWS are appearing on this front page, either edit the articles or unpublish them, to further customize your website.

Look through the other articles on the front page, if you are not going to use them then unpublish them or send them to trash, do this for all sections.

Side Note: When you have a long article, click the read more button at the bottom. This will break your article, where only a little content will show on the Front Page and if you click read more, it will take you to a new screen.

# Polls

Your website is coming along with your own content. Let's modify the polls to be a survey based on our website. My poll is going to be about "What is your favorite sport?"

To do this, you need to go to Components/Polls.
Step 1: Click the Joomla Poll under Poll Title
**Figure 90: Poll Manager**

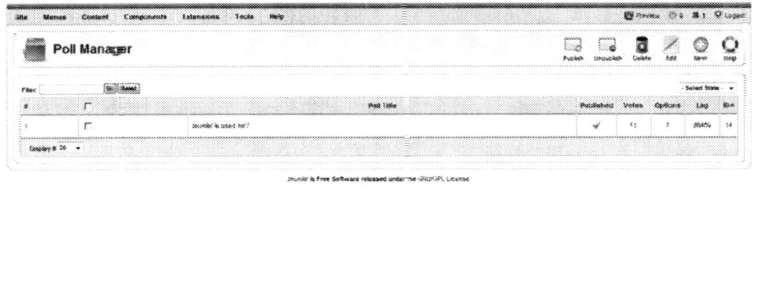

Step 2: Rename the title - mine is "What type of company are you?"
**Figure 91: Poll Detail**

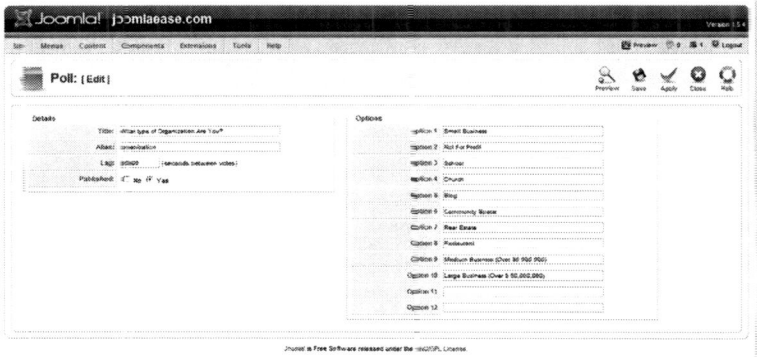

132    Joomla!™ 1.5

Step 3: Rename the alias; I am calling mine – business

Step 4: Replace the options on the right hand of the screen and click save.

Refresh your website, how does your poll look?

**Figure 92: Poll changed**

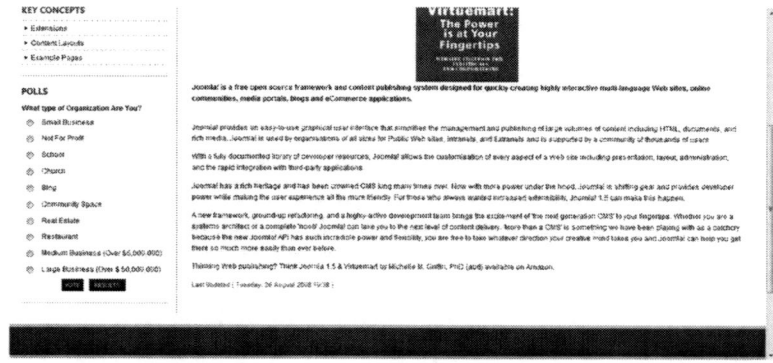

# Menu Manager Overview

Since we have customized the articles, let's now customize the menus. The first thing we need to do is change the "Welcome to the Front Page" statement, to something which fits our site. To change this statement we need to go to Menu on the Joomla Dashboard.

There are different types of menus
• Main menu – which is the main navigational menu on all pages
• User menu – which is setup for registered users to see special areas
• Top menu – special navigation or articles for people to go to.
• Custom Menu – you can create your own menu

Let's go through the columns on the Menu Manager screen. To access the Menu Manager go to Menu/menu manager.

**Figure 93: Menu Manager**

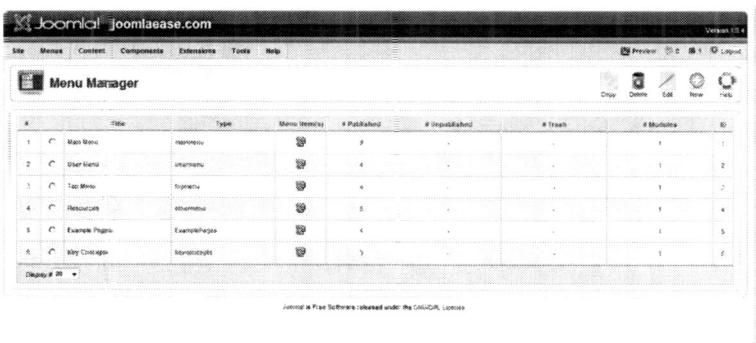

The columns are the following:
• # is the unique identifier of the menu, notice there are 6 menus. You can create as many menus as you would like.

- Title: is the name of the menu. To change the name just click the menu name.
- Type: is the type of menu this needs to be one word with no spaces
- Menu Items – allows you to edit the menu
- # Published – The number of menu items within this menu.
- # Unpublished – The number of menu items which are unpublished.
- # Trash – The number of menu items in trash
- # Modules – Modules tied to the menu. Main menus are article based, this tracks how many modules are tied to the menu.
- Id – a unique identifier

Let's click on the Menu Items and look at the detail menu screen for sub menu items.

Let's go to the main menu first, to change the "Welcome to the Front Page". Go to menu/main menu.

**Figure 94: Main Menu**

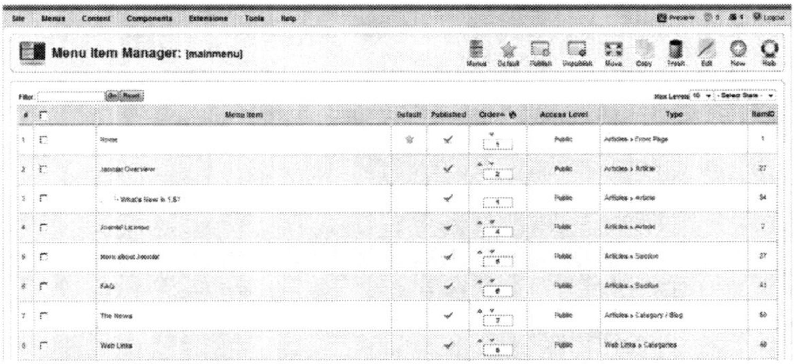

Menu Manager Overview 135

Note: Short cuts, instead of using the menu manager just go directly to the menu under the Menu dropdown.

Let's double click on the menu item "Home". On the right hand side there is the drop down arrows. The arrow we need to select is "system".

You will see the page title. Change this to something appropriate for your website.

**Figure 95: Home Menu Parameters**

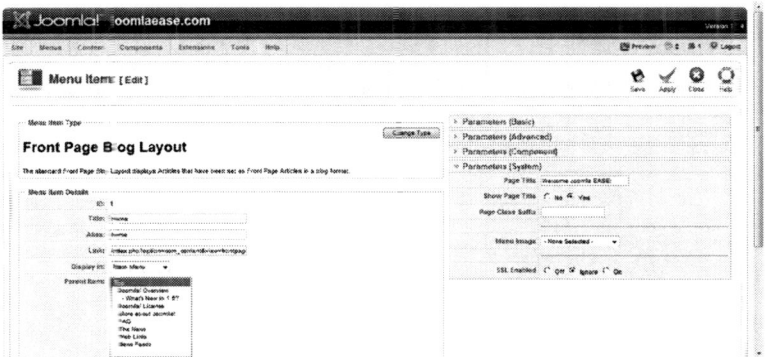

Since, I am building a business site, I am going to type: "Welcome to Joomla Ease!"

After you change it, click the save icon. Now, refresh your website.

Your website should now show your new title.

## Figure 96: Website changed to JoomlaEase

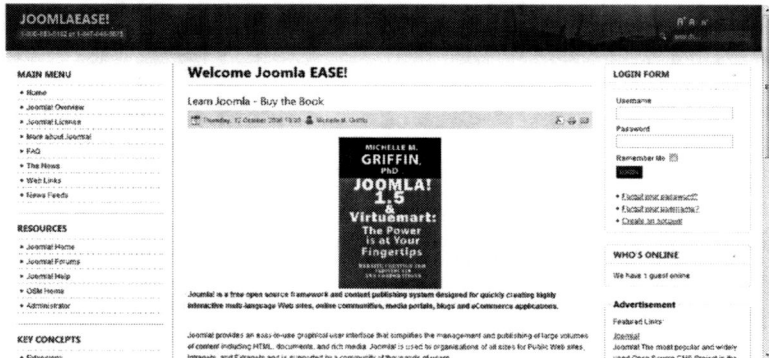

# Modify Main Menu

Let's start modifying the links on the main menu. This is the module box in the left hand column. Even though your template may be different, the websites should look similar.

**Figure 97: Website**

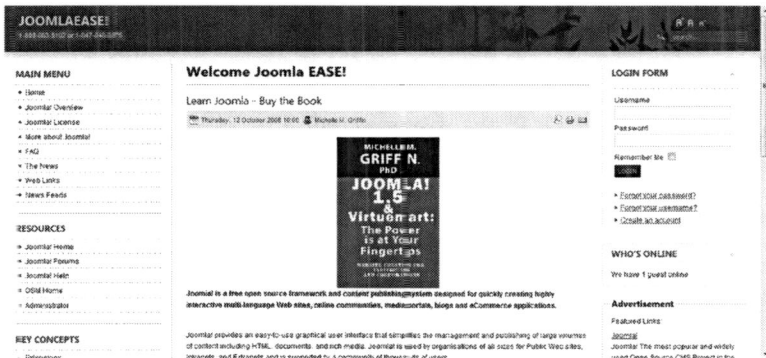

To do this we need to go to the Joomla Dashboard and highlight the menu toolbar. Before we went to Menu Manager this time we are going to go directly to the Main Menu.

**Figure 98: Main Menu**

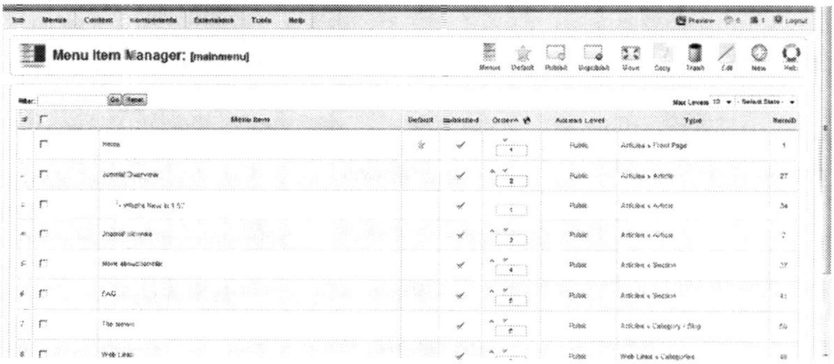

The Main Menu is your main menu. There must be at least 1 menu published within Joomla.

We can either trash the menu items which are there or modify them. In the case with the soccer website, I wish to set up teams,

Therefore I am going to delete a few. To delete you check the box in front of the menu item you wish to delete and press the trash icon. I am going to delete anything with Joomla in it.

Let's setup a new menu item called Teams. Click the New Icon. The following page pops –up

**Figure 99: New Menu Item**

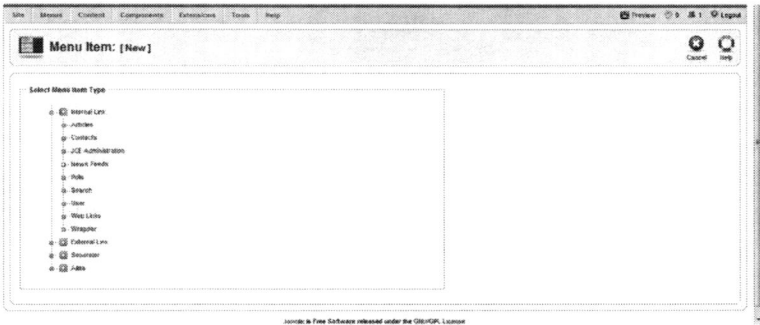

When creating a new menu item, there are many selections to choose from; below is a summation of the types of menus.
• Articles: This links to articles (Most used menu item)

• Contacts – this displays all contacts or a single contact

• Components – JCE Administration is a component, components can be setup as menu item if for instance you have someone else maintaining them or to access them the component it is through the menu. We will learn more about this when we install more components.

- News Feed – uses the component Newsfeed categories or it can display a single newsfeed.

- Poll – shows the component polls which we already have setup as a module. But if you had multiple polls this comes in handy as a menu item.

- Search – allows you to put a search link on your menu

- User – shows a list of users or a single user

- Weblinks – shows the Component Weblink which can be selected via categories or a single link.

- Wrapper – A wrapper allows you to have a link to an outside website but the frame is your site. The advantage to Wrappers is the viewer or customer never leaves your site, which means they come back to your site when finished. I use wrappers quite a bit.

- External Link – is similar to a wrapper, but they leave your site with no way back unless they hit the back button or re-type your site name.

- Separator – is placeholder for sub menu items

- Alias – An alias allows you to bring up similar content under a different name. Let's say you are running a blog. It allows you to have multiple blogs with different names.

Now, that we know the different types of menu items. We are going to create a menu item named Team. Since team is a separator of other categories for instance Boys teams and Girls teams we are going to select this.

Click New Icon to create a new menu item. Then let's click separator.

**Figure 100: Menu Item Detail**

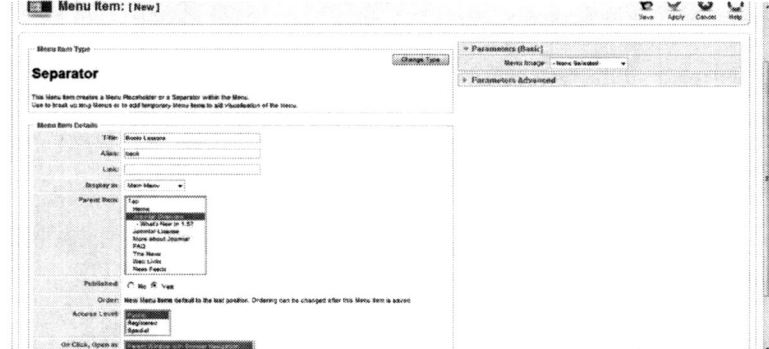

- Enter your title for you new menu
- Enter your alias (remember one word)
- Parent Item: You can link this item below another item as a submenu. If it is a main menu item then leave it Top
- Published – Yes or No
- Access Level – Is it open to the public or registered
- On Click, Open to: When your menu is clicked you can have it Open within the main window or open a whole new browser. Browser navigation means you can hit the back arrow key to go back to the previous site.

Go ahead and change all your main menu's to fit your site.

Now that you have added a few top level menus, let's add a

Modify Main Menu 141

submenu. To add a submenu you add a menu just like previously. But when you on the Menu Item Detail level, assign a menu level other than top in the parent item box.

**Figure 101: Sub Menu Detail**

By adding sub-items you are now developing drill downs within your site.

**Figure 102: Website**

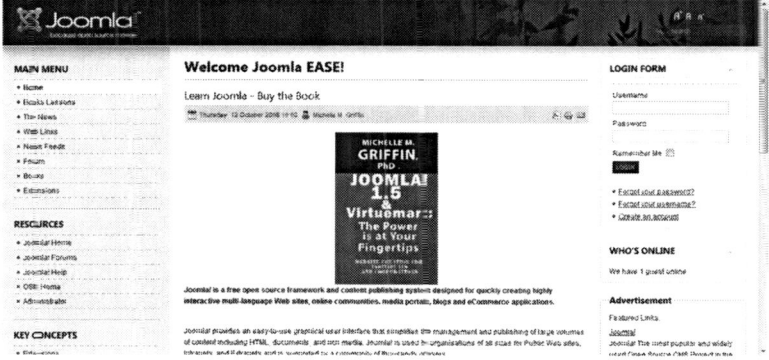

# Weblinks

Joomla is nice because you can setup Weblinks easily to your favorite sites. Weblinks are good, because it gives you more exposure within the search engines.

The first thing we need to do is go to our Joomla Dashboard and click on Component/Weblinks/Links.

**Figure 103: Weblinks**

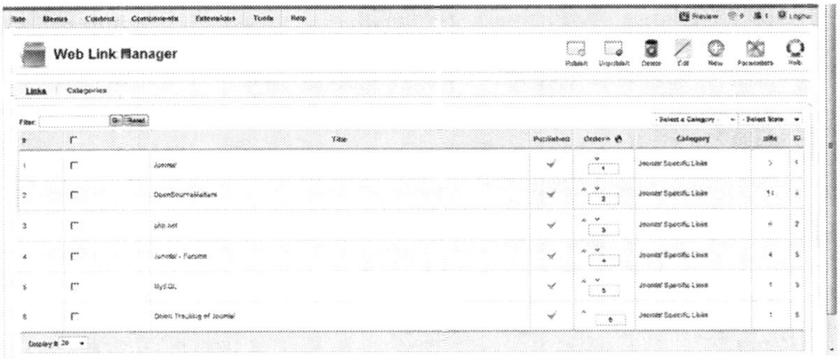

You should notice this screen looks the same as the other screens we have discussed.

If you notice there are two pages to Weblinks, Links and Categories. This is listed just under the Weblink manager name. Let's click on categories first and change the categories to what is appropriate for our site.

I am going to label my categories, soccer skills and coaching. Go ahead and click on the Category title and change the title, alias, description and add an image if you want.

**Figure 104: Web Link Categories**

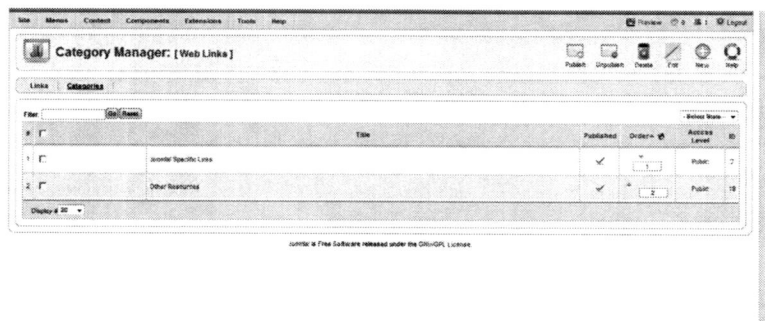

**Figure 105: Web Link Change Category**

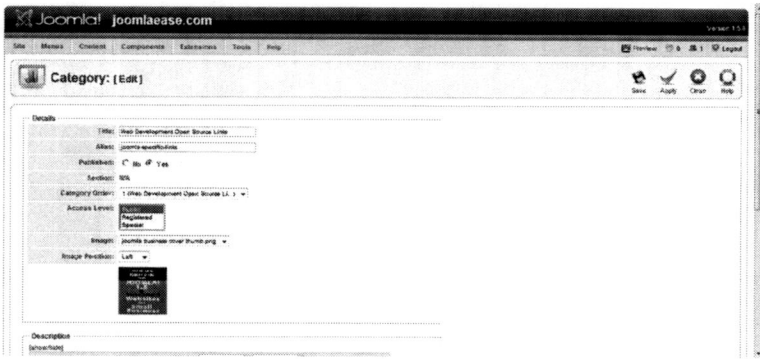

Now that we have changed the categories, let's now change the actual links. You will need the address of the websites you will like to have your site visitors' link to. The address looks like this:

> http://www.enterwebsitename.com

This is what mine looks like below.

# Weblinks 145

### Figure 106: Weblinks JoomlaEase

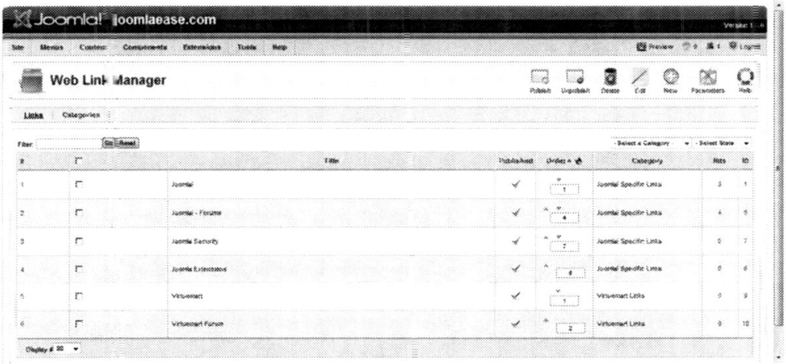

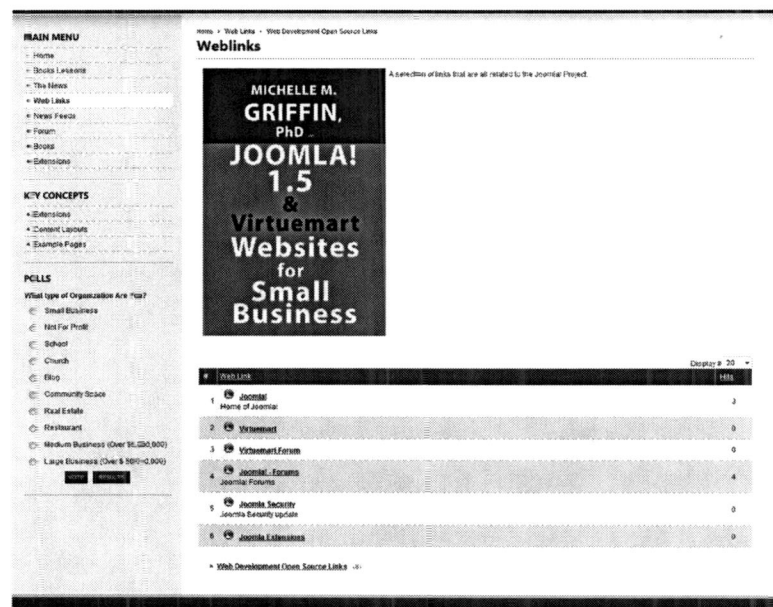

Now, refresh your site, under Weblinks on the main menu will show your new links.

### Figure 107: Website

# Wrappers

Wrappers are my favorite, I use them extensively because I want to be able to have links to other sites, but I do not want the person who comes to my site, to leave and go somewhere else. Therefore with wrappers, you hold their interest. Wrappers are similar to Weblinks, it just the new website they are navigating too, is incased in your website.

Let's play with the top menu for this tutorial. We are going to change all the top menu items to wrappers.

How you do this, go to the toolbar Resources Menu.

The resource menu is located below the main menu in the Purity template. The menu items begin with Joomla Home.

**Figure 108: Resource Menu**

Let's change this to all wrappers. Since there are already menu items, you can either put a checkmark on each one and click the trash icon or click the menu item name or open up each one and change type within the detail screen.

**Figure 109: Change Type**

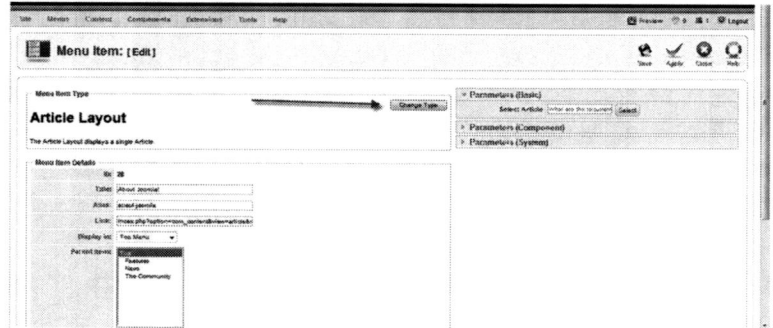

For my website, I am just going to click Change Type and change the menu item to wrapper.

**Figure 110: Menu Item Detail Screen**

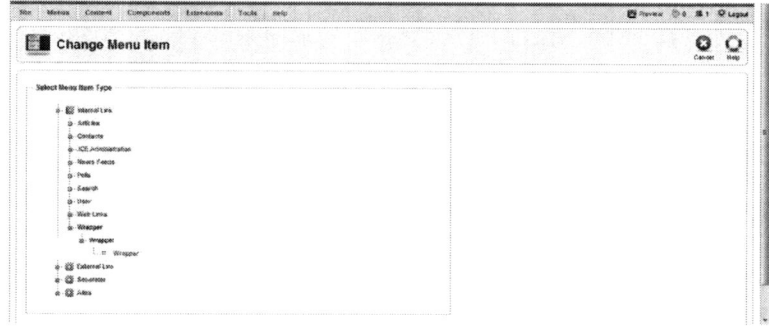

A wrapper is different than a Weblink, in that the link box you need to leave alone.

The wrapper website goes on the right hand side under link.

Wrappers 149

### Figure 111: Wrapper

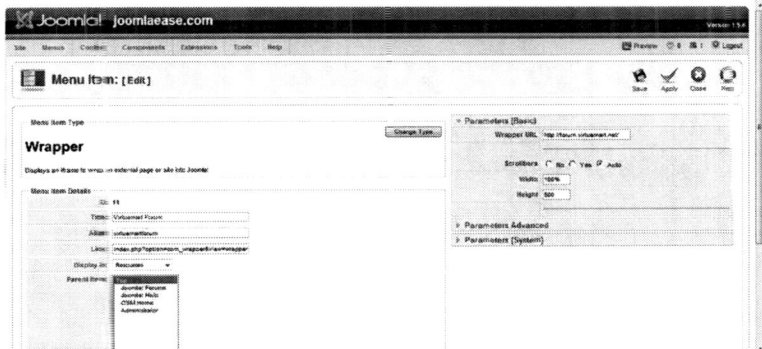

In the example, this wrapper is the Virtuemart Forum website; notice the link on the right hand side where the website address goes. Once you add your first wrapper and refresh your website.

If you click your you new menu item on the top menu the website which is a wrapper will open in the middle of your screen.

### Figure 112: Website Wrapper

Go ahead and change all your top menu links to wrappers, if you wish.

**Figure 113: Website with top menu changed**

# Updating the Logo

We need to change the logo from Joomla to your website name. Each template has a different logo name. Typically we would have to find it.

Since we are using the default template of JA Purity, we need to find the logo within the template file. The logo is located under:

Public_html/templates/JAPurity/images - logo.png

If you are using the rhuk_milway template then the logo is located under:

Public_html/tempaltes/rhuk_milkway/images - mw_joomla_logo.png

If you have already changed templates to another - you will find the logo in the template file under images. Everyone uses different names, so you may have to search a little bit.

To change logo you will need a program which can create .png or .jpg files. If you have Photoshop or another program the logo size is 1 inch (width) by .21 inch (height) using a transparent background. I assume that most people buying this book, may not have access to a program which creates .png or .jpg; I have enclosed a coupon at the back of the book, for you to have a professional logo created for you. All you have to do is provide proof of purchase of this book, and a Graphic Design artist will work with you to create the logo you need for your site.

I recommend you begin this process right away, once you read this because a logo takes on average a few days of back and forth to meet your desired look and specifications.

If you have a program, go ahead and create your logo. For the ja_purity or rhuk_milkway template you will need to name it mw_joomla_logo.png or the same name that the template calls it. I recommend keeping the same name when you save your file, then you don't have to go into the actual template and change the code.

The logo file is located within the Cpanel/File Manager. Go back to the Cpanel chapter if you don't remember how to access it. Once the File Manager opens go to the Template folder, then double click and go to the rhuk_milkway folder/images.

**Figure 114: Image Folder**

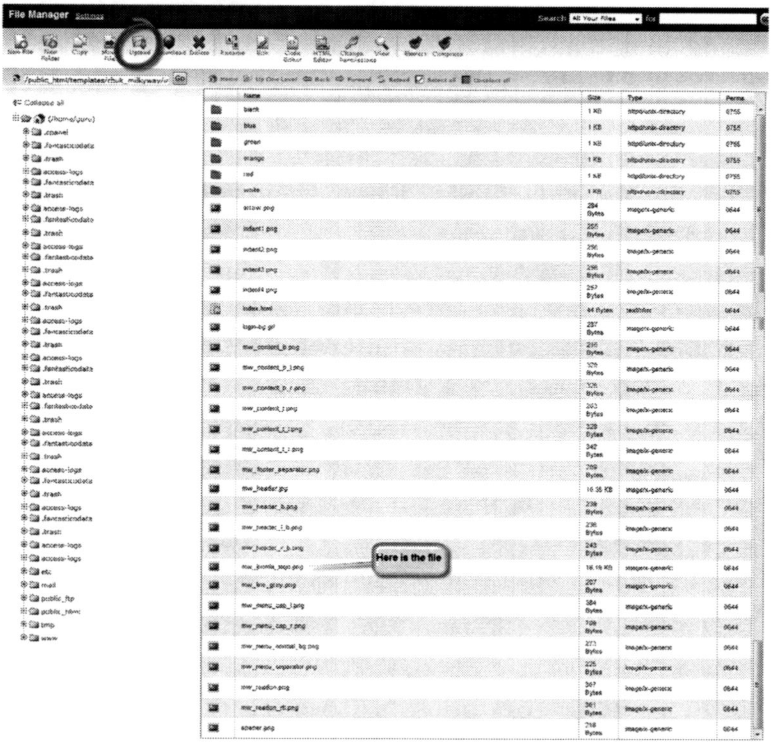

Logos 153

Do you see the mw_joomla_logo.png in the screen shot. At the top of the screen, there is a circle around the upload icon on the screen shot.

Click the upload button to browse and find your file. Then click upload. When it asks to replace file, click YES. The image will now upload.

**Figure 115: Upload**

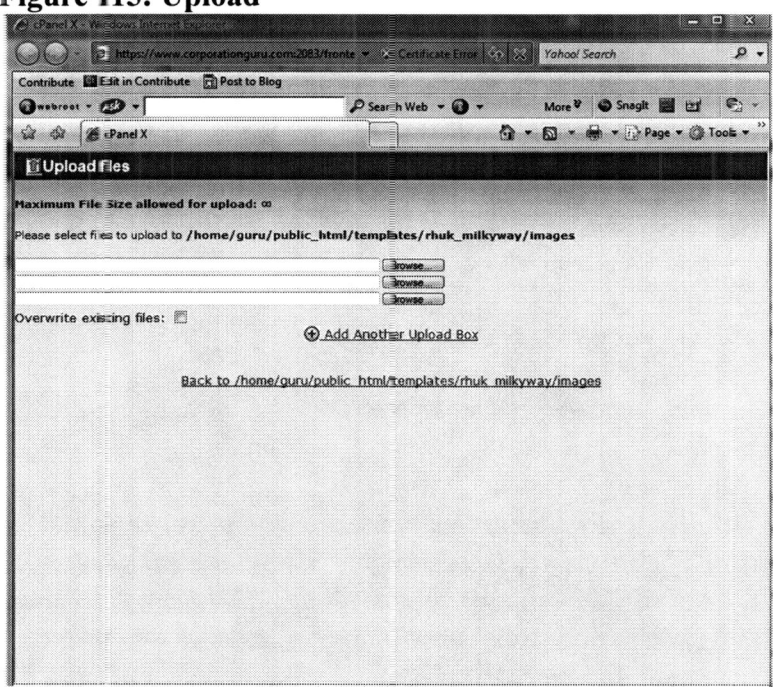

**Figure 116: Replace File**

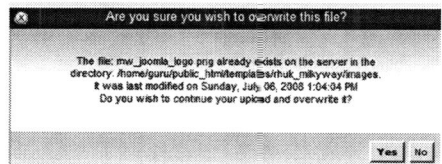

### Figure 117: Upload Complete

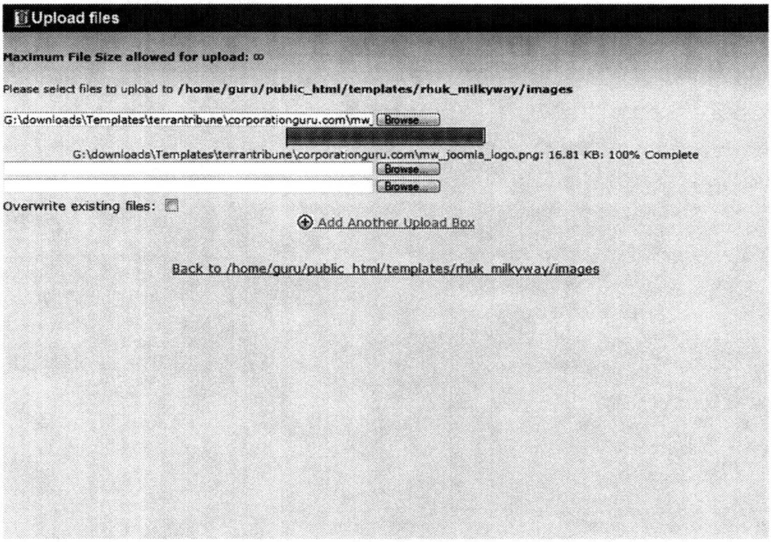

Go ahead and refresh your website your new logo should be there.

I am going to change my template completely to one from Rocket Theme called Meta Morph. Therefore our sites will be different but you can still follow along. If you wan to change your theme permanently, now is a good time to do it, since we are changing the logo.

On the theme I changed to, there were actually 2 logos. One at the top and one at the bottom. Therefore I had to modify both. Do you see the difference a template makes. I turned off some modules and rearranged others and the site is completely different.

**Figure 118: Website with new Logo**

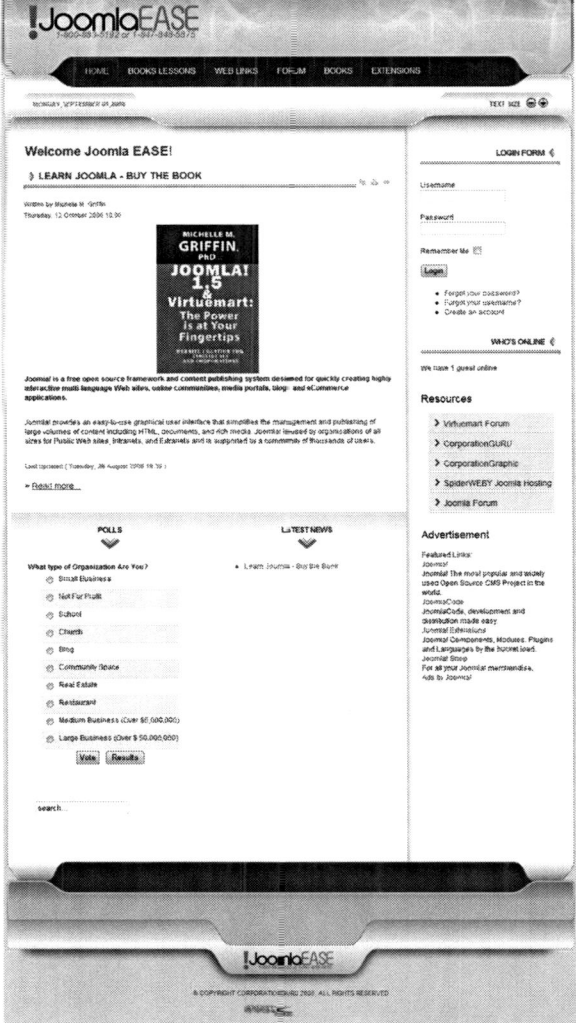

# Media Manager

Before we go too much farther, you need to learn about the Media Manager and adding images to your site. The Media Manager is located under Site/Media.

**Figure 119: Media Manager**

If you click the Banners folder on the left hand side, this is where the Banner images are stored. The banners will be discussed in the next section. But if you look at your website, the Joomla Shop is a banner at the bottom of your site.

**Figure 120: Banner Media Manager**

158   Joomla!™ 1.5

If you click on the image, it will enlarge it.
**Figure 121: Banner Image enlarge**

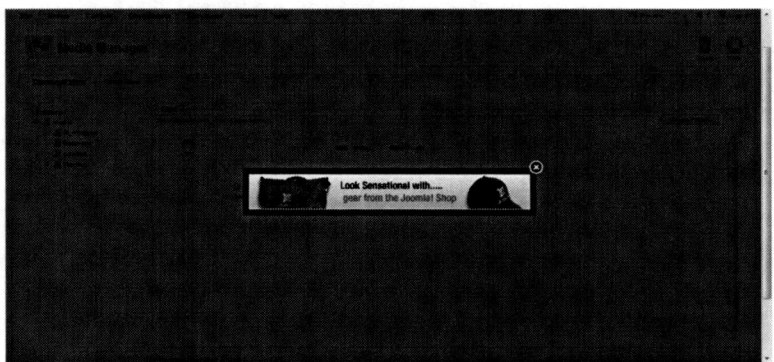

Clicking the green arrow on your screen will bring up to the next higher directory or you can navigate using the menu on the left hand side.

Let's click on Stories and look and see what images are in there. Under Stories is where the images you use in Articles are stored. You can delete any of the default icons or keep them. It is up to you.

**Figure 122: Media Manager/Stories**

Media Manager 159

Media Manager is important, because if you are going to use graphics on your website, you will want to load them through here. Do you see the browse button at the bottom of the media manager screen? This is where you upload.

To upload an image from your computer, click Browse and navigate to the folder where your image is stored. Press open and then click Start Upload. The file will upload and tell you when complete; you will also see an image with the other images. I uploaded a soccer ball in this example.

**Figure 123: Media Manager Upload**

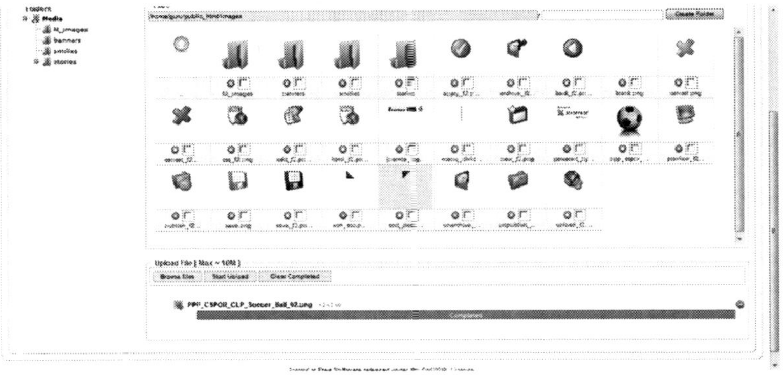

# Banner Manager

There is a neat feature in Joomla called Banners. Banners allow you to have advertising on your site, if you wish. Banners are changed under components/Banners and displayed through the Module Manager. If you refresh your website, you will see two Banners on your site.

**Figure 124: Website Banners**

The first on the right tool bar labeled Advertisement and at the bottom of the website showing a Joomla Store banner.

Let's update the Banner Categories first. Banners is located under component//Banners.

**Figure 125: Banner Manager**

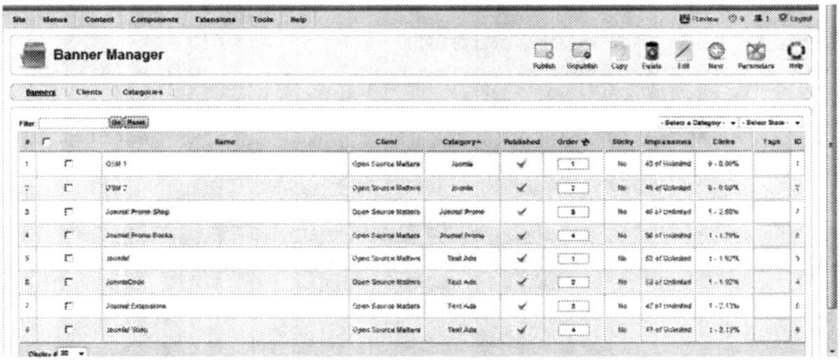

There are a number of default Banners. Let's modify some of the banners for your site.

Ultimately you will need to be able to create .jpg's or .png's in order to add images to your Banner ads.

But, we will walk you through the process, if you are not ready to mess with Banners, then you can go to the Module Manager (Extensions/Module Manager) and disable Banners.

First let's update categories for one of the banners. I am going to change the first category to Books and change the last category to Promo only.

Banner 163

### Figure 126: Banner Categories

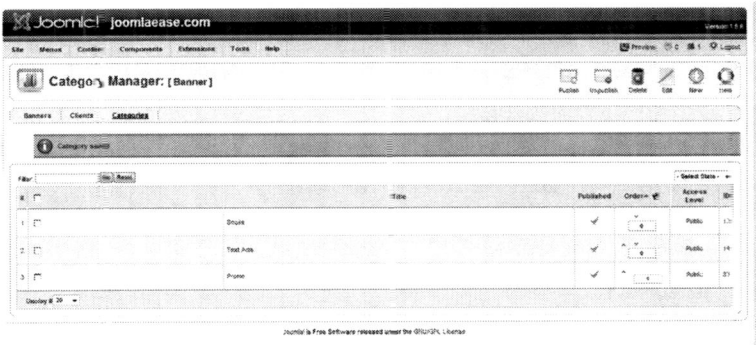

Let's click on the clients tab within the Category Manager. The link is just below the Category Manager name.

There is only one client, let's change it to something that fits your site.

### Figure 127: Banner Client Manager

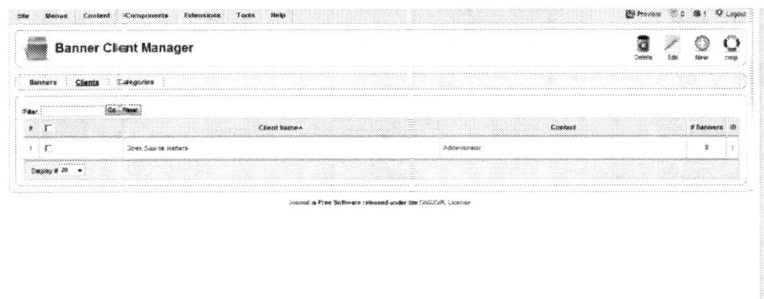

Click on the Client Name and change the name to something appropriate for your site. I am changing mine to "Soccer Advertising".

164 Joomla!™ 1.5

If you decide to sell space on your site, then you can set this up as actual client names, track hits and then charge them for space usage. Another cool feature you can have rotating banners, therefore you can have different clients and have different banners pop up based on settings.

**Figure 128: Client Manager Detail**

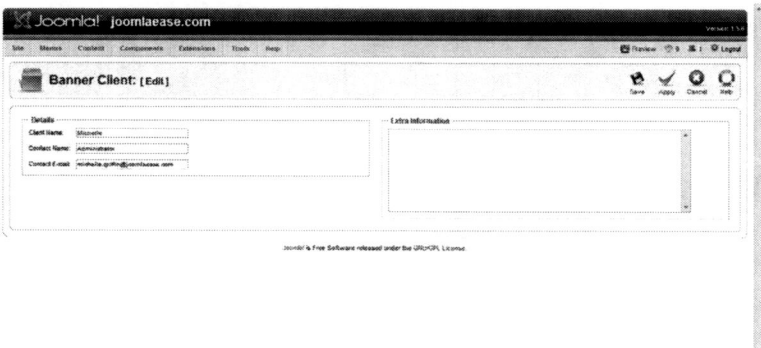

Remember to save your changes and your screen should be back at the Client Manager. Let's click the Banner link underneath the Banner Client Manager name.

**Figure 129: Banner Manager**

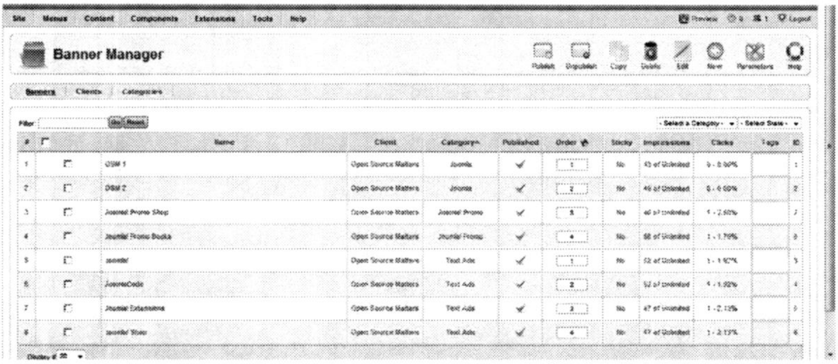

Click on the first Banner name in this case it is Joomla Promo Shop.

**Figure 130: Banner Detail**

Since I am interested in advertising the books. I have created a banner to do this. This will show you generally what you need to do for adding a banner campaign.

Banner campaigns' can be profitable; if you have a high track site those pennies add up. Look at where Google makes all their money. It is from the click through.

Fields:
- Title: Name of Banner
- Alias: Name of Banner with no spaces
- Show Banner: Yes or No
- Sticky: Yes or No ( Means it is a static banner and does not change)
- Order: position of banner compared to other banners.

- Category: The category showed in the Banner module is selected in the module detail for Banner. In this instance, I have it set as Promo.
- Impressions Purchased: How many times do you want the banner to appear before the end of the campaign.
- Click URL: If the banner is clicked what site does it navigate to.
- Custom Code: You can add html or Java Script code to have the banner do additional functionality.
- Banner Image: Select image which is stored in Site/Media Manager/Banner
- Tags: Keyword which are tagged by the search engines.

**Figure 131: Banner Detail Page**

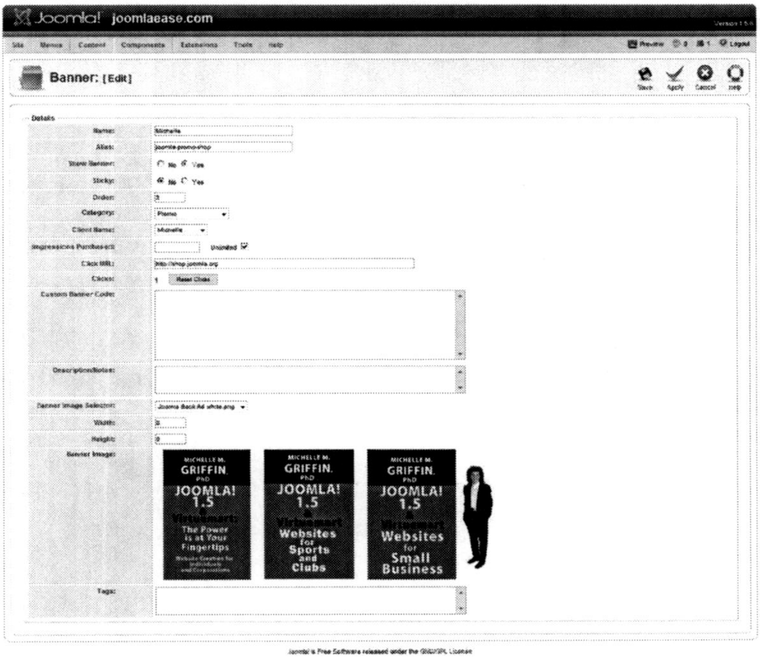

If you go to Extensions/Module Manager and open the Banner Module, you will see the detail fields which state how images from the Banner modules are transitioned.

**Figure 132: Banner Module**

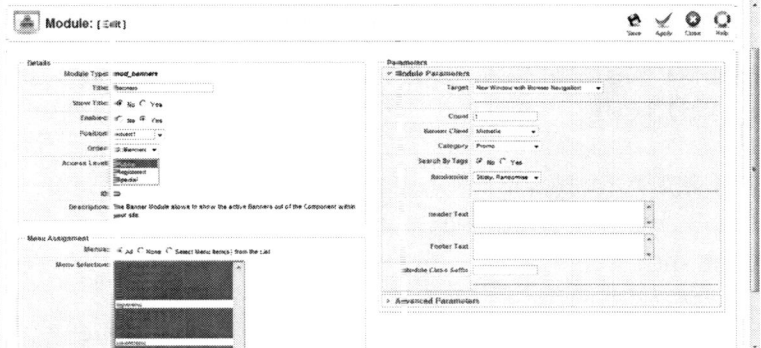

The right hand columns control how banners are displayed.

- Target: Do you want the banner when clicked to navigate to the new website or open a new session. When clicking a banner, you do not have the option of a wrapper. Therefore I recommend have the navigation open a new window. Then your website is still visible on the other session. If selecting new window, I recommend no browser navigation. Therefore they have a higher probability of exiting that session and going back to your site.

- Banner Client: Leave as Select Client if this banner does not run just a specific client.

- Category: Select what category the banner will be pulled from.

- Randomize: Sticky, Randomize or Stick, Ordering this is taken from the Banner where the order and stickiness were selected.

The bottom of the left hand column is selection of what pages the banner is to show up on. You can select all or select individual pages.

Change whatever fields you need to change to fit your website and click SAVE.

Now the Advertisement module is also tied to the Banner Component. The advertisement module looks similar to the Banner module.

If you open up the Advertisement module you noticed it uses a different Category. But, also notice that the default Joomla site add code into the footer text on the right hand side, this adds a link to a website with the text "Ads by Joomla". You can either delete this code or change it to navigate where you desire.

**Figure 133: Advertisement Module**

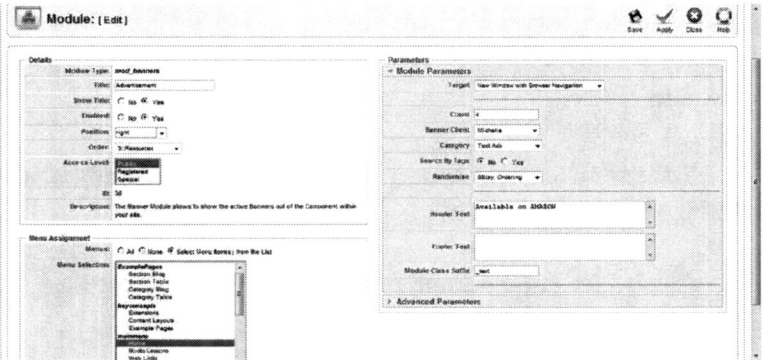

But for the website we are building, I am doing to disable this module.

Because in a few chapters we are going to begin adding modules from components we will download from www.joomla.com. If you need then alter it as you see fit.

While we are in the Module Manager, I am also going to turn off the Resources module, Extensions module and Example Pages.

Go ahead and re-arrange your page through the module manager to fit how you would like to see it.

Don't worry about spaces, we are going to be adding more modules to the website.

The demonstration website now looks like this.

170   Joomla!™ 1.5

## Figure 134: JoomlaEASE Website

# Search

The search component in Joomla is a handy tool. If turned on, then when someone searches your website, it records searches. Then you can modify your site to contain the items your customers would like to see on your site.

To turn this feature on, just go the search component under Component/Search.

**Figure 135: Search Parameters**

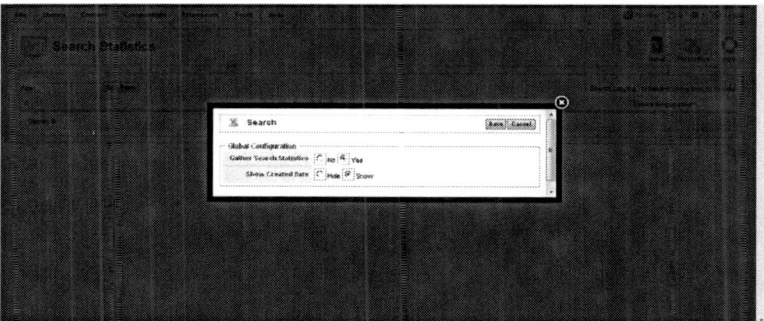

Let's go to your website and type in a key word to search.

**Figure 136: Website Search**

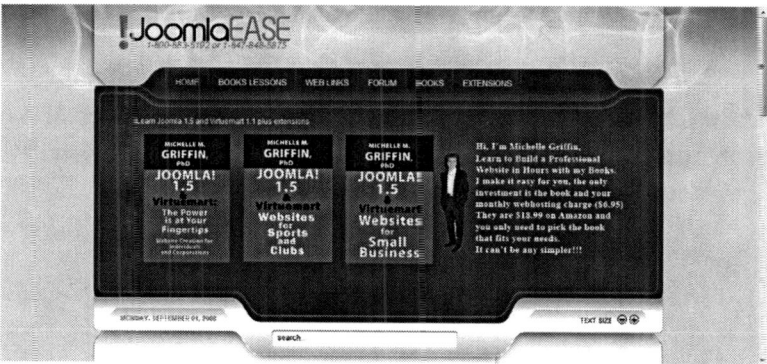

When I searched for joomla on mine, this is the results.

### Figure 137: Search Results

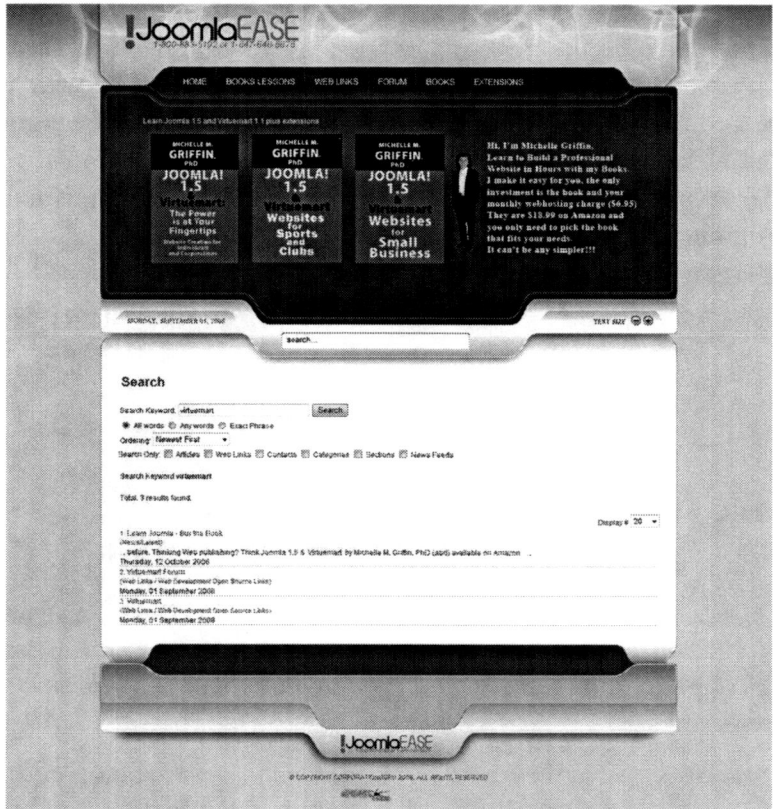

Once you change the parameter to Yes, go to your website and search for content. Then come back to the Search component and you will see that it recorded the search.

Coupons 173

## Figure 138: Search Recording

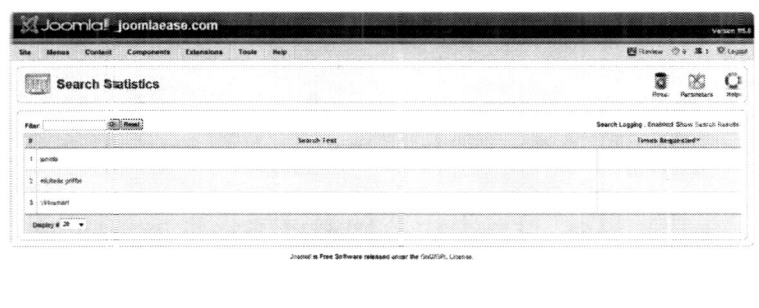

# User Manager

To access the User manager go to Site/user Manager.

**Figure 139: User Manager**

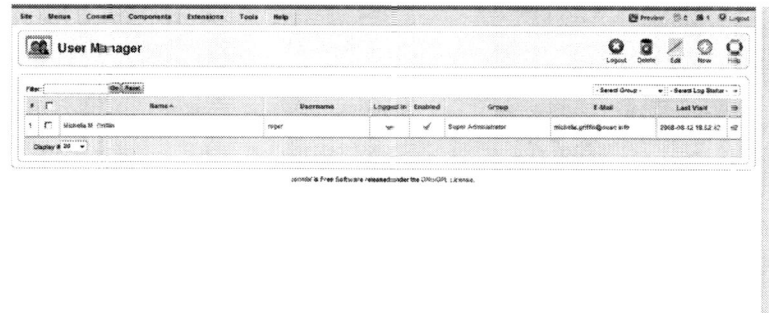

Let's look at the detail screen of your user. Click the User name and we will look at the details.

**Figure 140: User Manager Detail**

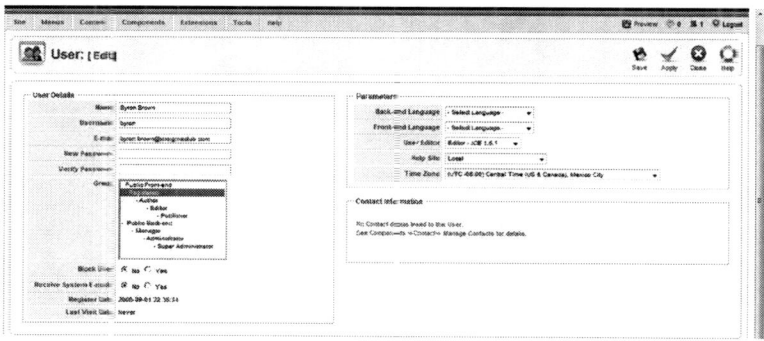

We briefly looked at the User Manager when we installed the JCE Component. But now we are going to add a user to Joomla.

**Figure 141: User Login**

User Manager 177

We are not going to add it from the back end, we are going to pretend we are a new user and add it from the login module on your website. Let's go to your website and Create an Account underneath the Login module.

The fields are very simple to register. You have to use a different email, then the one you are using for administration. Your hosting company allows you to setup additional email addresses. Go back to the email chapter in order to create a second email address to test your login module.

**Figure 142: Registration**

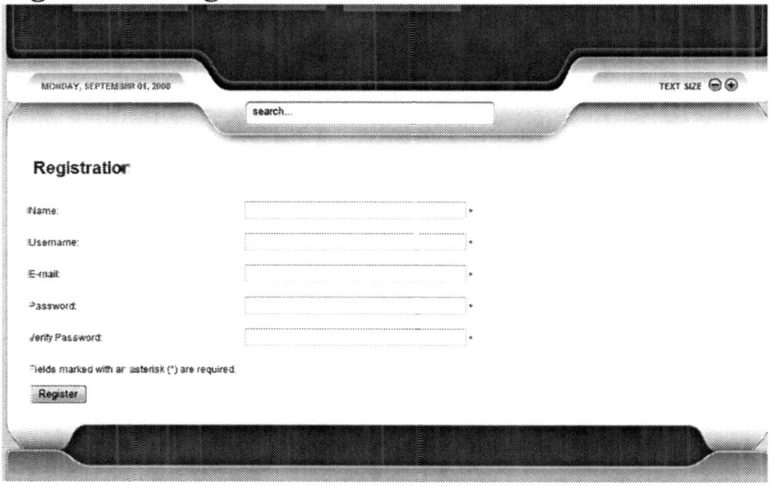

Let's fill this out. Click Register. If registration is successful the following message appears to your customers.

Now go back to your User Manager and refresh. Your new customer has just registered.

### Figure 143: User Manager with new registration

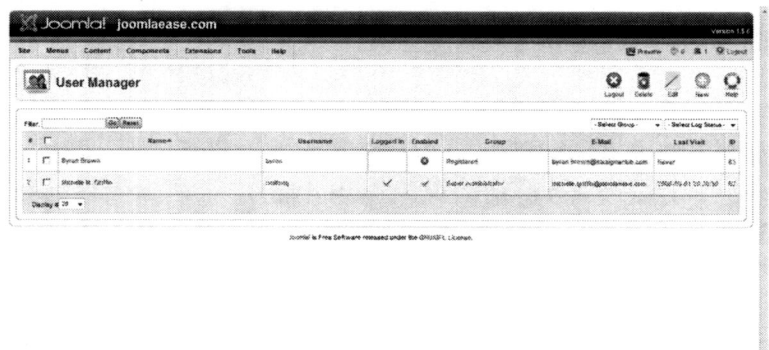

Now check your administration email. There will be an email stating a new user registered.

### Figure 144: Email notification of user registration

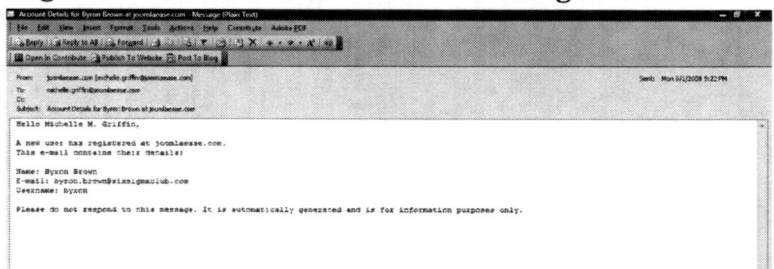

Now, check the email for the user there is a activation link. Click the activation link to activate the account.

User Manager 179

### Figure 145: Email Notification to New User

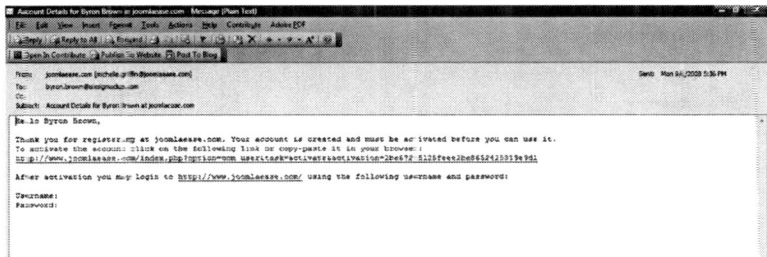

### Figure 146: New User Activation

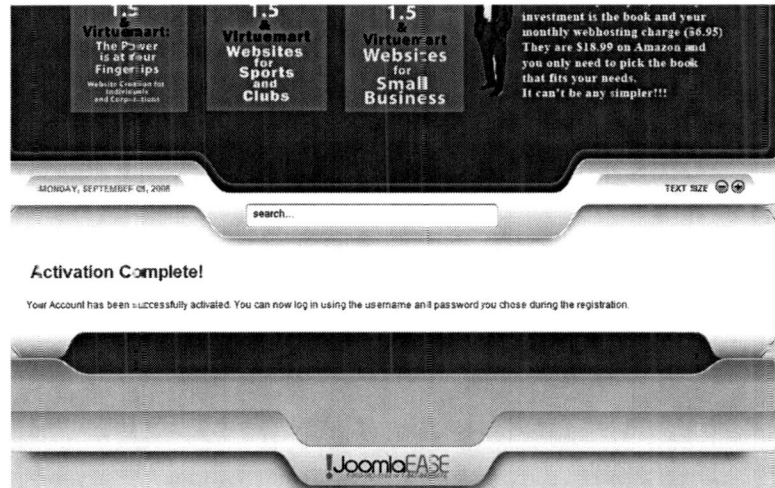

By using the icon, I made the registration appear friendly. Let's refresh the Joomla dashboard. The user is now enabled.

180    Joomla!™ 1.5

**Figure 147: User Manager Enabled**

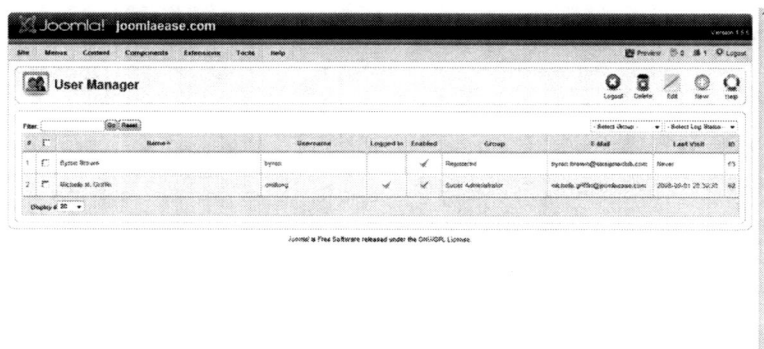

**Figure 148: User authorization levels**

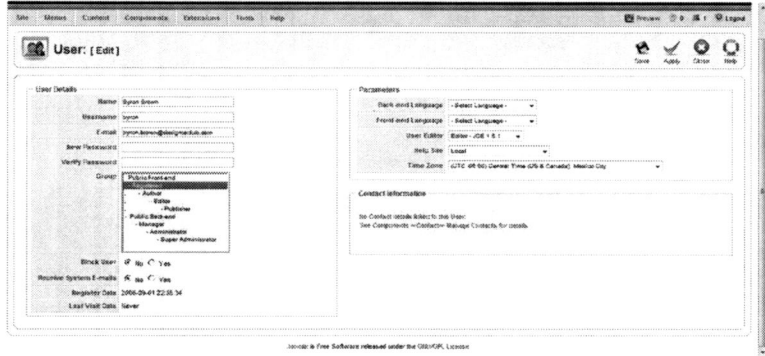

There are different Group levels within User management
• Registered: User can access the website and view registered only modules and content.

• Author: Can submit content to the website, typically through the Submit content menu item. Even though content is submitted it is not posted until a high level group approves the submission.

- Editor: The user can post and edit any content on the site. But cannot approve the content for publishing.

- Publisher: This user can post and edit as well as approve posting for content submitted by other users.

Back End Permissions:
- Manager: Similar to Publisher but able to access the Joomla Dashboard to create content. All modules and features in the back end are disabled except for what they are authorize to modify.

- Administrator: Can do everything in the Joomla Dashboard, except change Site Templates or edit the Global Configuration file.

- Site Administrator: Has all rights to the Joomla Dashboard.

We are going to leave this user you just created as Registered. But if you notice on the right hand column, it allows you to select User Editor.

This feature can be changed individually for all users or can be changed globally in the Global Configuration file. In order to change it in the Global Configuration file, you will need to go back to the Global configuration chapter and reset the permissions for the configuration.php file.

Then go to Site/Global Configuration and change the Default WYSIWYG editor to the JCE module or Tiny if that is what you are using. I am going to change it to the JCE module.

182    Joomla!™ 1.5

**Figure 149: Default WYSIWYG Editor:**

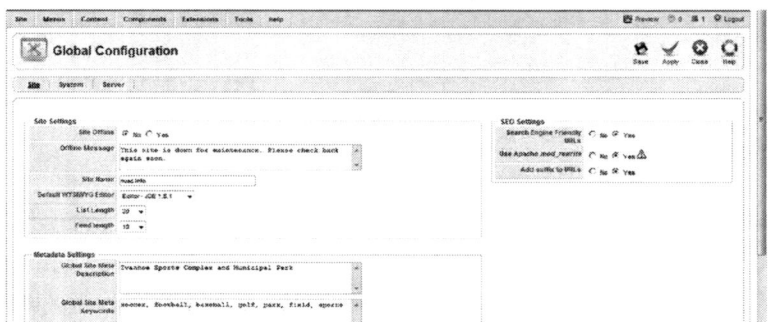

If you decide to set the Default WYSIWYG Editor then ensure you go back and change the default to 644 in the Cpanel. Once you change this all future users are given the default editor.

All you will need to do is grant access to their groups within the User Module.

# Upgrading

Every few months, it is a good idea to go back into your Cpanel/Fantastico to verify the version of Joomla which is available.

**Figure 150: Fantastico upgrade**

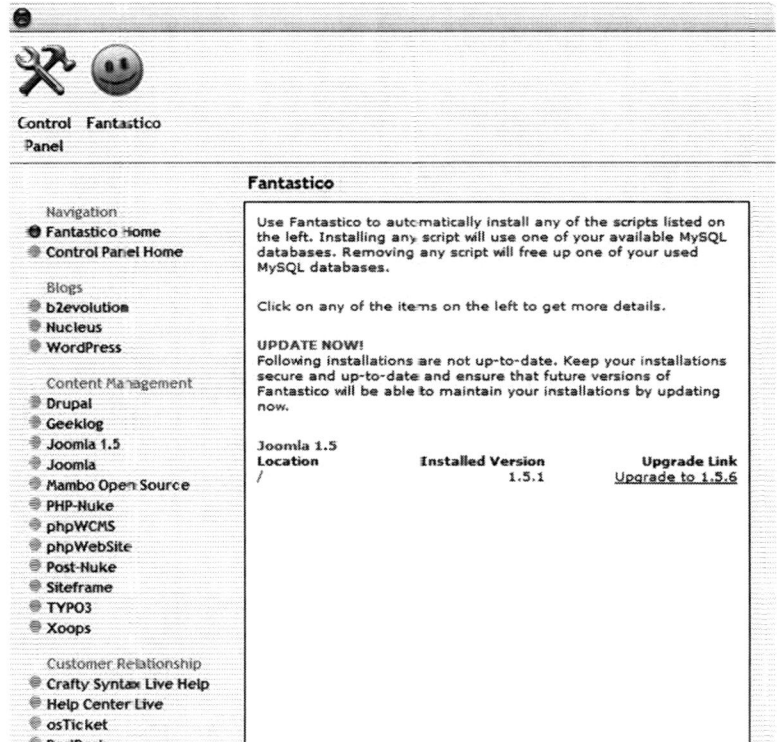

As you can see there is a stable upgrade to Joomla 1.5.6. Let's click the upgrade to 1.5.6

Realize when you upgrade, it means you may have to reinstall some components and modules for your site.

Any site templates you installed will also be lost and it will revert back to the original Joomla site.

Once you have re-designed your site a few times, you won't be initiated by upgrading. It is not something you do all the time, maybe once or twice a year.

**Figure 151: Continue Joomla Upgrade**

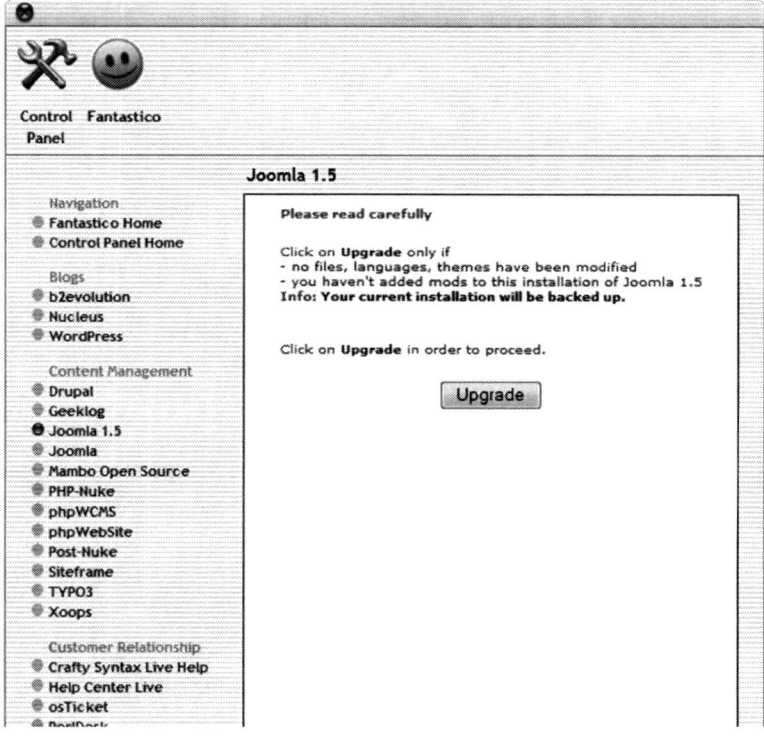

# Overview

In the first section of the Joomla! 1.5, we walked through how to create a basic website. You can be as creative as you wish. Now we are going to enhance a new website and create an e-commerce website which sells product.

For this section, I am going to build a website which I need for helping people to learn Joomla and the other components.

Before I install the Virtuemart components, I am going to spend sometime, adding articles and configuring the site.

Go ahead and change templates, add articles, and change menus. Next we are going to install Virtuemart shopping cart for team registrations as well as accepting donations for our teams.

The functionality is endless from this point; it is a matter of playing and trying different extensions and modules to see what works for your site.

In this chapter, I will show you how to install two extensions called Rokmininews and RokNewsRotator. I use both of these extensions frequently on some of my sites.

186 Joomla!™ 1.5

## Figure 152: JoomlaEase Website

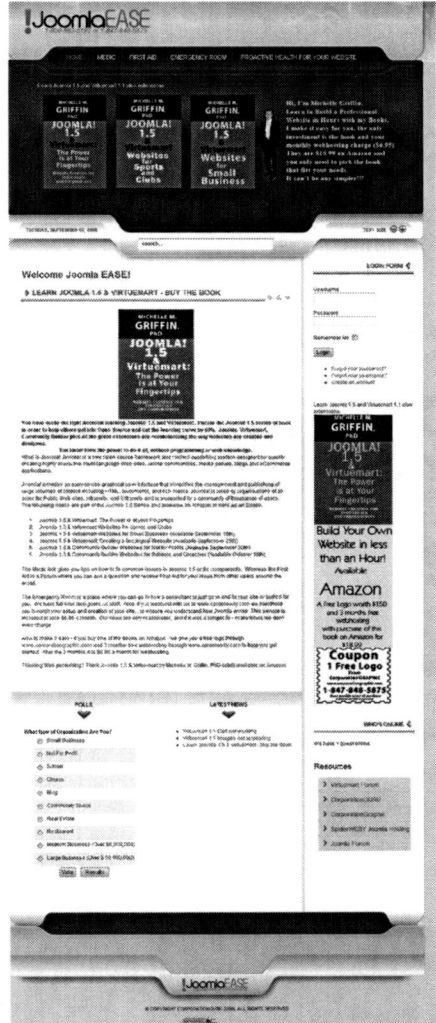

Overview 187

The Rocket Themes also have a number of module positions. Which allows the flexibility of moving items around in order to create a unique site.

The module positions give you unlimited functionality to create a site that is personalized to your individual sports team style.

The template comes with two additional modules which have to be installed separately from the template.

It also comes with a neat little module that allows your site to look like CNN. It is called "rokmininews". All you do is install the module and place it in the newsflash position and it picks up all the articles in a particular section.

To refresh your memory to install a module go to Extensions/Install.

**Figure 153: Install RokMiniNews**

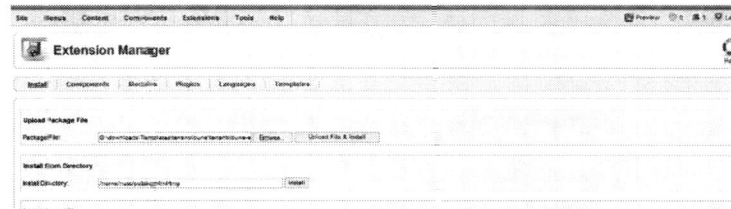

Once it the rokmininews is installed we then need to go to Module Manager, located under Extensions and modify the parameters.

### Figure 154: Rokmininews Parameters

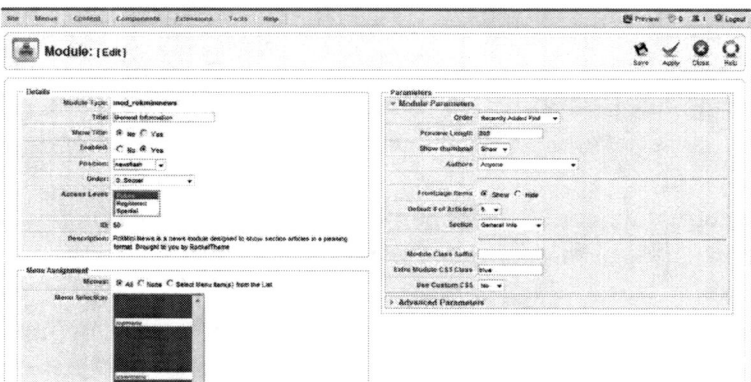

I recommend turning off the title. Since it will pick up the Section name.

The best place for this module is in the newsflash position. This is where multiple copies of this module can be used to show articles from different sections.

Change the Section parameter in the right hand column to the Section of your choice. This module works the best if you have a section with multiple categories and articles.

Under Extra Module CSS Class, you are able to type in a color with the Terra Tribune template. The available colors are red, blue, green, brown, purple and gray.

Lastly, you can change the preview length to whatever fits with your website.

## Figure 155: Rokmininews View

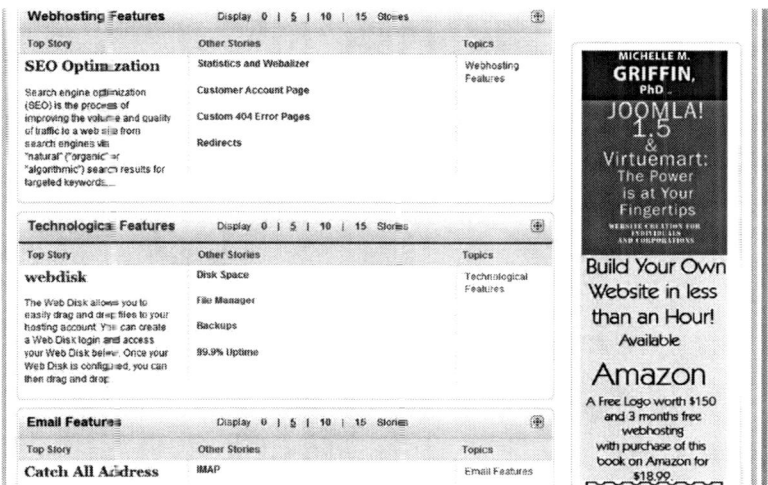

You are able to have multiple modules, just by copying the module or creating a new module in Module Manager. Just make sure they are all put in the same location of Newsflash in this template.

The other module we need to install is RokNews Rotator. This allows pictures with articles to transition on your site.

This is a little tricky, this is best placed in the Header of this particular template. If you noticed, on the previous screen print of the website, I placed the login form into the Header 2 position.

The header position gives you a clock with two positions for news or images. The clock is a parameter you are able to turn on and off. I like it, it is a nice feature to have, therefore I left it on.

**Figure 156: ROKNews Rotator**

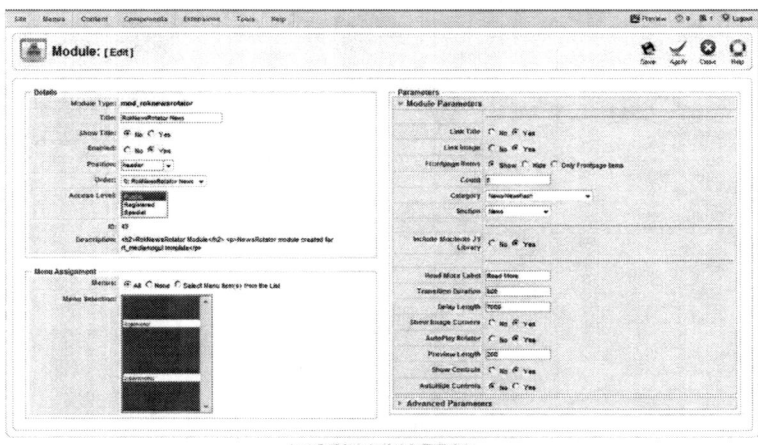

Once installed go to Extensions/Module Manager and find the RokNews Rotator module.

I recommend you turn off the title or change the name to something that fits your site. Then change the position to header.

On the right hand side, select your category and section to display and change the autohide controls to no.

Now for the tricky part. In order for this to work with an image, you will need to follow the following steps:

1: Go to User Manager/ User Detail for your login. Change the Editor from JCE to No Editor and save.

Overview 191

**Figure 157: User Manager**

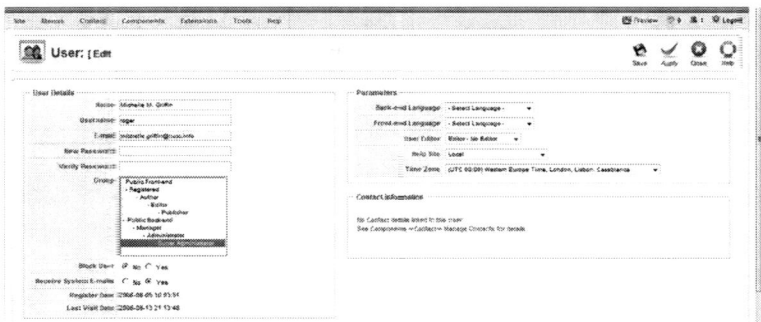

2: You need to go to the Media Manager and create a new folder under Stories. I used the name Lego, since this is the example on the rockettheme website. Then upload your image.

**Figure: 158: Media Manager**

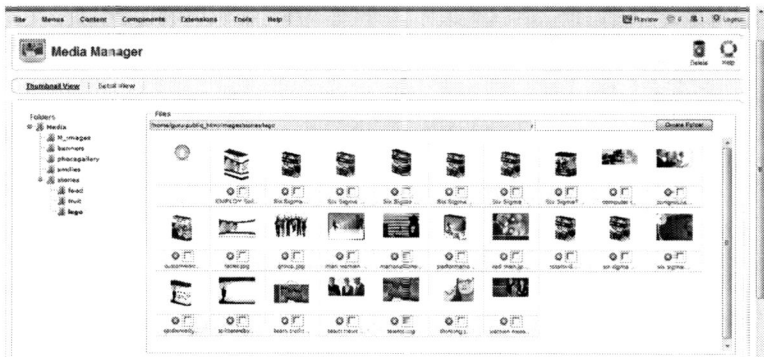

3: Go to Article Manager and open or create an article you would like to have appear in the rotator.

4: Ensure you select the Section and Category which matches what you setup in the Rotator module.

5: Add the following code to your article:
<!--IMAGE images/stories/lego/basketball.jpg IMAGE-->

Replace lego with your folder and basketball.jpg with your image name.

**Figure 159: Article**

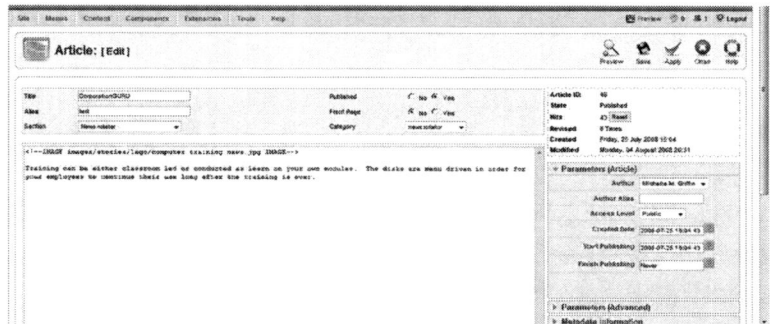

6: Once you have created all your image articles. Go back to the User Manager and change the editor back to JCE.

7: Go back to the Articles you added the image to and go to the second line, your image code is hidden and type in your text you would like to appear with the image.

You may have to play with this setup a little, it is very sensitive. Sometimes you will need to click on the image in order to have the control and text show up.

Overview 193

## Figure 160: Sample with Rotator News

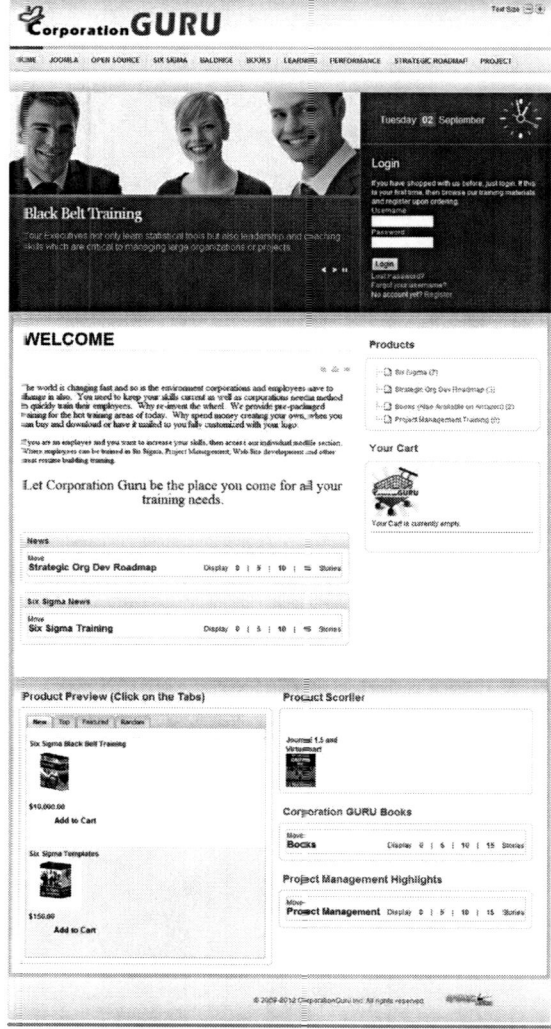

# Virtuemart Installing

Now let's add a shopping cart in order to pay for customer purchases. Go to www.virtuemart.net.

**Figure 161: Virtuemart Website**

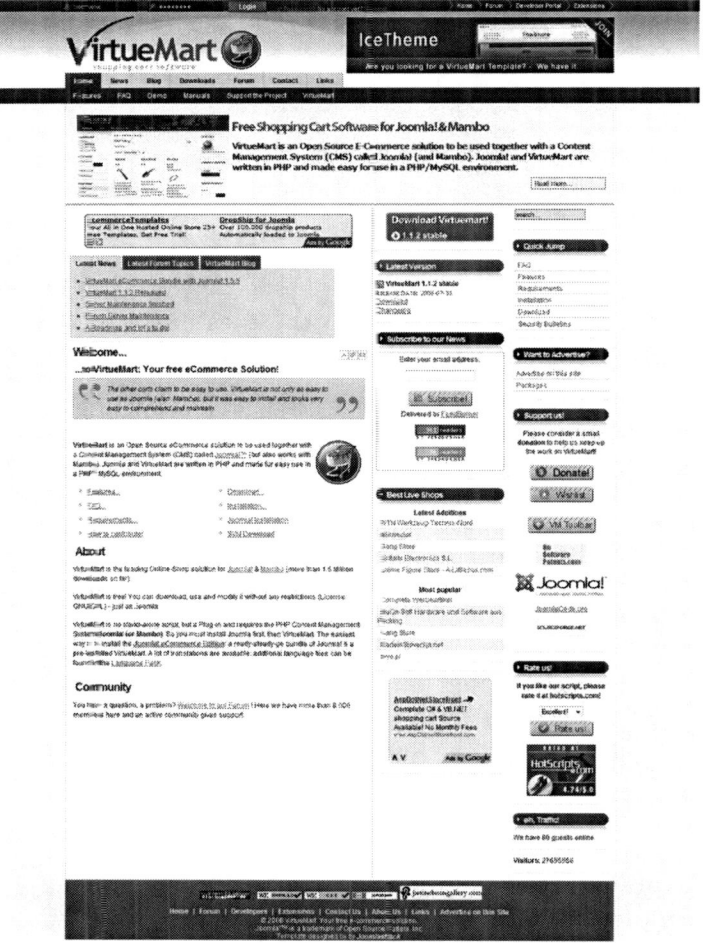

196   Virtuemart™

At the top of the website there is a box, stating download Virtuemart stable version. Let's click this button. It brings you to the download page. We want to download the Virtuemart version for Joomla 1.5.

**Figure 162: Virtuemart Download**

Click on the Virtuemart download for Joomla 1.5. If you look at the download page, there is VirtueMart 1.1.0 (stable) which is the core modules and then there is a patch upgrade also.

**Figure 163: Complete Package for Joomla 1.5 download**

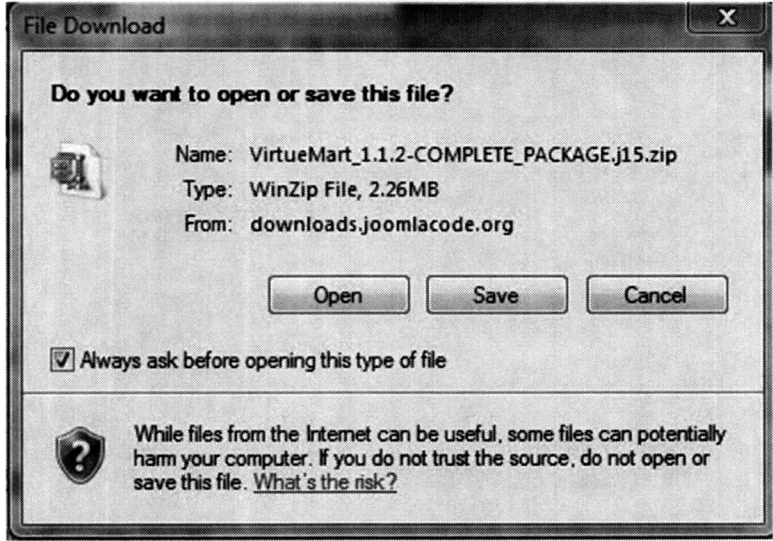

Click Save and navigate to where you would like to save the file.

**Figure 164: Virtuemart Save**

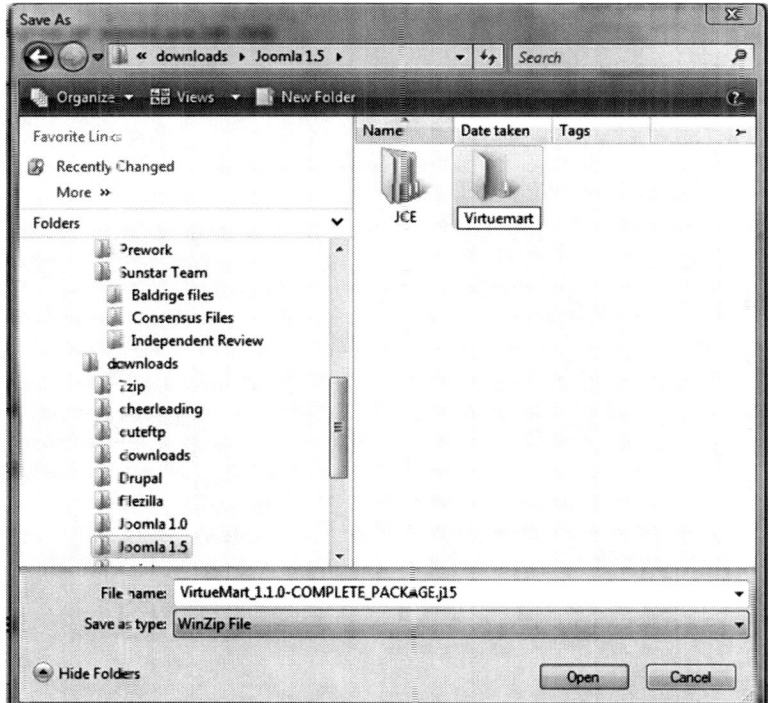

Let's download the core module and its components, and then we will add the patch before we begin building our site. Given we are building a new site it is easy to upgrade.

Just remember when you have a full site with your catalog and ordering setup, you must be cautious on upgrading in the future to ensure you don't have to re-enter all your data again.

Given we have already installed Joomla through Fantastico we

198   Virtuemart™

need to download the Complete package for Joomla 1.5. Go ahead and click on the link and let's download.

I highly recommend you create a separate folder for Virtuemart because there will be a number of files.

Do you see the New Folder icon within the explorer panel which opens when you click save? Click on New folder to save your file.

Once the file is downloaded it is a zip file; which needs to be unzipped. Open Windows Explorer and navigate to your Virtuemart folder.

If Windows Explorer is not on your desktop it can be found in your Windows Navigation/All Programs/Accessories/Windows Explorer.

**Figure 165: Windows Explorer Virtuemart Folder**

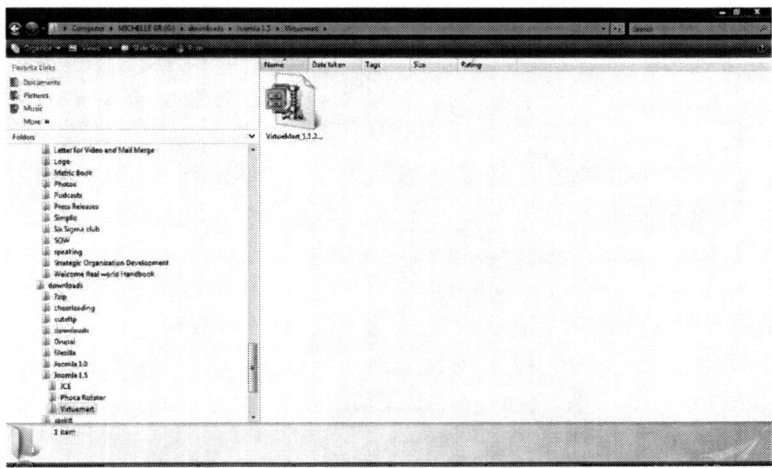

Virtuemart Installing 199

Double click on the Virtuemart file. On the navigation bar, it will stated Extract Files. If your Windows does not have and extractor installed, you can download Winzip or 7 Zip as a trial version to use temporarily or there is freeware zip programs also. Just do a search on your favorite search engine.

Once the Virtuemart file is unzipped your windows explorer looks like this:

**Figure 166: Virtuemart Unzipped**

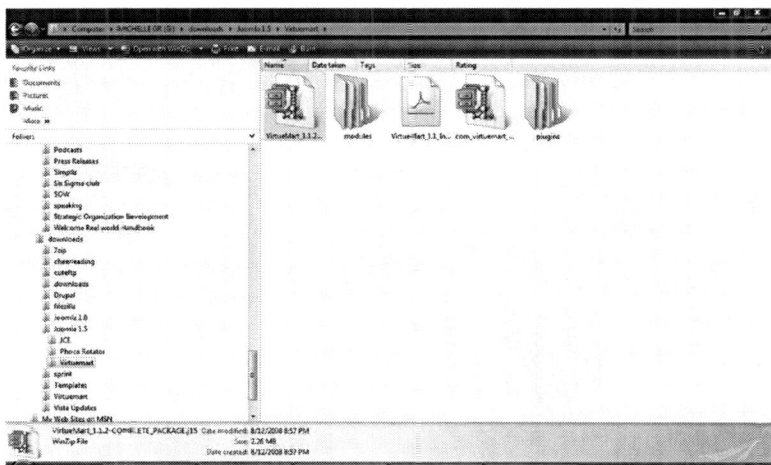

The first one we are going to install is the com_virtuemart_1.1.0.j15. Let's go into our Joomla Dashboard and install the file.

Go to Extensions/Install, then click browse and find the com file which you have in a folder.

### Figure 167: Install Virtuemart

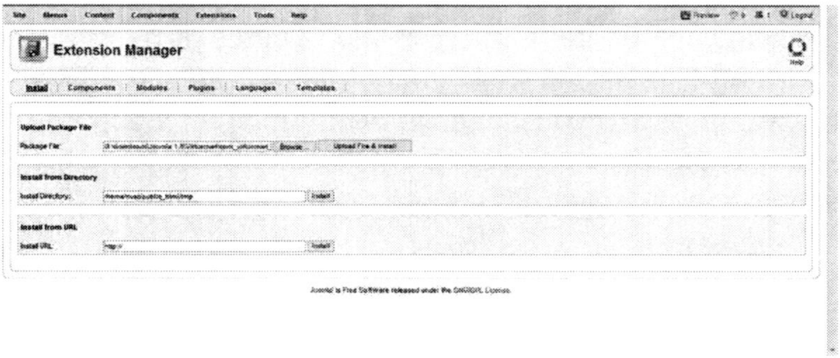

### Figure 168: Virtuemart installed

You have two choices to either install the sample data or not. I myself install the sample data then modify it. Mainly because then all fields are filled out and then I know what to change.

Without the sample data, you have to remember to do all the little things, like set up Tax, Country etc....it is easier in my opinion to just go change it.

## Figure 169: Virtuemart Store

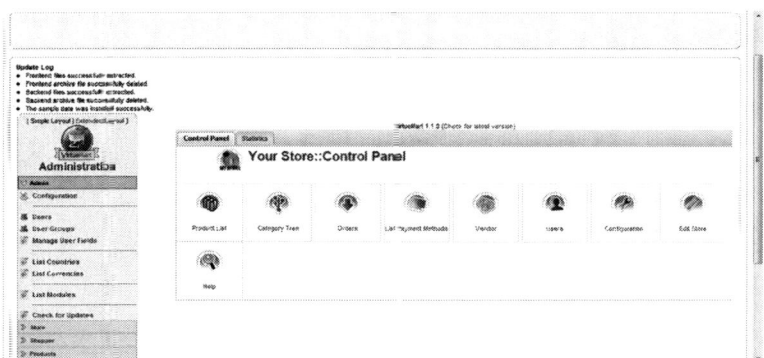

Now, before we do anything we need to install patches if there are any available. In this case we are at the latest version of 1.1.2, but I have provided directions in order for you to install a patch if a new version is available.

We need to go to the Virtuemart website and download the patch to the latest version or you can go to your Virtuemart Control Panel under admin/check for updates. I am going to show you initially how to download the patch.

## Figure 170: Virtuemart Download

We need to install the Patch for Joomla 1.5, click on the link.

### Figure 171: Virtuemart Patch Download

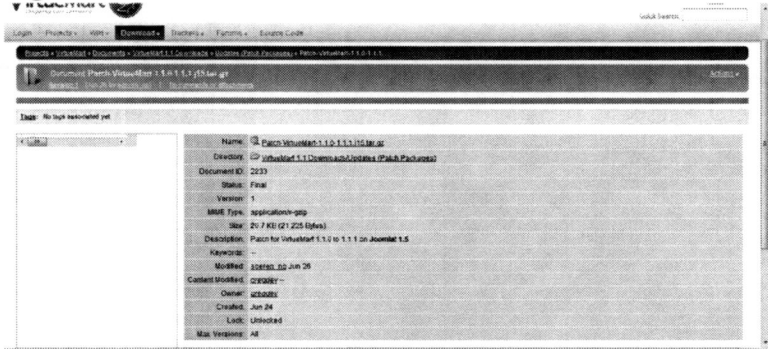

Click on the name of the patch to begin downloading. Save to your Virtuemart directory.

### Figure 172: Virtuemart Patch Save

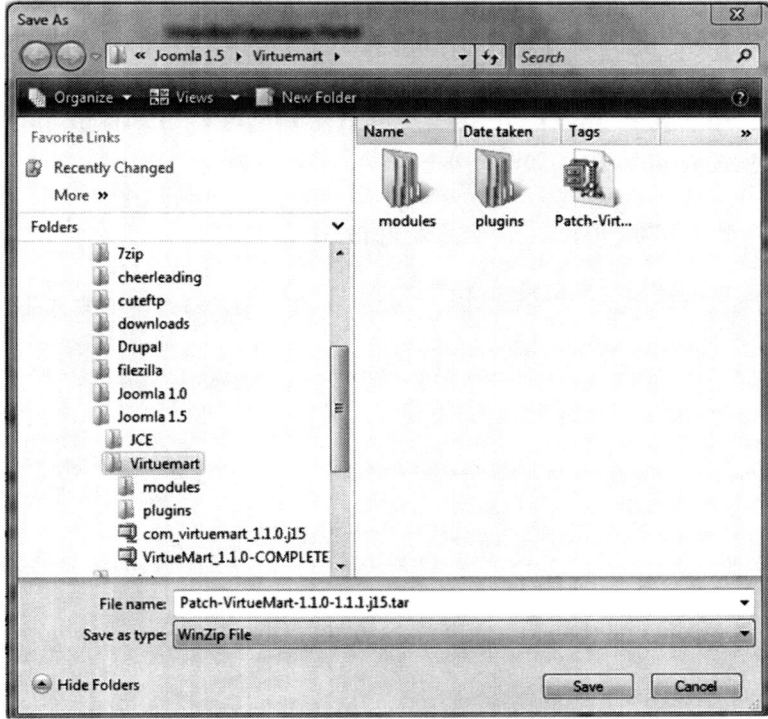

Virtuemart Installing 203

Now go back to your Virtuemart Control Panel. If you are not at the Virtuemart Control panel, it is found under Component/ Virtuemart. Virtuemart has made it easy to upgrade. On the left hand side of the Virtuemart control panel there is the admin. There is a little arrow in front of the word Admin, which opens and closes the navigation bar; click on Check for Updates.

**Figure 173: Virtuemart Check for Updates**

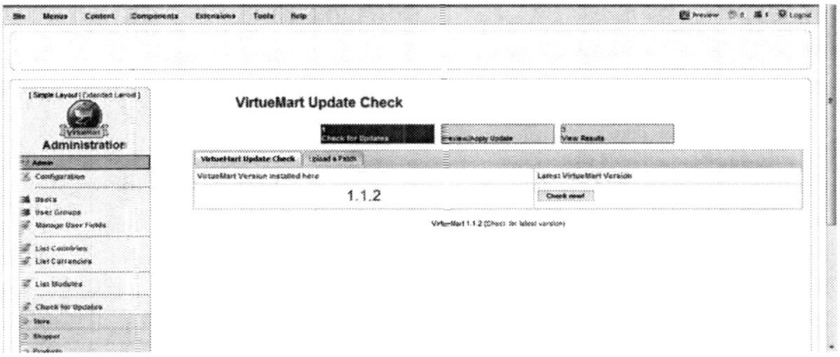

Click the button to check now. This will tell you what updates need to be updated. Sometimes, I receive connection fail when I try it. Therefore, since we already downloaded the patch at the Virtuemart site. We need to click the tab Upload a Patch.

**Figure 174: Upload a Patch.**

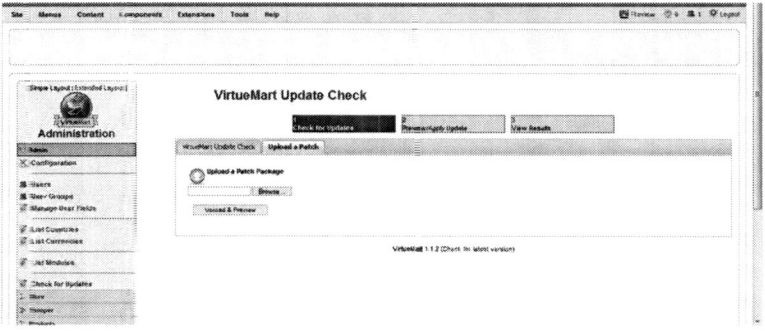

Browse for Patch file, that you just downloaded, then click Upload & Preview.

When you upgrade, realize that some of your content will be lost and you will have to go back and re-enter main Virtuemart screens, for instance Configuration, Store Summary, etc....

It does not typically lose order information, unless it is a major upgrade, just be very careful with upgrading.

**Figure 175: Virtuemart Patch Upgrade**

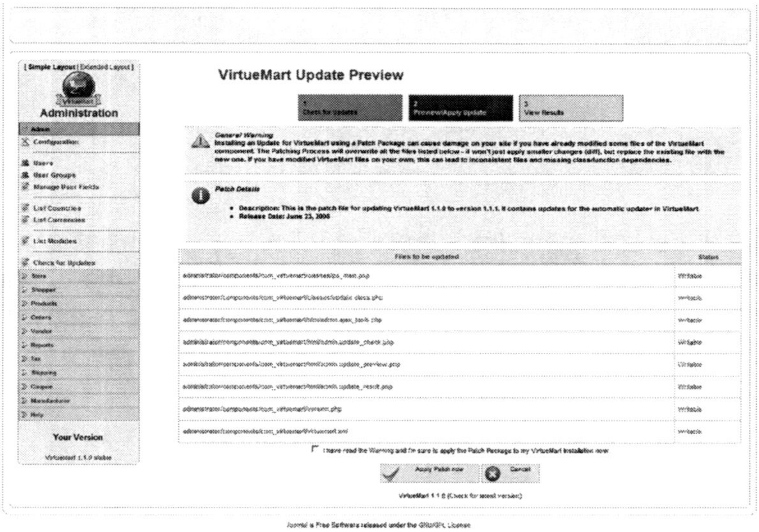

The list of files to be updated, will tell you basically what items you will need to re-update once the install is through.

Once you reviewed the patch then check the box stating "I have read the Warning" and click Apply Patch now.

## Figure 176: Virtuemart Patch upgrade Finished

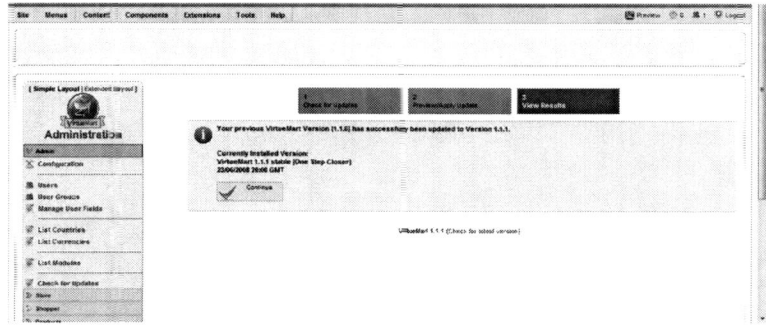

Press Continue and Virtuemart is now installed within your website. But it is not showing to your customers until we customize it.

# Virtuemart Modules

Before we enter product, let's install the Virtuemart modules. These modules were part of the zip file, which came in the original download. You can install all of them and use what you want or just install the one's you need. I typically install all of them, and then uninstall the one's I do not use.

**Figure 177: Modules**

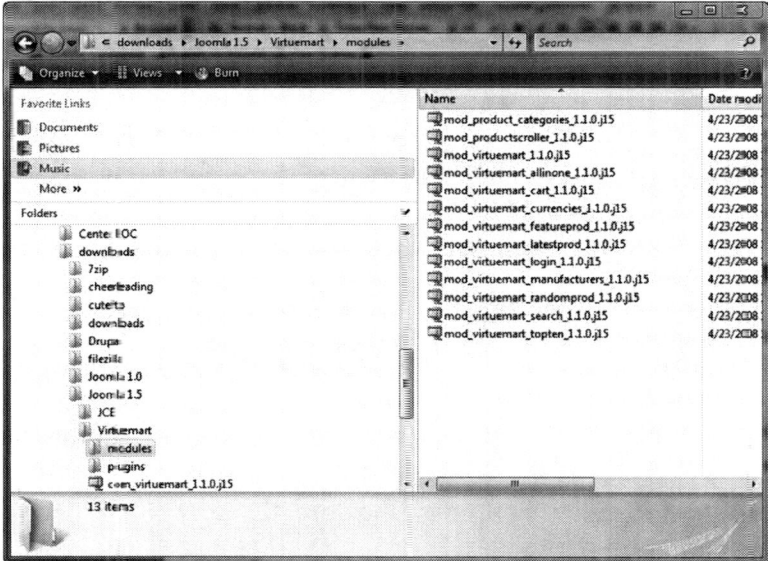

To install, we go to the Joomla Dashboard, click on Extensions/ Install.

Module Descriptions:

• Mod_product_categories – Displays a listing of product categories

• Mod_productscroller – This scrolls your products on the front page of your website.

- Mod_Virtuemart: A combination module with Shopping cart, product search, Administration link, account maintenance link and link to the download page.

- Mod_Virtuemart_allinone: A combination module showing best selling, latest products, featured products and random products.

- Mod_Virtuemart_cart: This is the shopping cart for your customers to make purchases.

- Mod_currencies: Allows customers to select different currencies to pay for their product.

- Mod_Featured Products: Shows a listing of featured products.

- Mod_Latestprod: Shows a listing of the latest products.

- Mod_login: Virtuemart Login replaces the Joomla login.

- Mod_manufacturers: Shows a listing of manufacturers for products.

- Mod_randomprod: Shows a list of random products.

- Mod_virtuemart_search: Allows the customer to search for product.

- Mod_virtuemart_topten: Shows the most popular products.

Browse to the location where your Virtuemart modules are stored and Click on each module to install.

**Figure 178: Install**

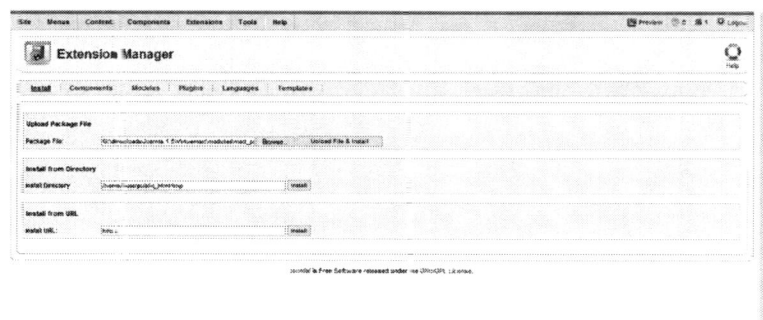

We also need to install Plugins. Within the installer, click browse and go to the Plugin folder. Let's install the plugins.

• Vmproductsnapshots: shows product thumbnails of your product.

• Vmsearch: This is an extended search feature.

Now that everything is installed, let's start activating the modules.

The first one is the Shopping Cart.

Now, you can play around with the module order just by changing the module position in the Module Manager.

210   Virtuemart™

### Figure 179: Module Manager

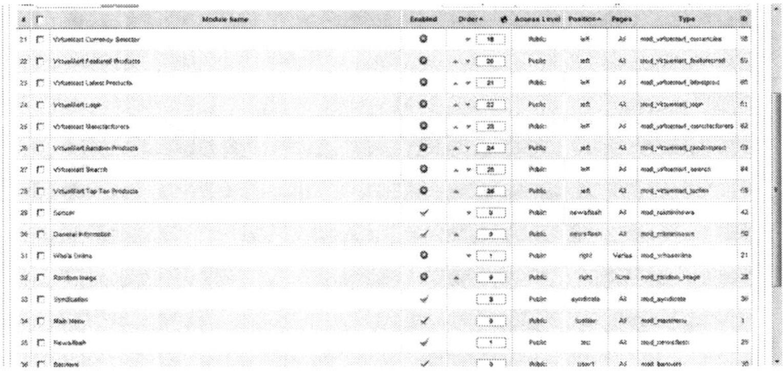

Find the Virtuemart cart module; (Virtuemart Cart) it could be on the first or second page. Click on the module name for the cart and go to the detail page. The first thing we do is change the Cart name to something which fits your site. I usually just rename it "Your Cart".

### Figure 180: Virtuemart Cart Detail

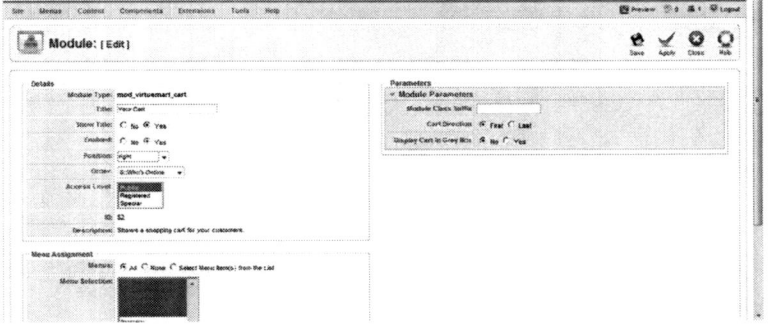

You also have to assign it a position. I have assigned it to the right column in the first position. Based on your template you will need to assign it to where you would like the module to appear.

Virtuemart Modules 211

Under Module parameters on the right hand side, you can set individual parameters for the cart.

- Cart Direction: First or Last – meaning which product is displayed first the first product added to the cart of the last product.

- Display Cart in Grey Box – is just cosmetics, try it and see which way you like best on your website.

Now let's save the cart and refresh the website. Your cart should now appear in the position you put it in. Mine is on the right hand column.

**Figure 181: Website Cart**

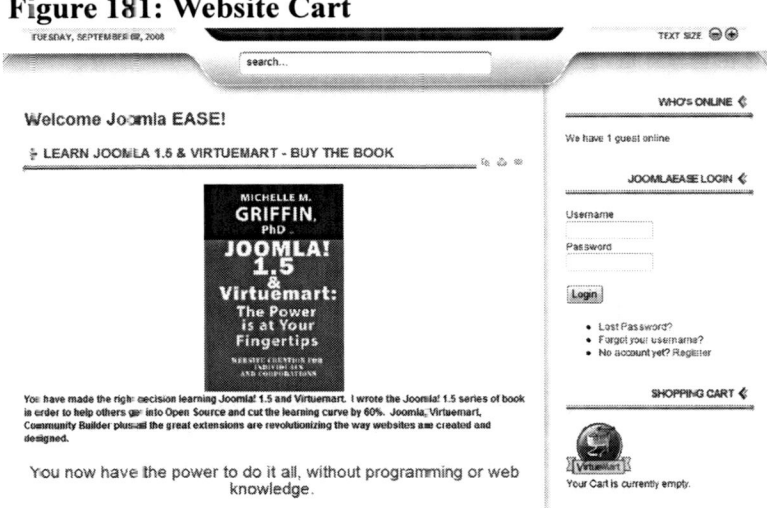

Now let's turn off the Joomla login module and turn on the Virtuemart login module.

Go back to the Module manager and disable the Joomla login. Find the Virtuemart Login module and click the name to go to the details.

## 212 Virtuemart™

**Figure 182: Login Module**

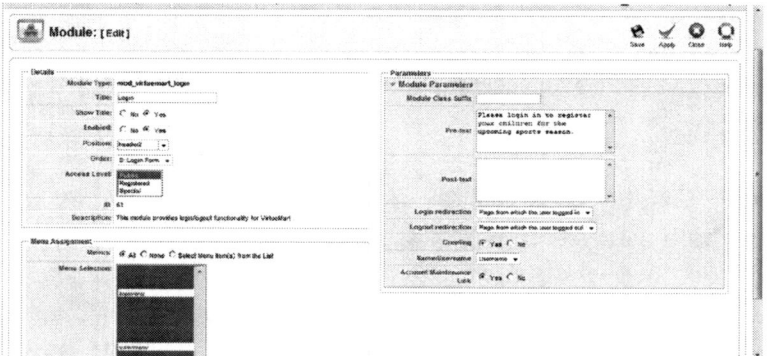

I have changed the title to just Login and entered Pre-Text on the right hand side.

The Account maintenance link, I recommend leaving YES. This is how your customers can review their information and pending orders once logged in. The Account maintenance feature does not appear until the customer is logged in. When done making changes, remember to save and refresh your website.

Now I would like to show Product categories.

**Figure 183: Product Categories**

Virtuemart Modules 213

Back on the Module manager listing, let's find the Virtuemart Product Categories modules. Click on the name and let's look at the details.

I changed the Title to Products I also modified a few of the parameters on the right hand side.

Where it shows JSCook Type: I changed it to Tree from Menu. The Menu option shows the categories with images of the product in front. I personally like the tree. Try them both see which you like.

I also changed the JSCook Menu Orientation to Vertical from Horizontal.

**Figure 184: Tree**

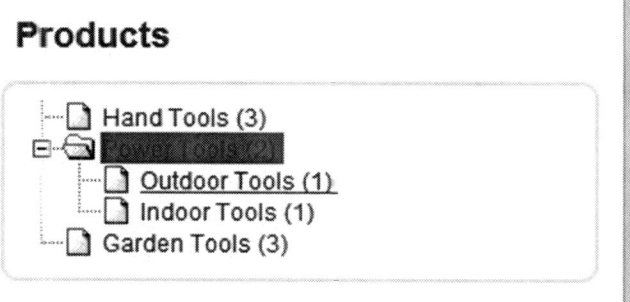

Remember the website template changed a few chapters ago. Therefore I provide a website view just for your comparison.

214  Virtuemart™

# Figure 185: Revised Website

### Figure 186: All In One

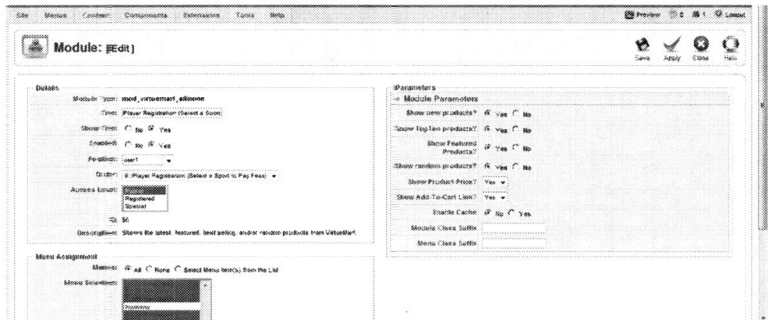

I am going to add a product scroller and the Virtuemart all in one module. I am going to place them in User 1 and User 2.

You need to look at your module columns, to know what available positions you have.

I have also changed the title to Player Registration.

First, I changed the title, notice I wrote (Click on the Tabs). The reason for this is this is a tabbed module and I wanted to ensure customers noticed this feature.

Next, drop down the box for Position; you are able to see the available positions. I place this in User 4. I also need to enable this module. One the right hand column under Module Parameters you can modify the settings. I will leave them as default.

Now I am going to add the Product scroller to my site.

**Figure 187: Product Scroller**

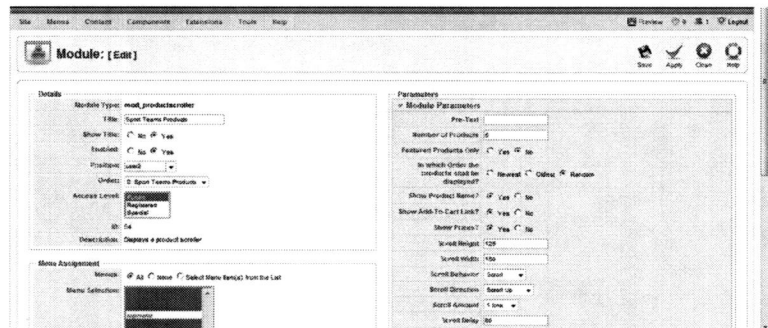

I changed the title to just Product Scroller. I placed this module in User 5 position.

Under Module Parameters, I added pretext letting the customer know to click on the image to view the product. I changed the number of products to 10. But, if you have a lot of products, I would change it even higher unless you have only a few products you want to focus the customer on.

There are many settings for this module. Play with it, until you find the settings that are right for you. Refresh your website. How does it look?

I noticed on mine, it is off balance, therefore I am going to move modules around until it is balanced.

Then I need to add more content to the middle section. Go ahead and modify your website, to give it the appearance you are looking for.

Since we have not setup any products, the modules cannot

be displayed correctly. Therefore in this instance a different website is displayed in order to demonstrate the scroller and login modules. This site is at www.corporationguru.com

**Figure 188: Website Revised**

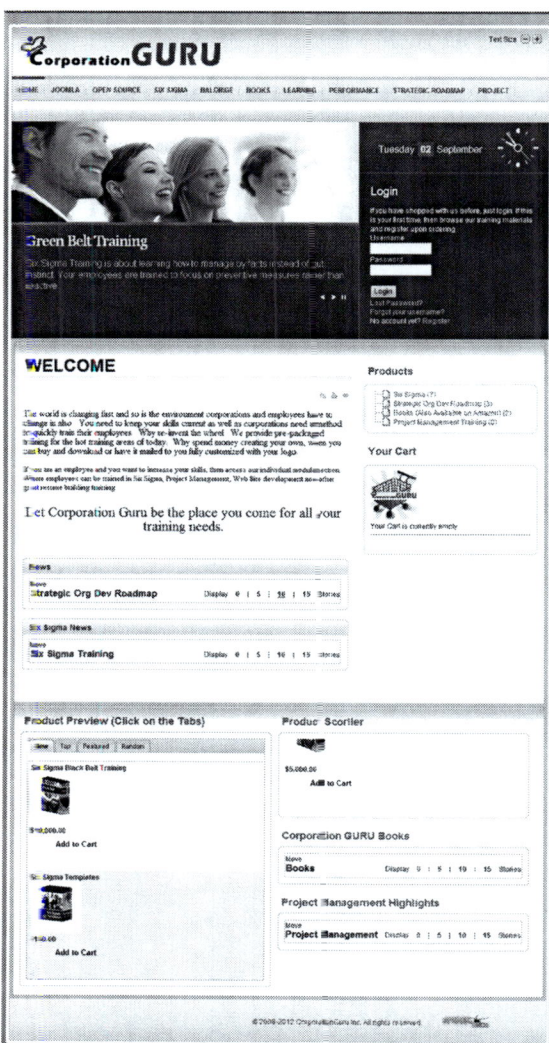

# Virtuemart Configuration

Now let's go to the Virtuemart Control Panel and select Admin/Configuration.

**Figure 189: Virtuemart Admin**

Before we get started, take a look at the control panel. There are two different Virtuemart Control panel layouts. The figure above shows the simple layout. If you look above the shopping cart on the left hand side there are links for Simple and Extended.

If you click on the extended layout, it changes the look of your control panel to drop down menus. Set the layout to how you like it.

Now, we are going to modify the configuration file. The configuration file is located under Admin/Configuration.

I recommend staying with the defaults, but changing only a few items, because there is quite a few buttons. If you change something in the future, change one item at a time save and see how it functions.

### Figure 190: Extended Layout

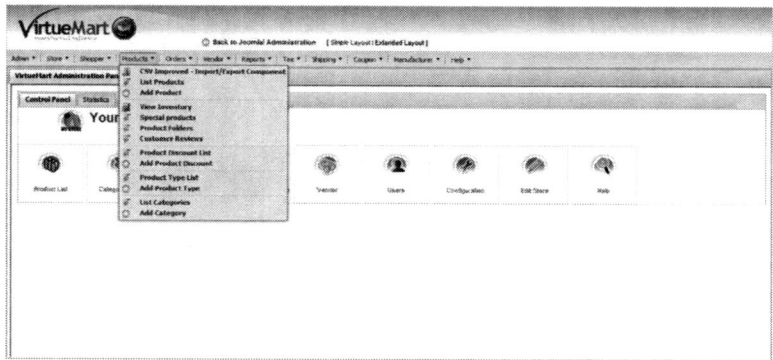

### Global Features:
Shop Offline: Check this only if your shop is offline.

Shop Offline Message: You can customize this to a personal store message.

Use only as Catalogue: Check this if you would customers to be able to view your products but not place an order online. Maybe you would like to have them call in their order or fax it in. This disables the cart functionality.

### Front End Features:
Enable Content Mambots/Plugin Descriptions: This takes the descriptions from the Plugin versus from Virtuemart.

Coupon Usage: This allows customers to enter discount codes to receive discounts. If you are not offering discounts then Uncheck this box.

Enable Customer Review Rating: This allows customers to rate your product. If you don't require ratings then turn this off.; if you don't know then leave it on for no.

Auto Publish Reviews: Only check this box, if you do not care to review comments on your products. I recommend this stays unchecked. This gives you the control of whether a review is published, which is unfairly negative.

Comment Minimum Length and Maximum Length: How much detail do you want from a customer posting a review.

Affiliate Program: At the writing of this book, this future does not fully work. Please do not check.

**Figure 191: Virtuemart Configuration**

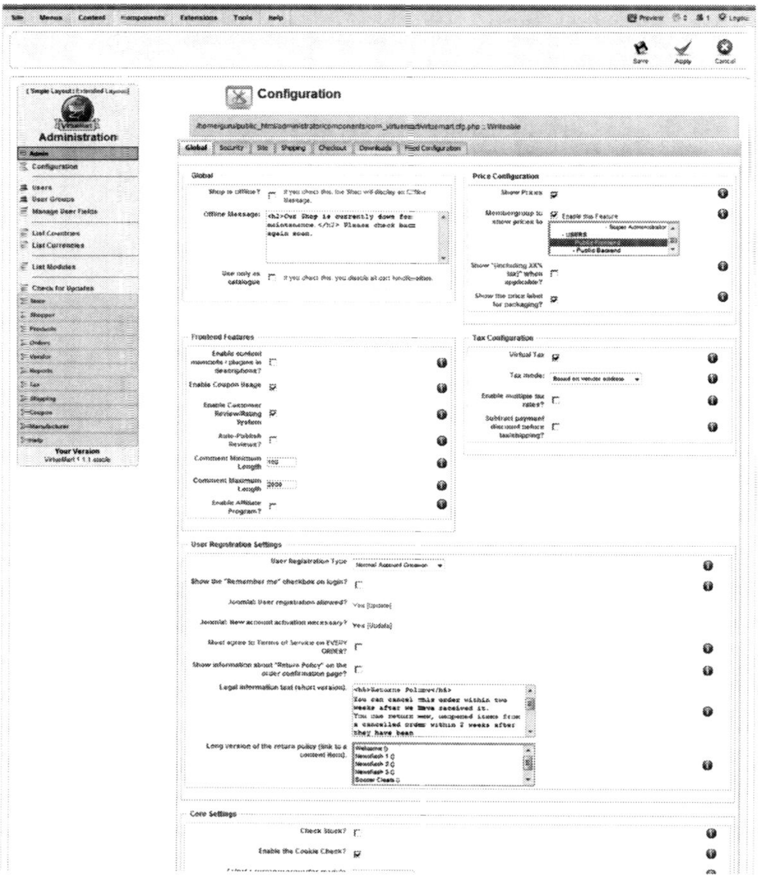

## Price Configuration

Show Prices: Allows prices to show with your product.

Member group to show prices to the default is "Public Frontend". Public Backend is registered users can only see prices.

Show tax when applicable: Customer will see the tax to be added on.

Show the price label for packaging: Shows customers the pricing per package versus unit.

Show Prices including tax? Customers will see the price with tax included. This I usually check.

## Tax Configuration

Virtual Tax: This feature determines if items with zero weight is taxed.

Tax mode: The tax rate is used for calculating taxes for the customer. The tax rate is based on either the Vendor's address or the Customers Address.

Enable multiple tax rates: This you need enabled if you have different taxes for different products.

Discount before tax/shipping: Subtracts the coupon discount prior to calculation of tax. If you are offering discounts or coupons then you want this checked.

## User Registration Settings

User Registration Type: There are four different types of User Registration:

- Normal Account Creation: This is a standard

registration where the customer must register prior to placing an order.

- Silent Account Creation: This method is a username and password is automatically generated based on the email address. I don't recommend this, because customers are constantly forgetting their passwords, if they do not change it to something they remember.

- Optional Account Creation: A customer can optionally create an account.

- No Account Creation: Checkout occurs within an account.

Show the "Remember me" checkbox on login? This feature sets a cookie on the customers' computer, in order for them to not have to login each time. This is a security threat and not recommended to be turned on.

Agree to Terms of Service on EVERY ORDER: Check this only if every time a customer purchases you want them to agree to your terms of service. This is personal, and based on the type of website you are running. I personally will not have it turned on.

Show information about "Return Policy" on the order confirmation page? If you are selling a product, by law you must have a return policy. This should be checked.

Legal information text (short version): This is your Return policy, read through the standard and make changes which fit your product you are selling.

Long version of the return policy (link to a content item): This is the actual return policy with all the caveats. This is an article written in the article manager, and selected here to be published.

### Core Settings

Check Stock: Verifies there is stock available for this item.

Show Products that are out of Stock? Allows you to show Out of Stock product.

Enable the Cookie Check? Allows you to check and see if a customer accepts cookies. I do not set this.

Currency Converter Module: Looks to convert currency, I recommend you leave this as default.

Order-mail format: The setup of your order confirmations either text or html email is sent.

### Logging:

I would leave off, logging could create a large file and could deteriorate your server response time.

Let's click on the Security tab and set these parameters. For my site, I am not changing anything on this page.

### Figure 192: Virtuemart Global Custom Settings

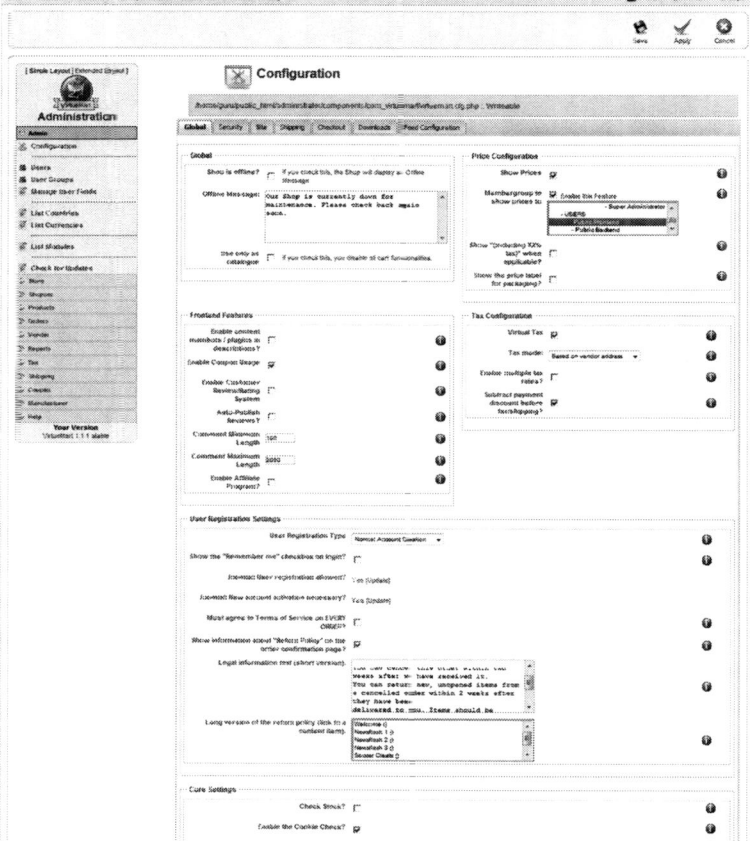

I recommend leaving the security page as the default setting. The only setting you may want to check is the Allow Frontend Administration for non-backend users.

If you have a lot of products to manage, you may want to grant access to users with special privileges' to update the products.

Click on the Site tab now, in order to review these settings.

226  Virtuemart™

### Figure 193: Virtuemart Security

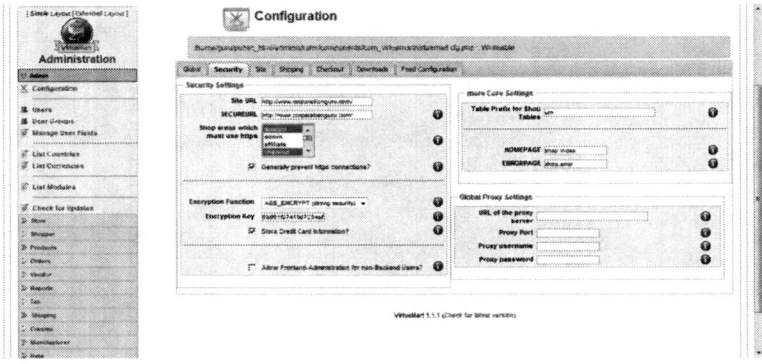

### Site Configuration

PDF - Button : Show or hide the PDF button

Show the "Recommend to a friend" button? Show or hide the link to recommend a friend

Show the "Print View" link? Show or Hide the link for the print view page.

### Figure 194: Virtuemart Site

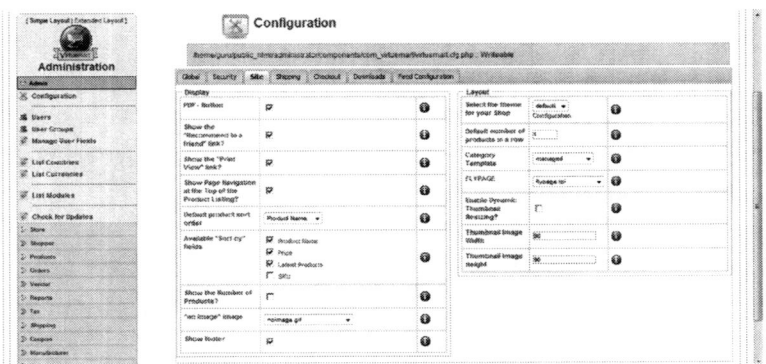

Show Page Navigation at the Top of the Product Listing? Similar to Breadcrumbs in Joomla shows page navigation when down multiple product levels.

Default Product Sort Order: Allows you to select the default sorting of either Product, Price, SKU or Latest Products

Available "Sort-by" fields: The customer can sort their products by Product, Price, SKU or Latest Products.

Show the Number of Products? Shows the number of products in a category; a good feature to have turned on.

"no image" image: Image shown when there is no product image.

**This is located in /components/com_virtuemart/themes/default/images/noimage.gif if you wish to replace the generic image.**


Show footer "powered by...": This displays a VirtueMart Footer image.

### Layout

Global Shop Theme: You can add custom themes for your Virtuemart Shop.

Default number of products in a row: The number of products per row. I recommend setting this after you site is setup and looking at the best layout.

Category Template: Defines the category template for displaying products. Again, I would wait until your site is setup before changing this, in order to see what looks best.

FLYPAGE: This displays the page which appears when displaying your product. I would wait to modify this until you site is setup.

Dynamic Thumbnail Resizing? This dynamically resizes the thumbnail images for you, this creates higher quality images.

**Note: you must have PHP's GD2 enabled on your server.**

You can check if you have GD2 support by going to your Joomla Dashboard and navigating to

**Help/ System Info, click on the tab for "PHP Info" and scroll down until you see gd.**

Thumbnail Image Width and Height : Width and Height of Thumbnail image. Leave as default.

**Figure 195: Virtuemart Site**

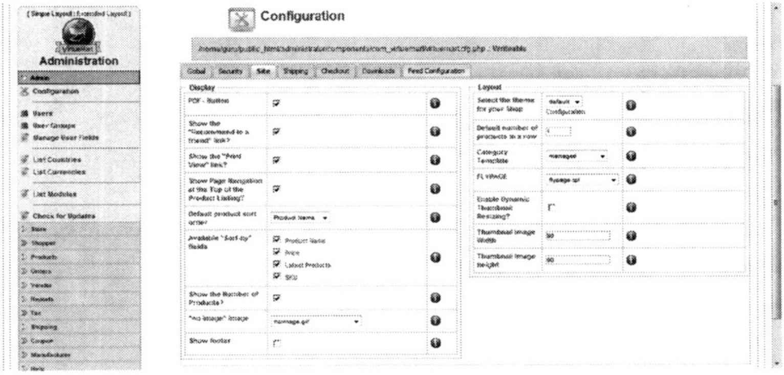

Virtuemart Configuration 229

Let's stay on the Site tab, under layout do you see "Select a theme for your site?" Underneath there is a configuration button. Click on this button.

**Figure 196: Virtuemart Site Configuration Button**

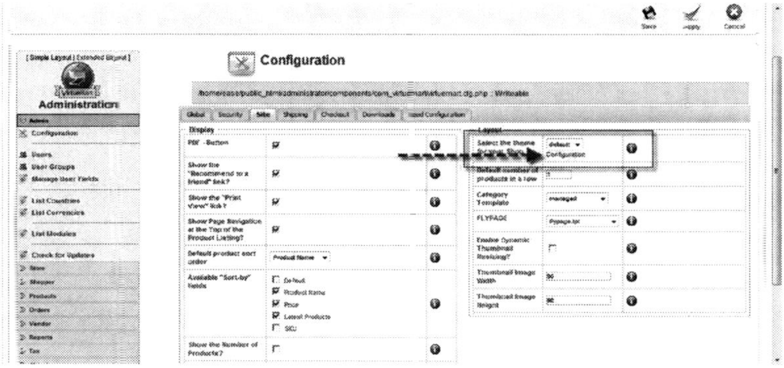

Your theme settings are found here.
**Figure 197: Theme Settings**

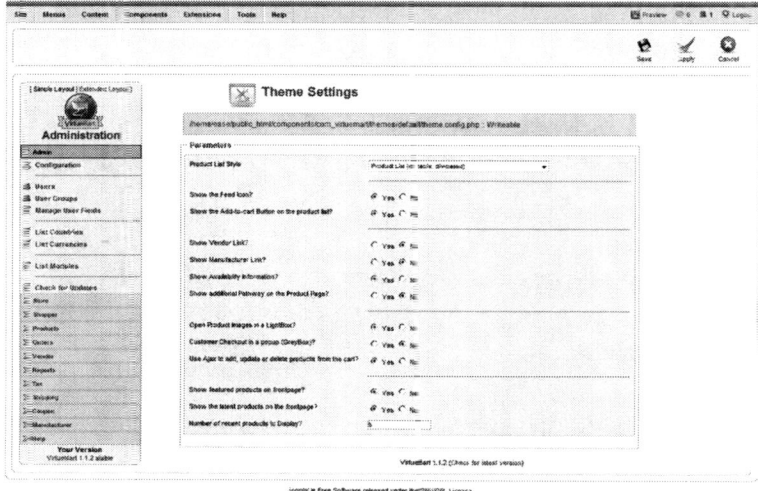

230  Virtuemart™

The theme settings is where the ajax which runs the cart is found.

Also show Featured products and random products on the Virtuemart frontpage, you may want to turn on or off. Since if you have a lot of products they run together on the page.

The next tab is Shipping, let's look at the parameters for this screen.

**Figure 198: Virtuemart Shipping Config**

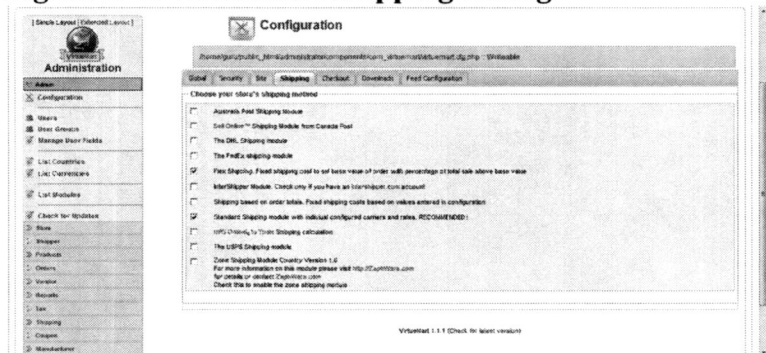

The shipping module is very flexible and if you have DHL, FEDEX or UPS accounts you configure them to access your account for rates and billing.

You will need to go to the Virtuemart site for configuration of these accounts.

If you will not be charging shipping then you need to disable this module as well as in the Checkout process change the shipping verification.

At this time, I will leave everything default for the demonstration site. Let's click the next tab, which is Checkout.

Virtuemart Configuration 231

On the Checkout page, I recommend leaving this as a default, unless you do not offer shipping then you would uncheck the second box.

The Checkout Bar tells customers what stage of the ordering process they are in, it is very handy for customers.

**Figure 199: Virtuemart Checkout Config**

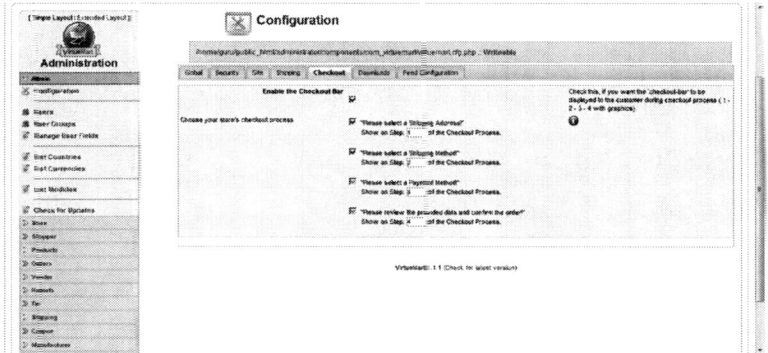

The stages are numbered, and you can change the order of the stages by changing the number assigned to the stage.

Now let's proceed to the Download configuration page.

**Figure 200: Virtuemart Download Config**

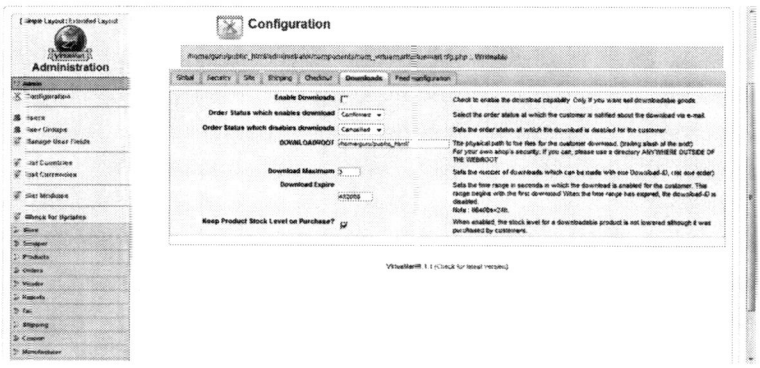

The download page is only for those who sell downloaded products. Since this site will have downloads. I am going to check this box.

You also need to create a folder where your downloaded products will reside for the automatic download process to work.

The last configuration file is Feeds. This is found on the last tab.

**Figure 201: Virtuemart Feeds Config**

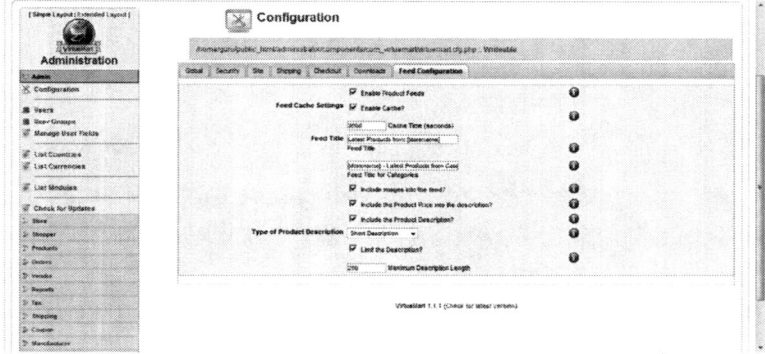

This feature is pretty cool, your customers upon registration can subscribe to a feed, which would send them product updates automatically. For now, let's just leave the default in place. That is it for the configuration file. Make sure to save.

Now we need to go back to the Virtuemart Control panel. Under Store click on summary. This takes you back to the main control panel

Virtuemart Configuration 233

### Figure 202: Virtuemart Control Panel

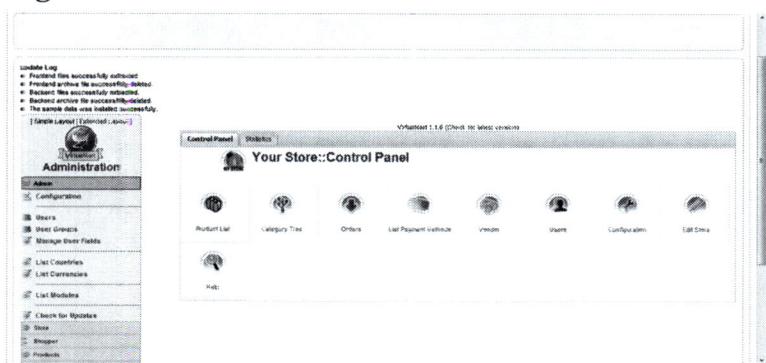

If you look at the center of your screen there is a tab for Statistics. This is a handy little screen to track your number of orders and statuses. It is a nice little Executive summary.

### Figure 203: Statistics

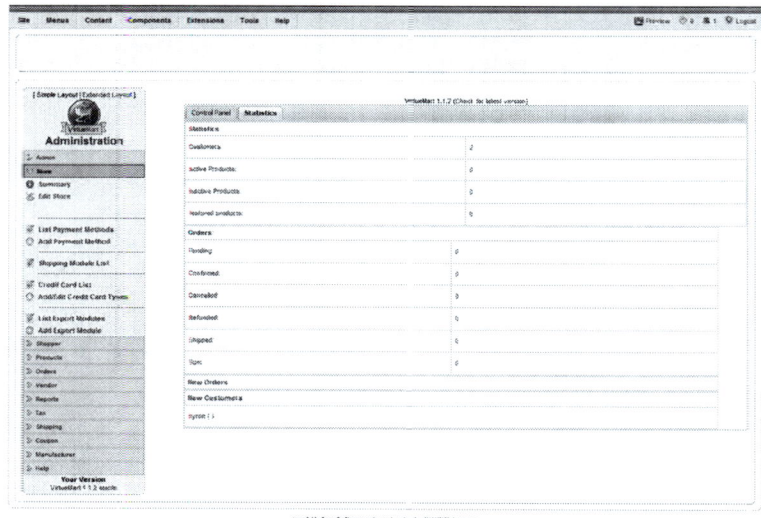

Let's set up the store information now.

# Virtuemart Store

Let's update the store information. The store information is located on the left navigation under Store.

**Figure 204: Store Navigation**

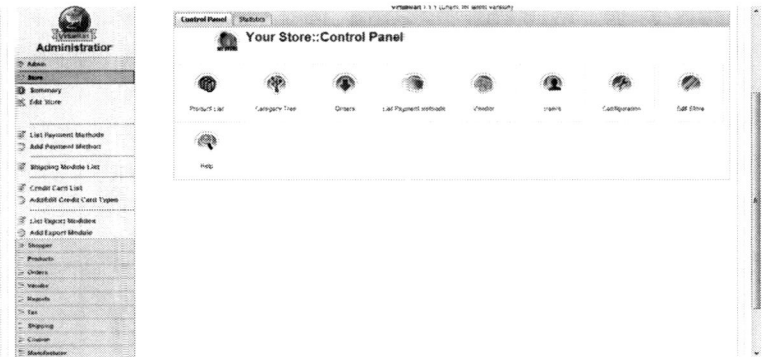

Let's click on Edit Store

Go ahead and change the detail information in the Store to your information.

**Figure 205: Store Summary**

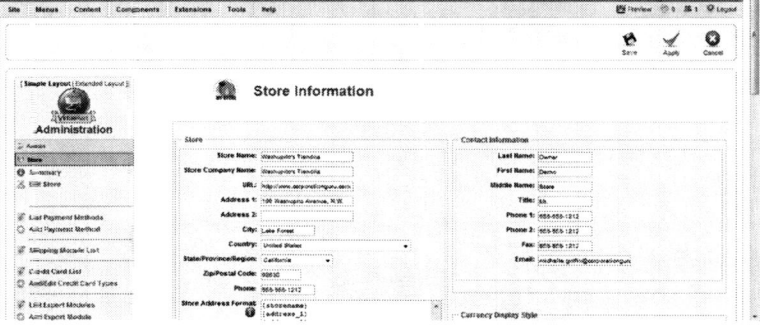

Then click on the image field and browse for your logo from your website, click save.

Your Store information is shown, if you still need to finish editing then re-click on the Edit Store link.

236  Virtuemart™

Don't forget to scroll to the bottom of the Edit store screen to update the description of your company.

One last thing to do, under Currency Display Style in the Thousand separator field you need to enter a comma.

**Figure 206: Store Information**

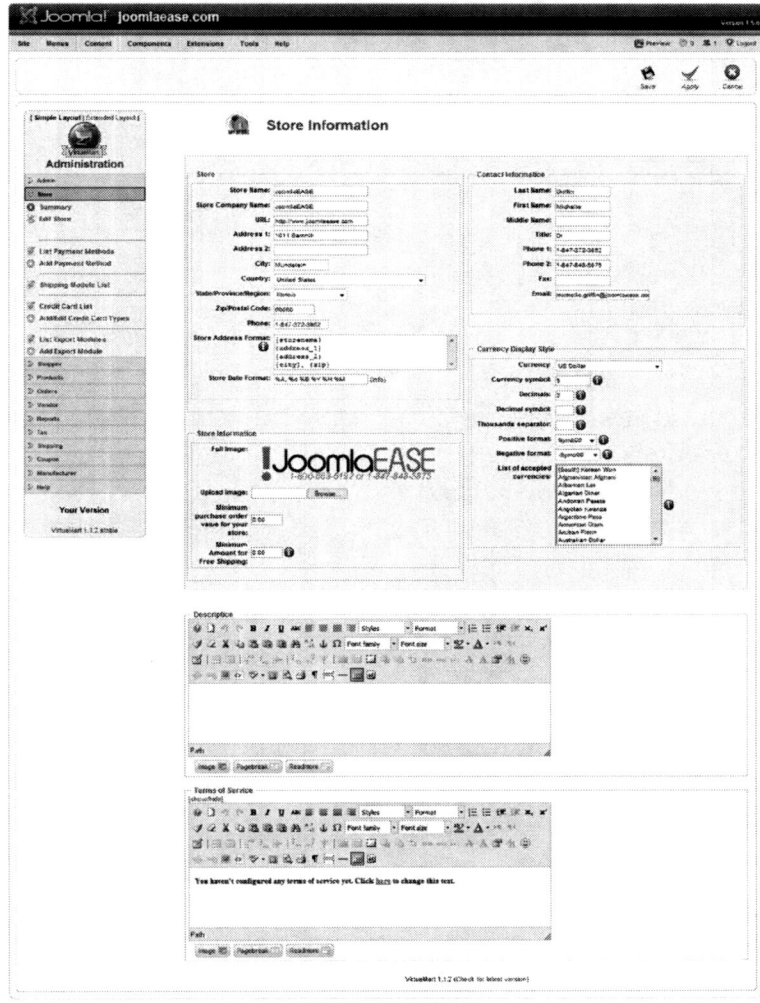

# Virtuemart Payment Methods

Payment methods are important to configure. If you are a corporation dealing with other corporations, you may need to take Purchase Orders. If you are a company which sells products to customers you may need to take credit cards. But, if you don't have your own credit card processor then you may need to use PayPal.

**Figure 207: Virtuemart Control Panel**

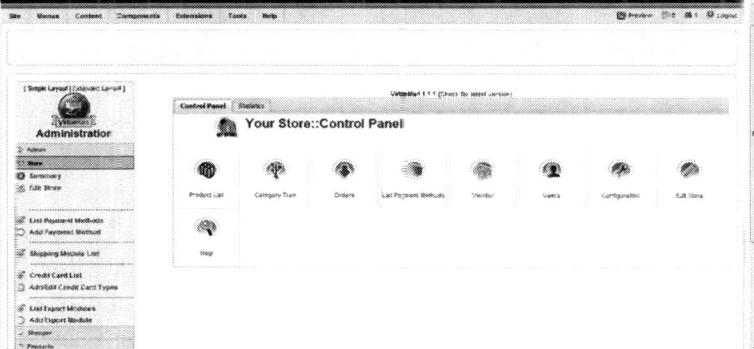

Once the Virtuemart Control Panel opens, on the left hand side under STORE, click on Payment Methods.

As a default the Credit Card, Epay, PayPal, Verisign, Purchase Order and Cash on Delivery are published. For the CorporationGuru website, I will be using only PayPal or Purchase order for right now, therefore I am going to unpublish the other options.

Go ahead and Publish or unpublish what you need for your site.

For this example I will show you how to configure PayPal. To begin, let's open the Virtuemart Control Panel; when in the Joomla Control Panel/Component/Virtuemart.

238   Virtuemart™

### Figure 208: Payment Methods

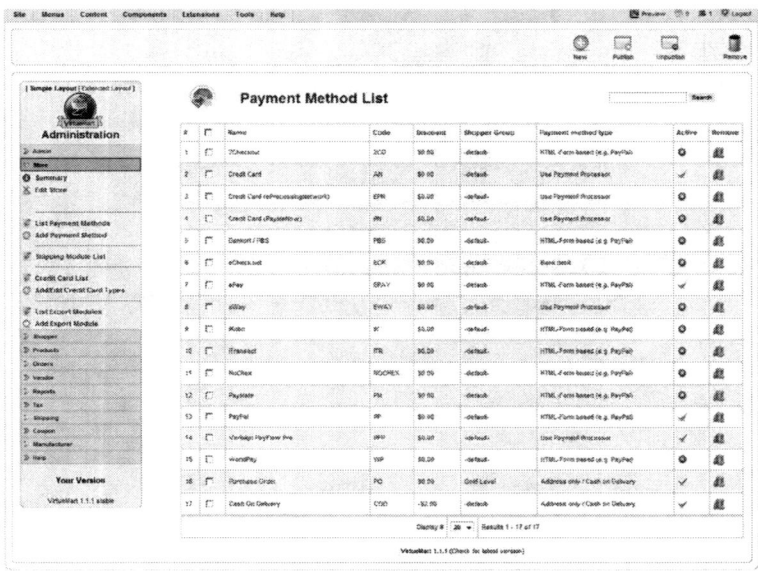

Let's click on Purchase Order and update this first. Since this is a sports website, registration can be handled by check. Therefore we are going to modify this to handle checks.

### Figure 209: Check Detail

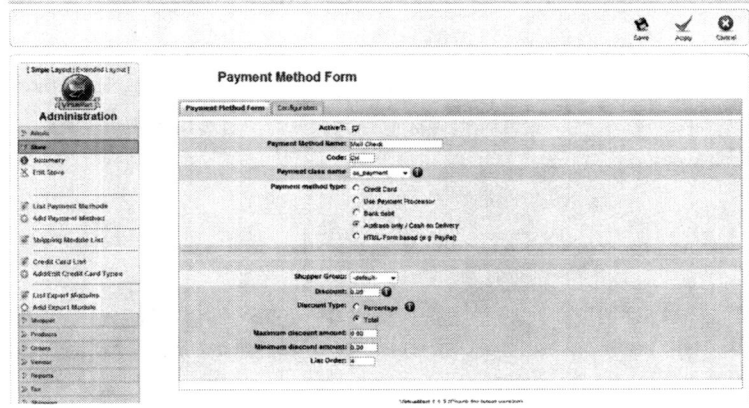

Virtuemart Payment Methods 239

Click the 2nd tab under Configuration and add a little blurb age about this payment method.

**Figure 210: Check Configuration**

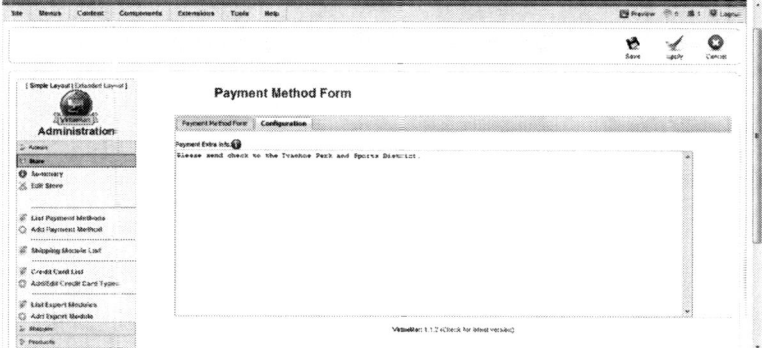

Now, let's configure PayPal. Click on the PayPal link and on the detail page go to Configuration.

Change PayPal Payment email to your email used to access your PayPal account, click save.

Now go back into the Paypal Payment screen and click on configuration again.

**Figure 211: PayPal Configuration**

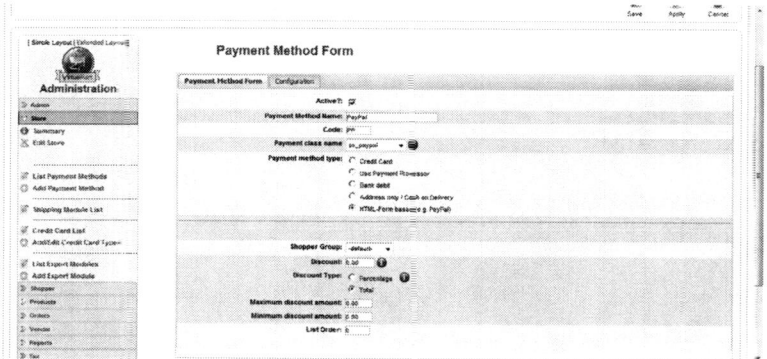

240  Virtuemart™

The test mode website for Paypal is down at the time of this writing. You need to change Test Mode to NO.

**Figure 212: Paypal Test Mode**

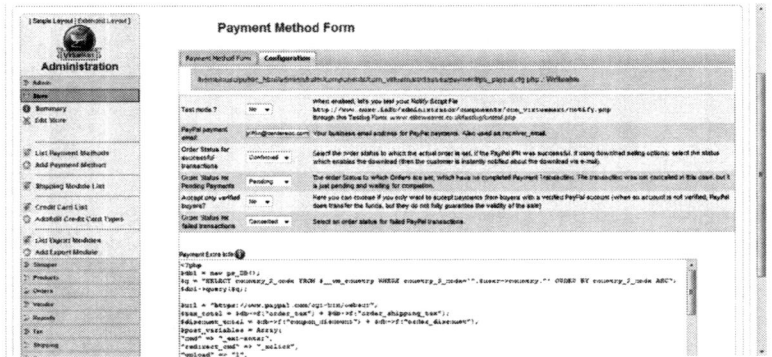

# Virtuemart Tax Rate

Let's set the Tax rates for your store. If you go to the Virtuemart Control Panel on the left hand navigation go to Tax Rate, click on list tax rates.

**Figure 213: Tax Rate**

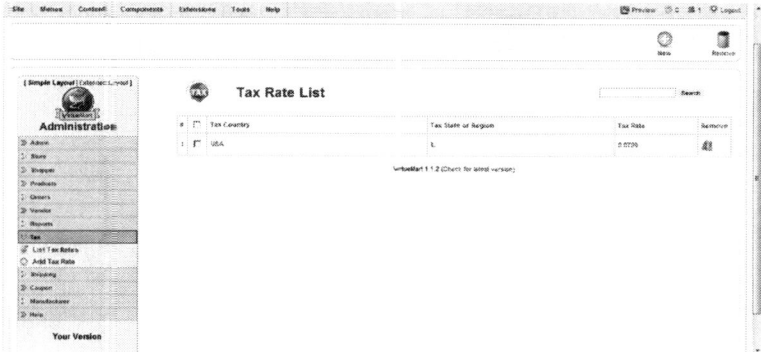

Now click on the USA rate and change the default to your home state. You will need to know your tax rate for your state also.

**Figure 214: Tax Rate Detail**

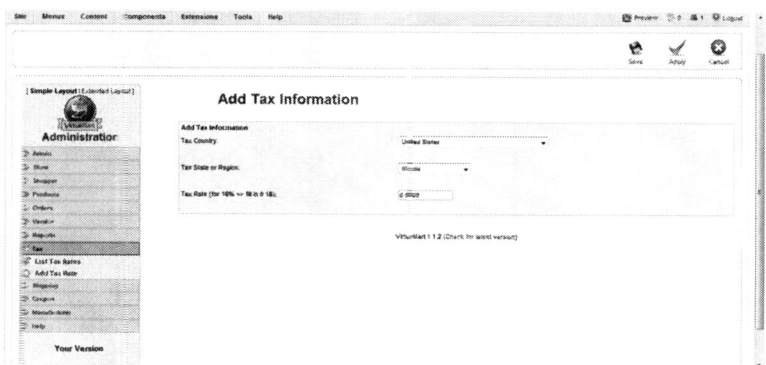

# Virtuemart Categories

The product categories are located in the Virtuemart Control panel on the left navigation under Products.

**Figure 215: Product Categories**

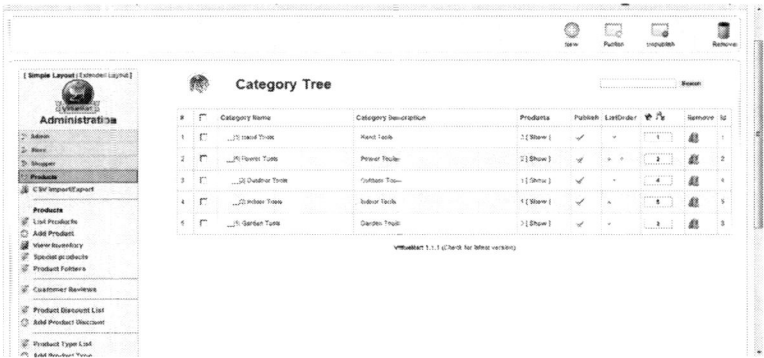

You can either change the categories that are there or delete them and create new ones.

I am just going to change the categories, because then all the fields are filled in. Click on Hand Tools and let's change this one.

At this point I am only changing the name and description.

Once we done, we will come back and adjust the Number of products per row and the Browser page. Browse Pages will be discussed in one of the next chapters.

Click on the 2nd tab and insert an image.

## 244  Virtuemart™

### Figure 216: Category Detail

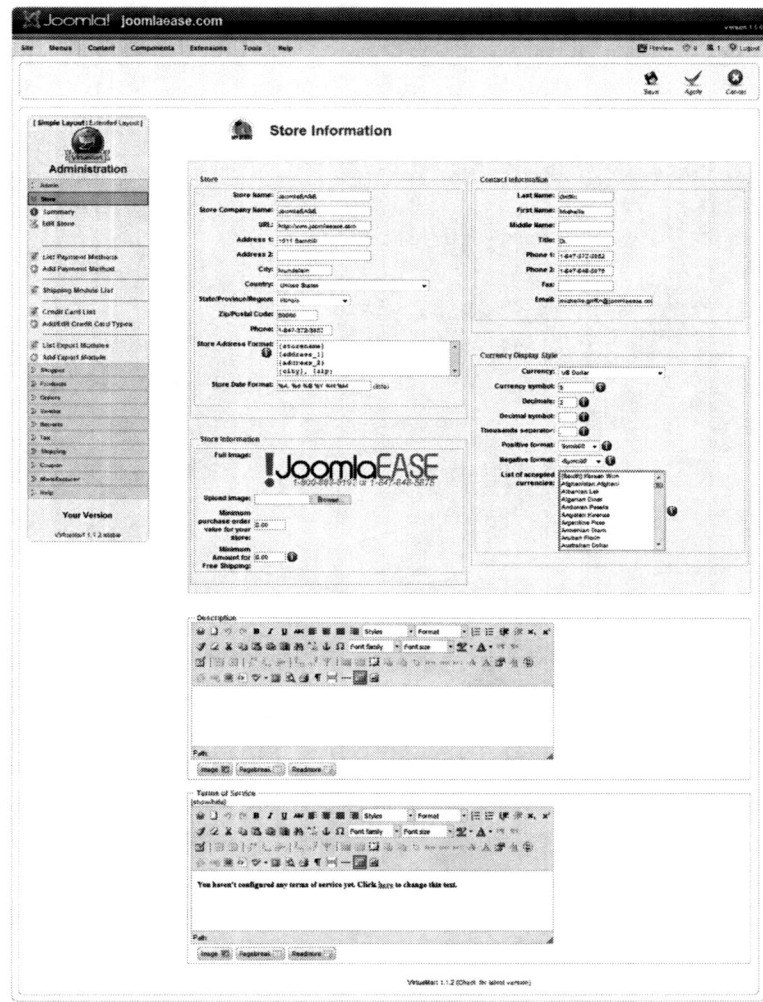

Virtuemart Categories 245

### Figure 217: Category Image

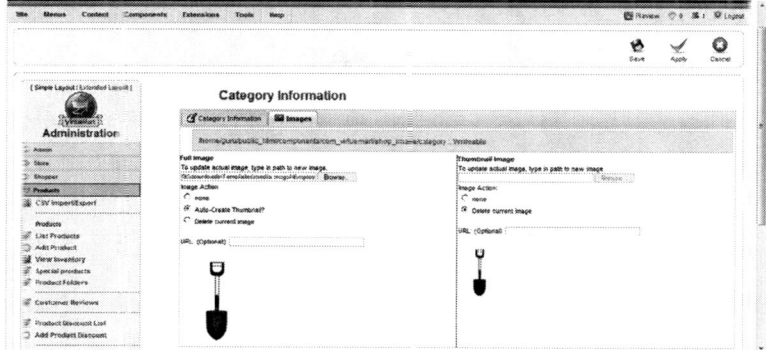

Browse for your image file and check the radio button for Auto-create thumbnail. Then check the radio button for Delete current image under thumbnail and save.

You will exit this screen and go back to the category listing

Go back in and verify your images appeared.

### Figure 218: Image update

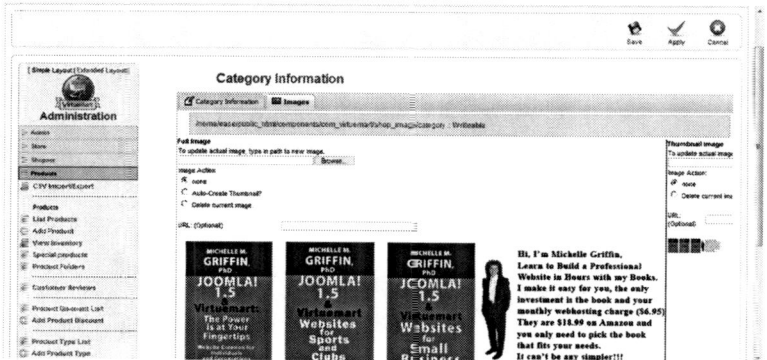

Now go change the rest of the categories to your topics.

246  Virtuemart™

**Figure 219: Category Tree**

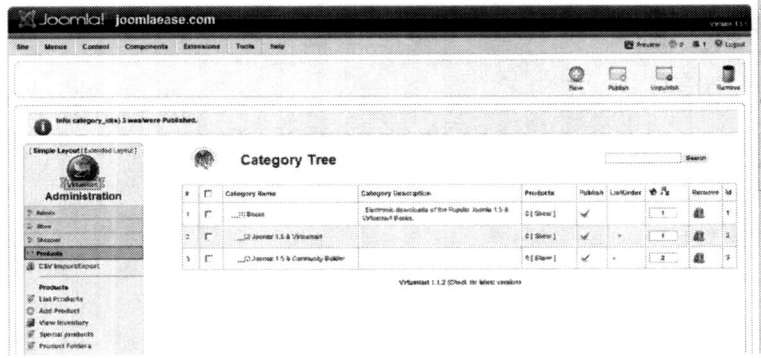

If you notice some of my cateogories are indented. This is because they are sub-categories. To create a sub-category you need to go into the Category to the bottom of the page and change the Parent listing for it to fall underneath a parent item.

**Figure 220: Category Parent**

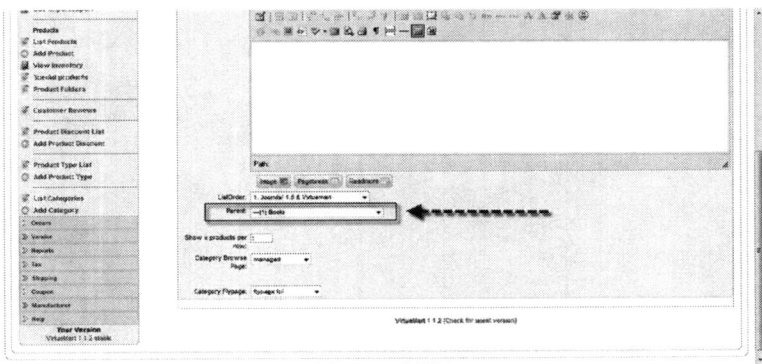

# Virtuemart Manufacturer

We need to add a manufacturer. This is optional but looks nice on the website. Go to the Virtuemart Control Panel on the left hand navigation menu click on Manufacturer then list manufacturer.

**Figure 221: Manufacturer list**

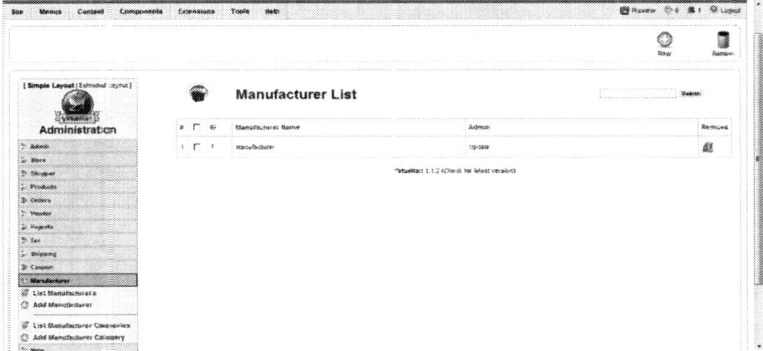

Click on Manufacturer Name to go to the details and add your manufacturers information.

**Figure 222: Manufacturer Details**

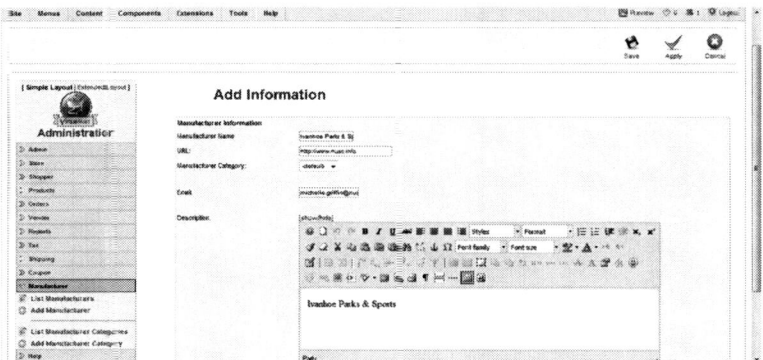

# Virtuemart Products

There are three ways to add products (Product List, Product Folder and CSV). I will show you all two ways, in this chapter we will cover only the Product List and Product Folder. The CSV improved module is still not Native 1.5 complaint and therefore I do not recommend using it at this point. So you have to load your products by hand. I expect it will be available toward sthe end of 2008.

The first way is to go to the Product list. First go to the Virtuemart Control Panel and on the left hand navigation go to Products/List Products

**Figure 223: Control Panel**

The second method is via Product Folders. If you look on the left hand navigation Product folders is located under Products.

When you click the item, it will go directly to the Product detail page, described in the next section.

Choose which method you like best and then we will begin to create a product.

250    Virtuemart™

### Figure 224: Product Listing

### Figure 225: Product Folders

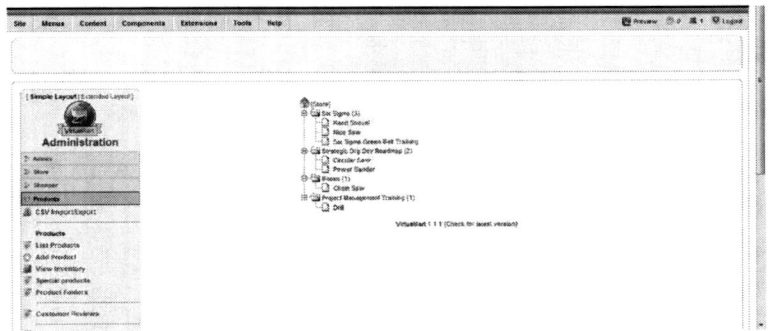

I use the product listing myself, since if I have a lot of products I can filter on a product category. Just remember if you use the filter, because you may get nervous when all your products are not showing and accidently re-add them back in creating duplicates.

The filter needs to be set as Select a Category to turn it off.

# Virtuemart Products 251

### Figure 226: Product Listing Category

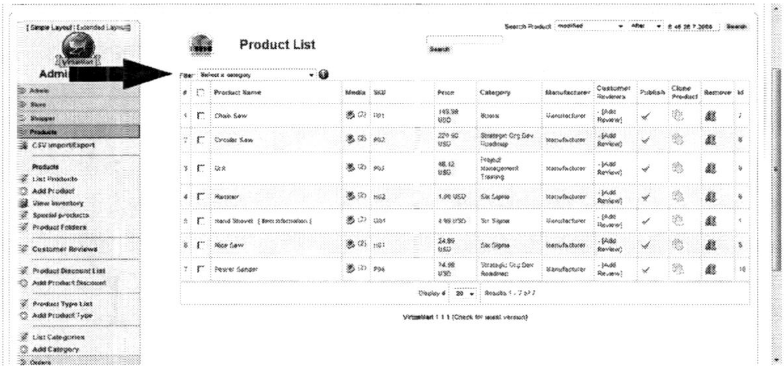

Let's go into the detail of one of the default products and change it to one of our products. The Product Detail page is basic product information.

### Figure 227: Product Details

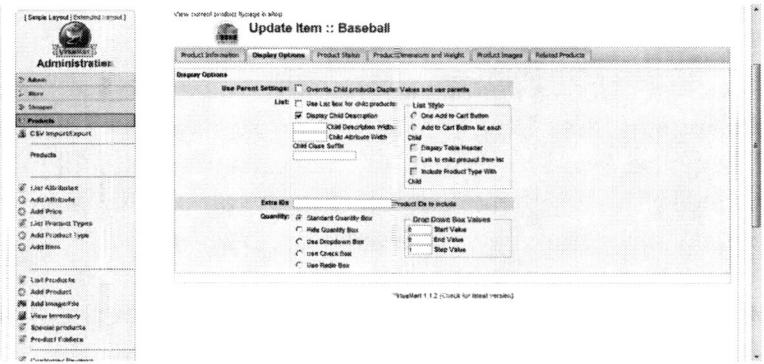

You will need to come up with a numbering scheme for your products in order to track inventory. These SKU numbers need to be unique.

There are two different philosophies in business. You will have to decide the proper method for your company. Once you decide on a direction it is hard to change within a fiscal year.

Therefore think through this process, especially if your website is for a growing business. Inventory numbering schemes:

• Smart Numbering, as your products structures grow with a large number of products you may want to use smart numbering. This could be alpha, numeric or a combination of both. For instance for my Six Sigma line, I have 6 products, therefore I could number the products: SSGB, SSBB, SSL, SSYB or SS01, SS02, SS03 where each number means a particular product.

• Consecutive Numbering, many large corporations use consecutive numbering because when you are dealing with 1000's of products, it becomes complicated to add new products to maintain consistent coding. Many organizations start with a 6 digit numbering scheme which goes up to 999,999 products. This leaves you plenty of room to grow and you may never max out on numbering.

Personally for JoomlaEase, we are going to use Smart Numbering, just to keep products segmented and also to think to the future, once a segment of the corporation is sold off or separated in to a separate corporation, the product lines can be separated apart from the rest of the product lines.

Again, this is a personal decision, but once set it is very difficult to change as a company direction in the future.

For your product add your SKU number, Name, Category, Price, Discount (if applicable), Short Description and Long Description (at the bottom of the form).

I recommend you save after the first screen and then go back in to the next tab which is Display Values. I would hate for you to enter all the information then your session times out.

**Figure 228: Display Values**

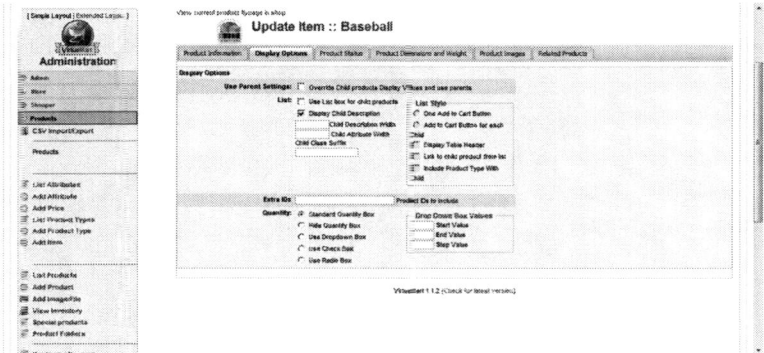

The default is focused on the Parent items. You are able to uncheck this box and individually configure the items for child items. For initial design of your website, I recommend leaving this as default. As you build your products then you can tweak the settings.

The Quantity boxes are nice, because you can play with the way your customer selects product. You will need to play with the settings to see what works best. Since my products are bought individually then I will stay with the default. But if you sell products where customers could buy multiple units then a drop down box may be a better choice. Let's click on the next tab, product status.

The Product Status page is packed full of features. Again, you will need to play with to see what works for you. I basically get all the products in and then begin to tweak them, as I work the website, in order to make it customer focused.

**Figure 229: Product Status**

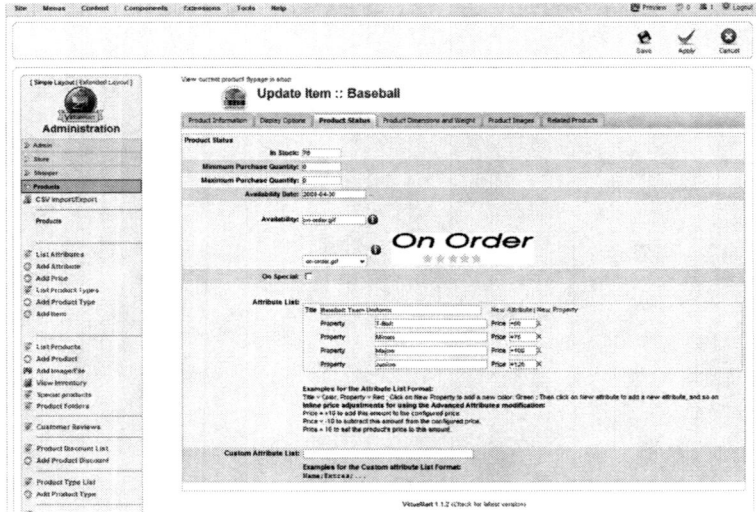

For JoomlaEase, I am not using attributes therefore we will work with another site in order to demonstrate. The site is www.bdsimply.com. This company is a catering company which serves sandwiches and party platters for lunch.

In the attribute space type in the name of the attribute and then add the property and if there is a price associated. If there are additional properties then click add.

The prices are added with a + or - in front. Therefore in this example, T-Ball is a +50. When this item is selected it will add the registration price of $100 to the T-Ball Uniform price giving a total of $150 dollars for registration.

Once you are done with the first attribute then click add attribute to add another. Make sure you save frequently. Below is an example of a number of attributes for a sandwich company.

## Virtuemart Products   255

### Figure 230: Product Attributes setup

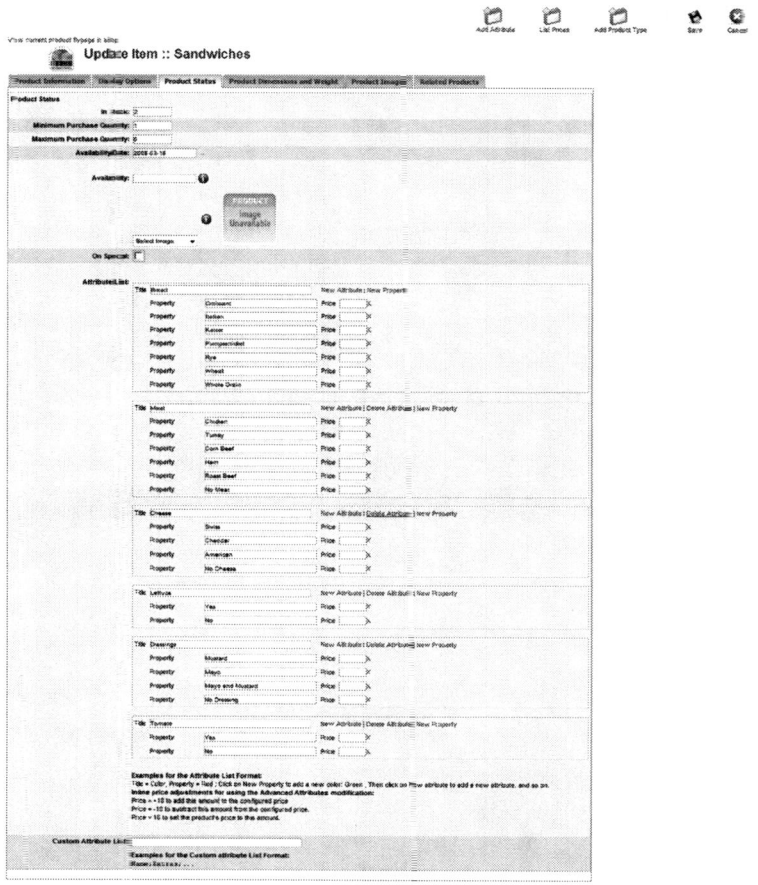

The next figure shows a website with a number of features and options for their products. Even though it is not sports related, you can get an idea of how it works.

This is a site, that one of my customers built by themselves. They had no programming experience and built it in about 3 hours.

Each attribute is a drop down box, this way the customer can select exactly what they want.

256  Virtuemart™

### Figure 231: Website Products and Attributes

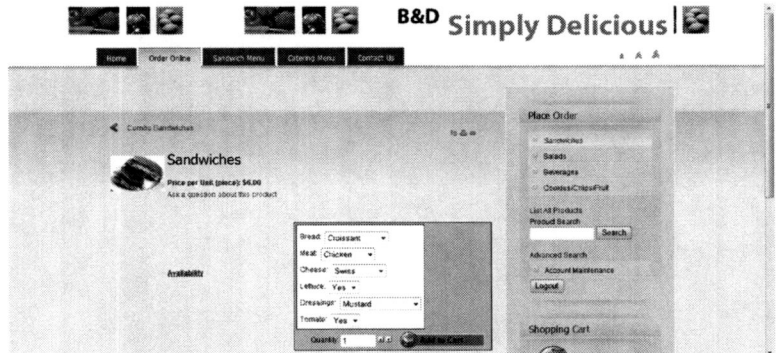

The sample invoice shows what an order looks like once a customer selects all their items.

### Figure 232: Sample Invoice with Attributes

## Virtuemart Products

**Figure 233: Product Status Date**

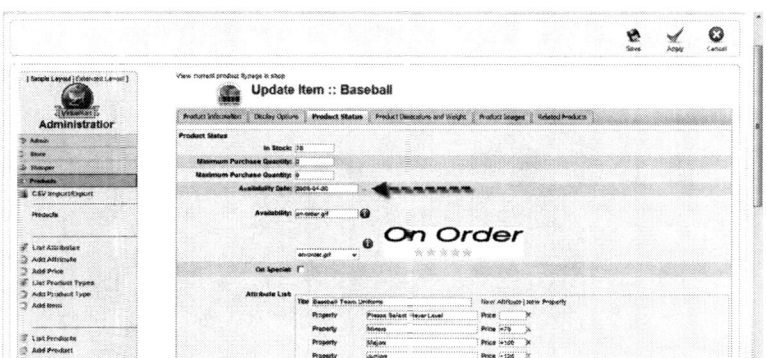

Now, we are going to jump back to the www.joomlaease.com website. Next to Availability date there is ... - click on this for a calendar. Make sure you have you product with a date in the past. Otherwise your product will not show up until the date it shows. On Special is a neat little feature, this need to be checked if you want your product to show up under Featured.

**Figure 234: Product Dimensions**

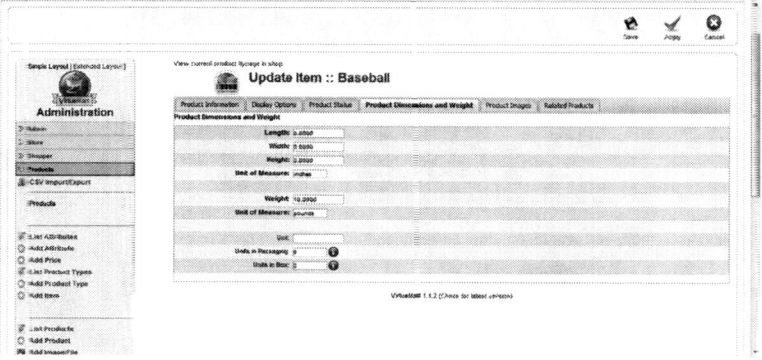

Let's go to the next tab. Product Dimensions is an optional screen, but if you use the shipping modules it is good to have the dimensions entered.

258  Virtuemart™

The next tab is product image. This is similar to how we handled loading images in the Product Category chapter. Go ahead and load your image.

**Figure 235: Product Image**

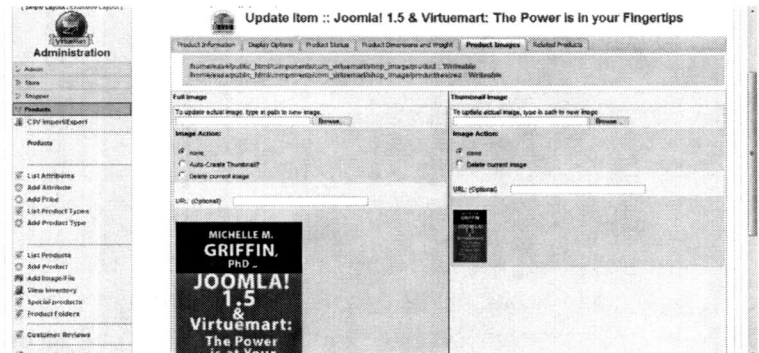

The last tab, Related Products you will need to fill out after you enter many of your products.

**Figure 236: Related Products**

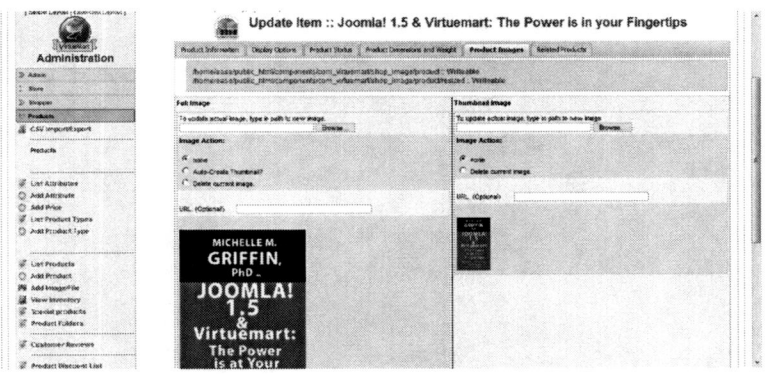

Virtuemart Products  259

To use this feature, just type in a key word for instance one of your categories and the selections come up.

Then click on the products which are related (customers who bought this product also bought this product). Go ahead and update, a few more products in order to have an understanding how this area works.

**Figure 237: Product Overview**

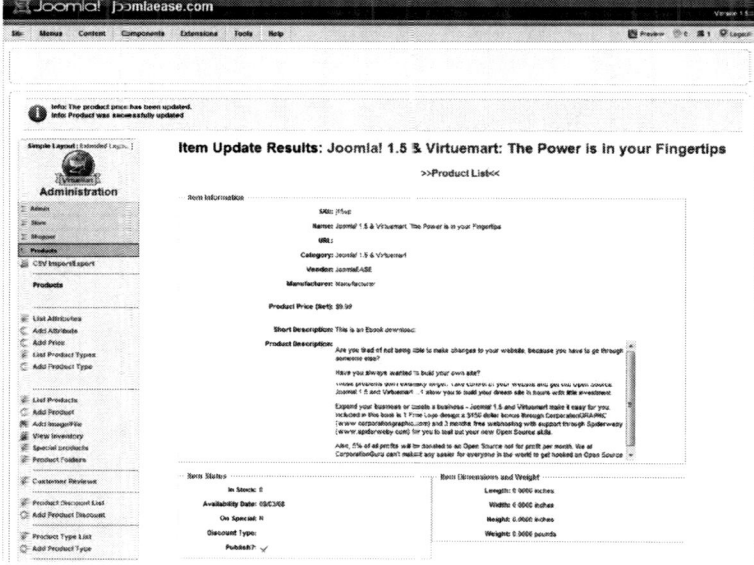

## 260 Virtuemart™

## Figure 238: Product View

# Virtuemart Configuration Update

Refresh your website and notice how your Product Scroller and Product features now show your products and listings.

Now that we have activated the Virtuemart Login versus the Joomla login we need to make a few changes before we test the ordering process.

Now that Virtuemart is installed we need to change the Activate user account to NO. We do not want a customer placing an order then having to go back and approve their registration account. They could become frustrated and not place the order. Therefore we need to limit the frustration level.

We need to go to Cpanel and change the permissions on the configuration.php file to 777. Refer back to the Global Configuration chapter for changing the permissions.

**Figure 239: Global Configuration update**

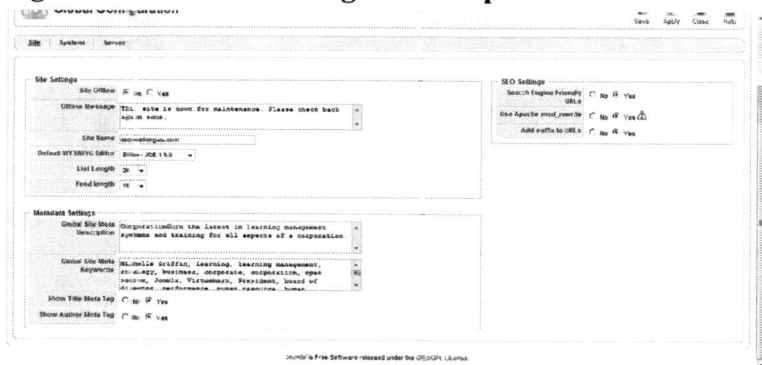

Make sure once you change the files you need to go back into Cpanel and change the permissions back to 644. Due to Security concerns, never leave this file writeable.

### Figure 240: Virtuemart Configuration

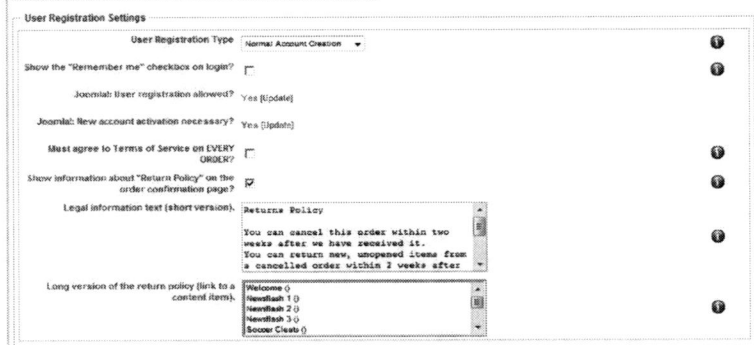

I recommend this be changed within the Virtuemart Configuration and not in Joomla Configuration.

Open the Configuration file under Admin in the Virtuemart Control Panel. Scroll down to User Settings and click on the update link for Joomla! New account activation necessary.

### Figure 241: Virtuemart Configuration updated

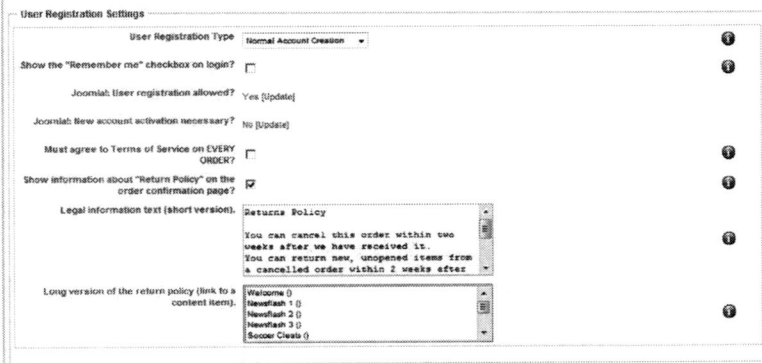

Virtuemart Configuration Update 263

Figure 242: Joomla Global Configuration

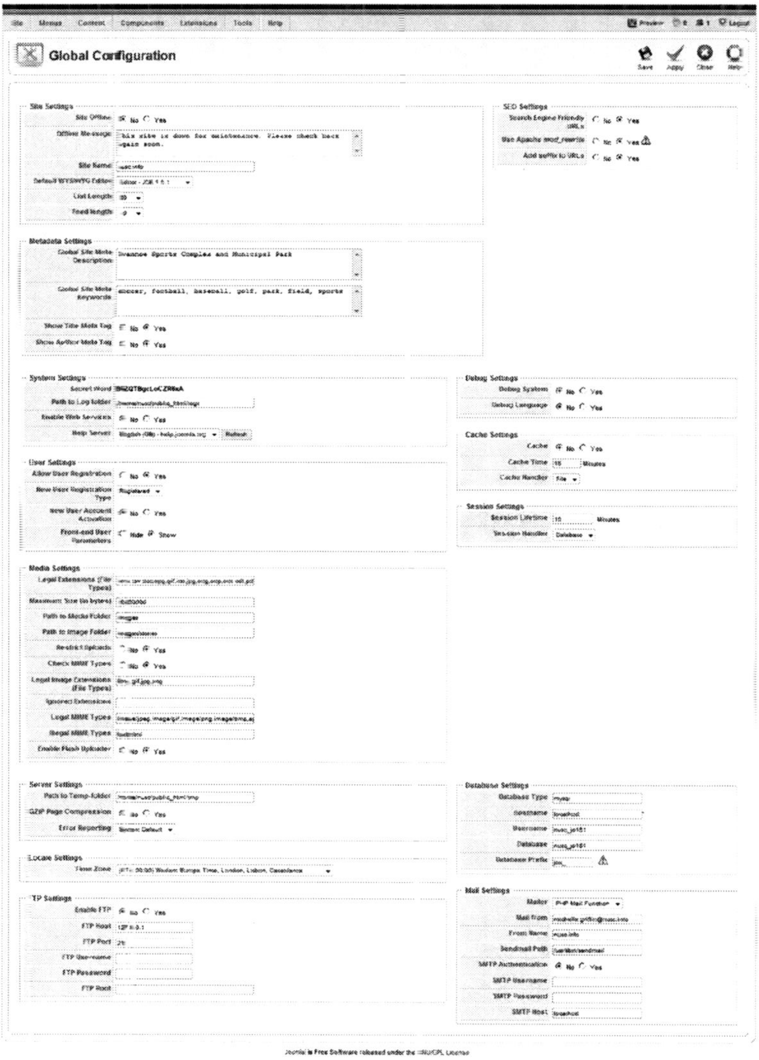

# Virtuemart Product Layout

Refresh your website. Let's click on the product category in order to look at the ordering process.

**Figure 243: Website**

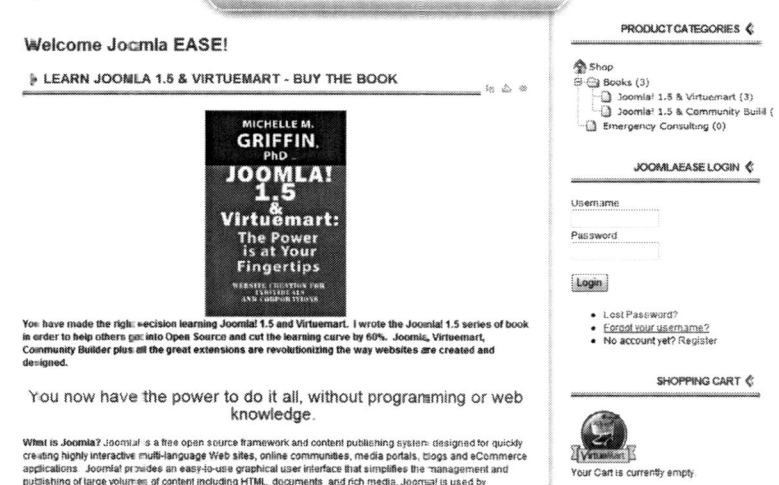

I clicked on the books link and then the Joomla Link. I looked at the page and the 3 across product listing looks cluttered. So let's walk through and clean up this page.

**Figure 244: Website 3 across**

266 Virtuemart™

First, let's change the view to be 2 across. We need to go into the Category Listing and change the display.

**Figure 245: Category Tree**

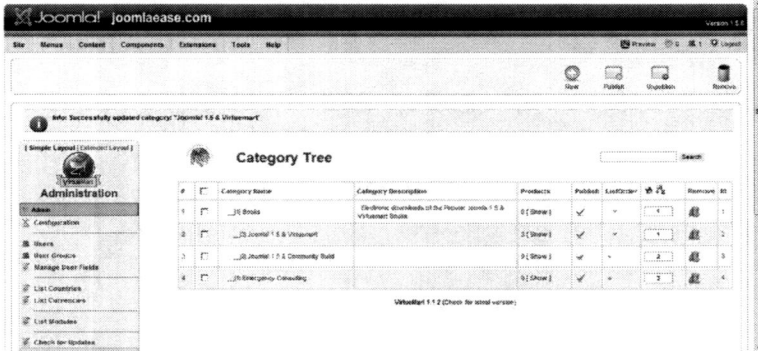

We are going to adjust the field "Show x products". I am going to change it to 2 across and then save and refresh your website.

**Figure 246: Category Detail**

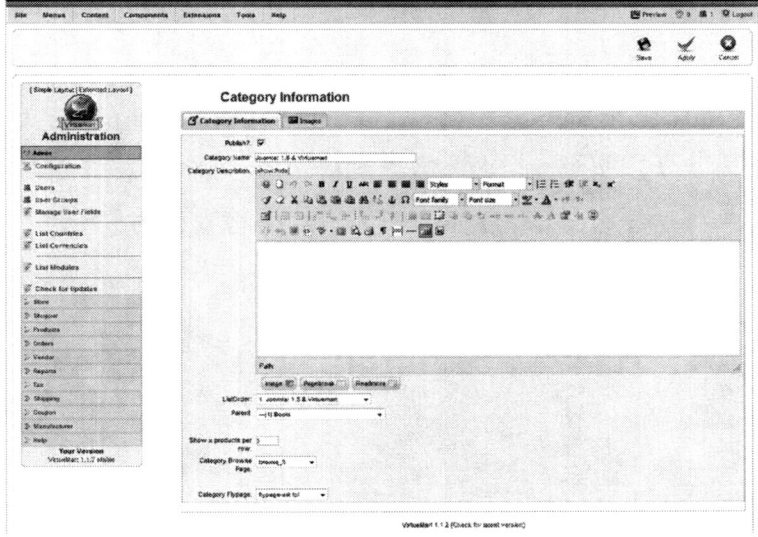

## Figure 247: Website Products 2 across

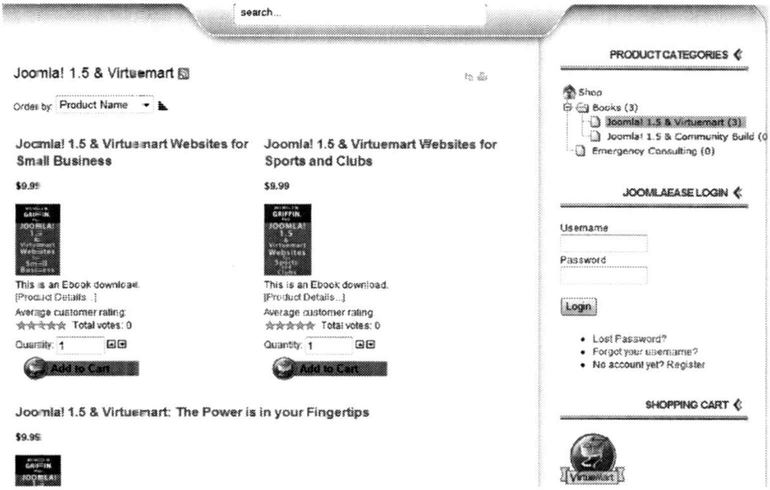

Play with changing the number across until you find the view you like.

# Virtuemart Browse Page Layouts

We are going to cover the browse page layouts located in the Category manager. There are just subtle differences.

But, you may find one you like better then the Browse_3 which is the default.

First let's go to the Category Tree this is located in the Virtuemart Control Panel under Products/List Categories then click on your main category and go to the detail page.

**Figure 248: Category Detail**

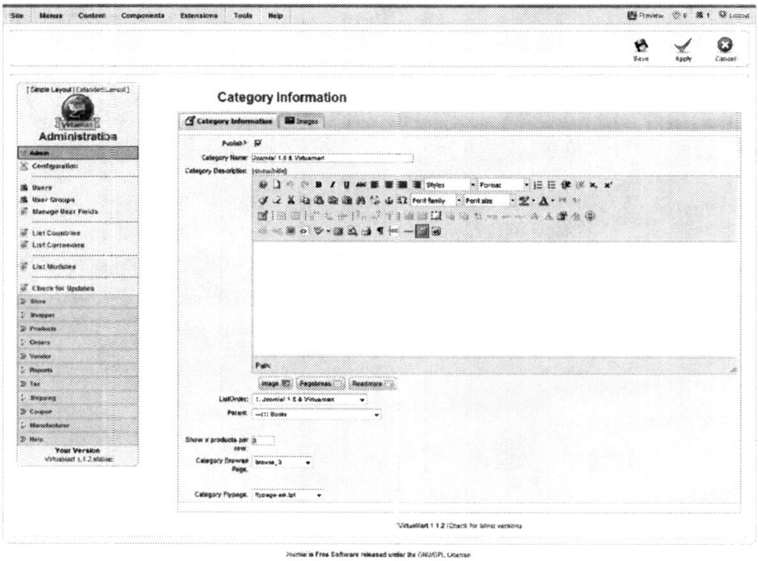

The Category Browse Page is set to Browse_3. We are going to change the browse pages and show you the differences.

### Figure 249: Browse_3

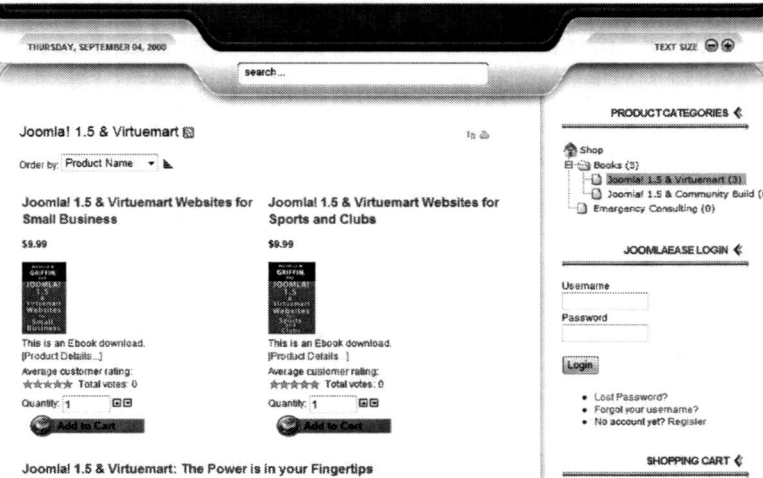

Let's changed it to Managed, and then refresh your website. Notice the Tax moves to below the image, the product details in next to the image and the Add to cart is moved to the right side.

### Figure 250: Managed

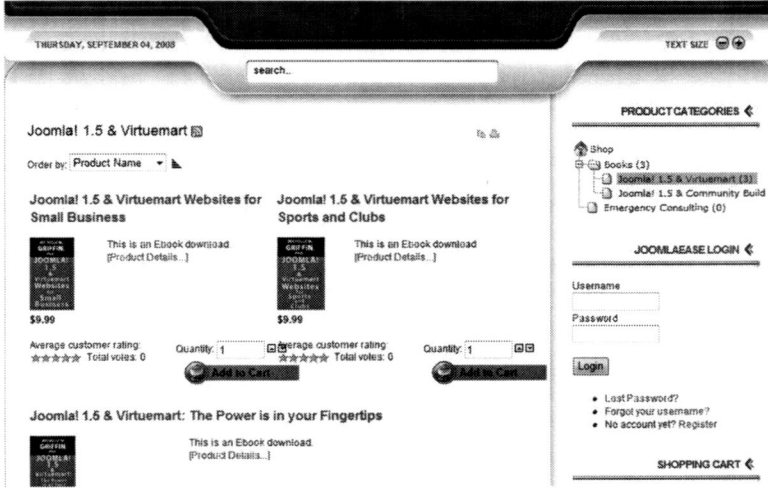

Browse Page Layouts 271

Now change it to Browse_1 and refresh your website. Notice the image moves up next to the name.

In order for this browse page to work you would need to disable the tax included in the configuration file.

**Figure 251: Browse_1**

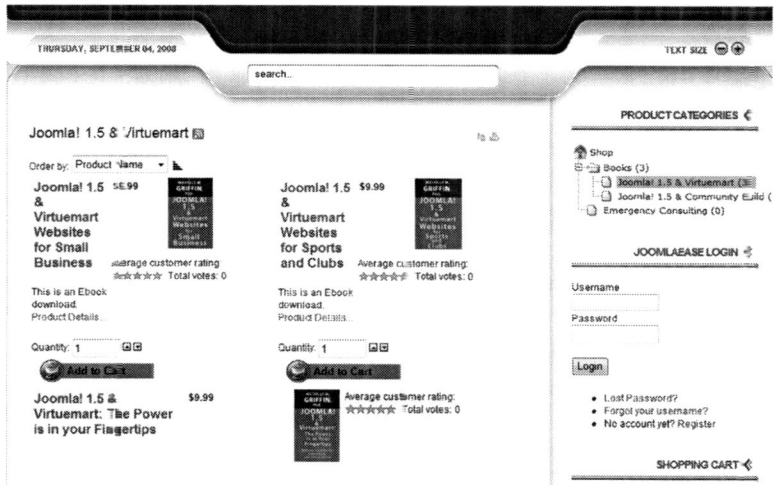

Let's try Browse_2 and refresh your website. The browse_2 looks like Managed, if there are differences it is very slight. Therefore let's look at what Browse_2 looks like as 1 across.

Go back and change "Show x products across" to 1 then refresh your site. This makes the site pretty clean looking for customers. But, if you have a lot of products using this view, you would need to categorize your products a little more. For me I seem to like this view so far.

### Figure 252: Browse_2

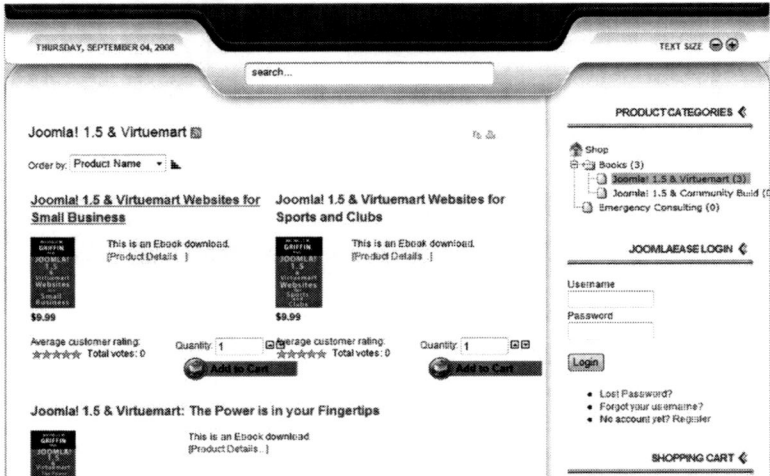

Let's try Browse_4 and change it back to 2 for products across.

### Figure 253: Browse_4

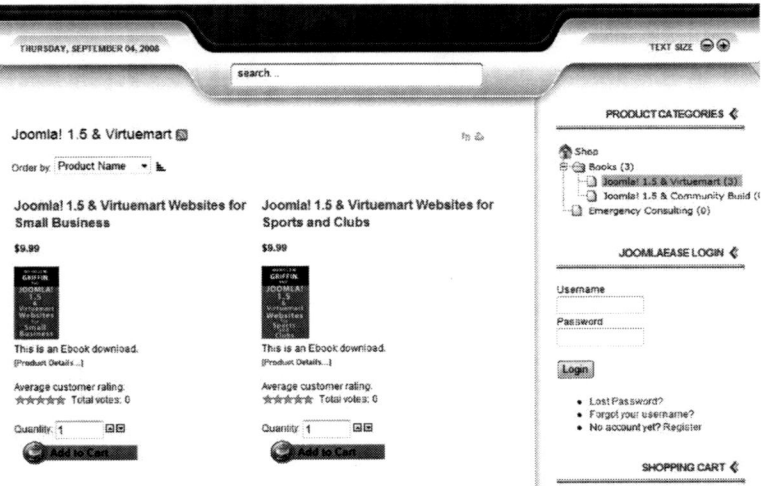

Change it now to Browse_5 and refresh the site. I like this but, it is missing the add to cart buttons. Therefore will not work for me.

Browse Page Layouts  273

### Figure 254: Browse_5

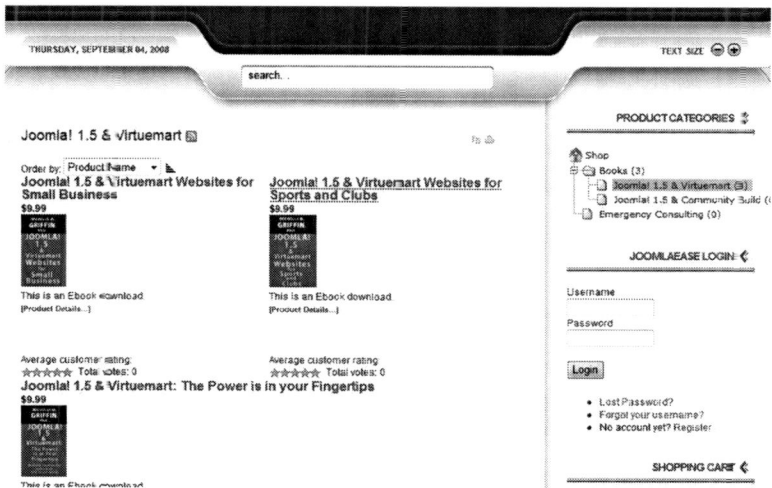

Lastly, let's change it to browse_lite_pdf. This one increased the font but is still missing the add to cart button.

### Figure 255: Browse_lite_pdf

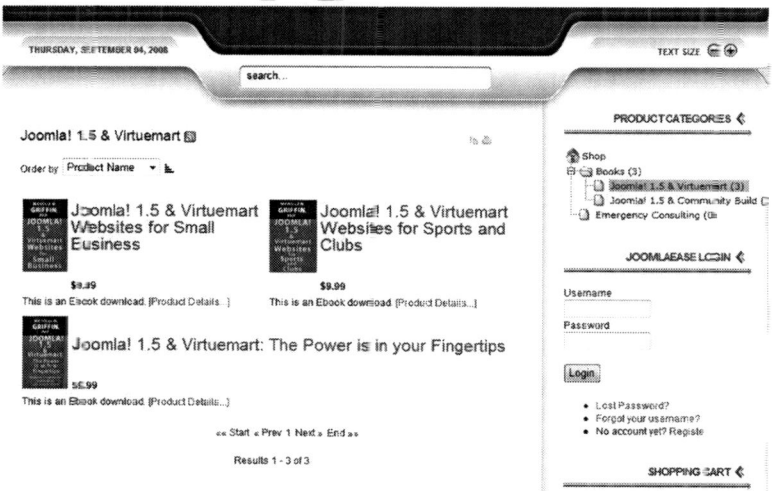

Go ahead and change your browse page to what fits your website.

# Virtuemart Order Process

Let's place our first order and see how it looks. Go back to the home page of your website and let's start at the beginning of the ordering process. Then click on a products category.

**Figure 256: Home Website**

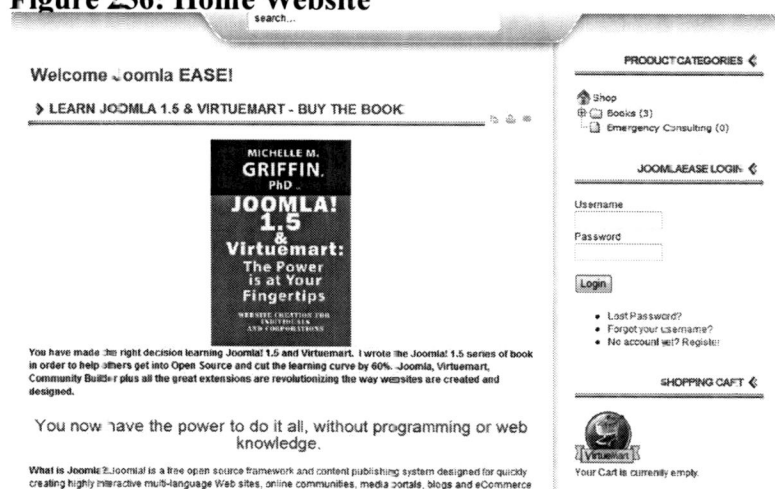

**Figure 257: Products Category**

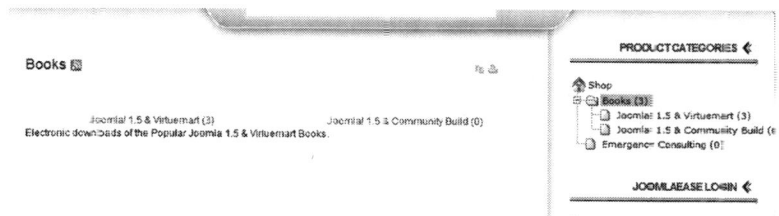

276   Virtuemart™

Add a few items to your cart. I am going to add 2 items to my cart. There are now 2 items in my cart. Notice the YOUR CART module now shows product. Next click on Show Cart

**Figure 258: Add Items to Cart**

**Figure 259: Update Cart**

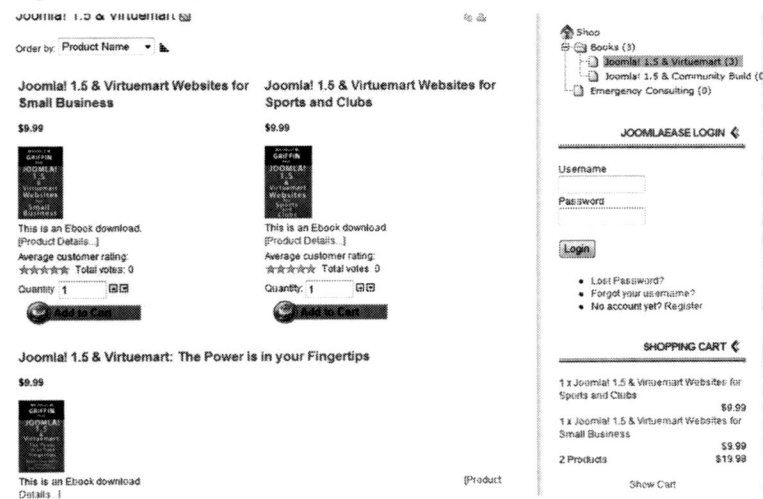

## Figure 260: Update Quantity

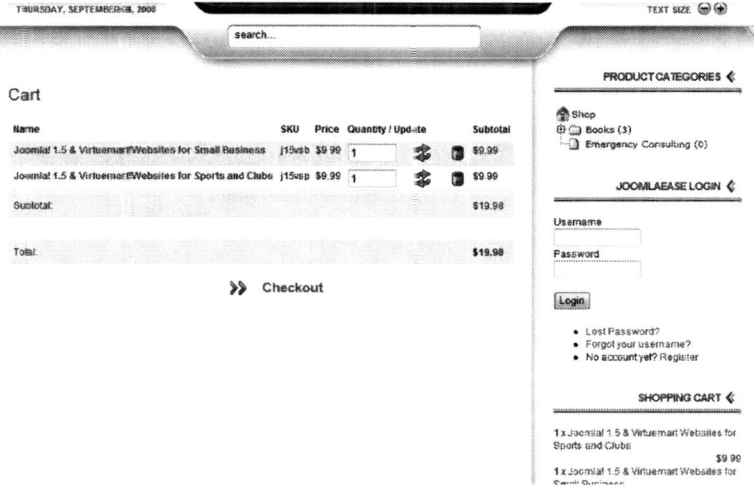

Looks nice so far, now update quantity for one of your items and click the refresh button next to the quantity (arrows). I am going to change mine to 2. Let's delete one of the items to ensure the delete functionality works correctly.

## Figure 261: Delete Item from Cart

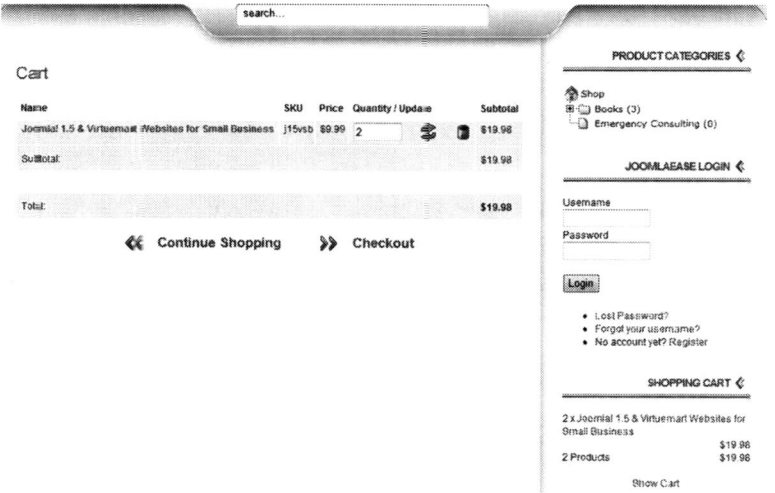

Now let's Checkout, click the Checkout button.

**Figure 262: Registration**

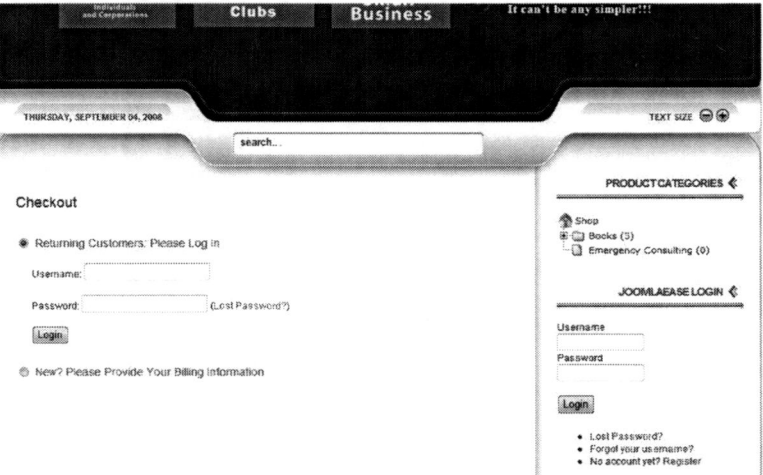

Click on NEW, and the registration fields' popup. Fill out the registration form with a user you had created an email for in the Cpanel or use a friends email.

You need to verify the registration process works therefore you need have access to the email.

The fields with stars are required. The one's without are not. If you want to change the required fields, this is done in Manage User Fields under Virtuemart Admin.

Once done, then press Send registration.

Order Process 279

## Figure 263: User Registration Form

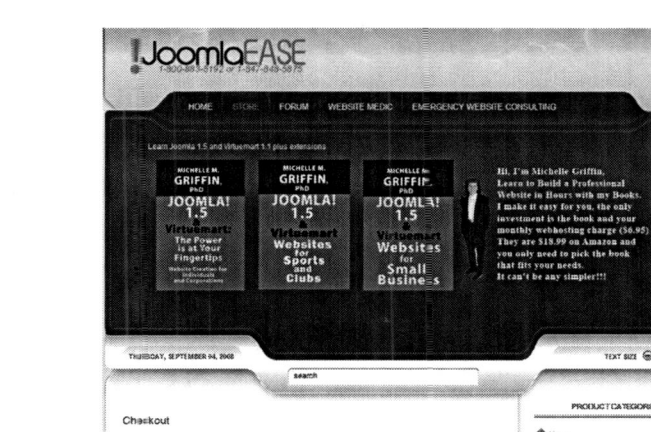

### Figure 264: Manage User Fields

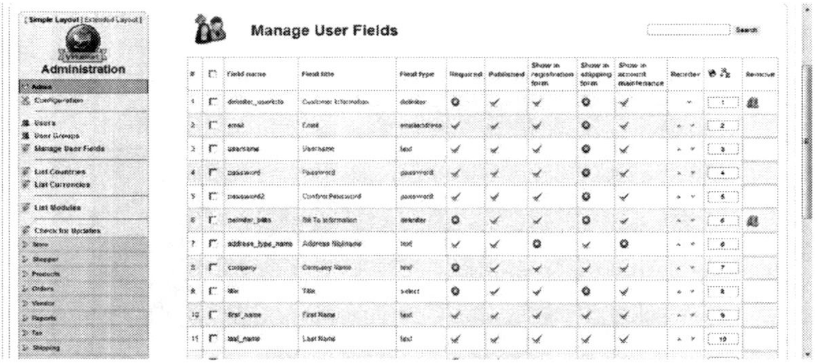

To make a field not required, just disable the required field check mark.

Also notice the columns the other columns:
- Publish a field,
- Show in Registration form,
- Show in Shipping Form
- Show in Account Maintenance

You are also able to change the order of the fields by re-numbering the fields and clicking the small disk at the top of the A/Z column.

Note: The Reorder column does not work at the writing of this book, therefore you will need to re-number using the next column.

Once the registration form looks the way you like then press send registration.

We have proceeded to checkout step 1, once the registration was sent. Your customer will receive an email that they registered and you as the administrator will receive an email also.

Order Process 281

## Figure 265: Checkout Step 1

### Figure 266: User Registration to Customer

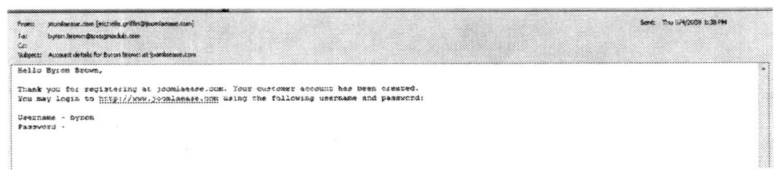

### Figure 267: User Registration to Administrator

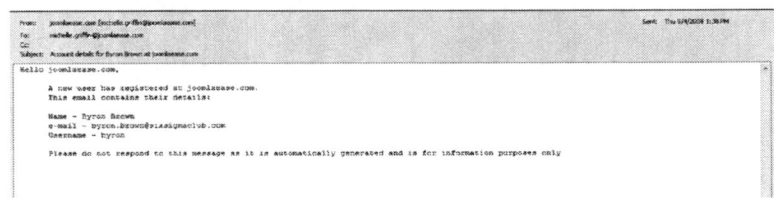

Click Next to proceed to Step 2. This is the shipping page. The shipping is showing up as $12.97, which tells me I have Flex Shipping on. I would like the shipping to be a flat rate. Therefore I am going to set the Shipping rates. Go to Virtuemart Control panel, under shipper. Click on Create Shipper link.

### Figure 268: Create Shipper

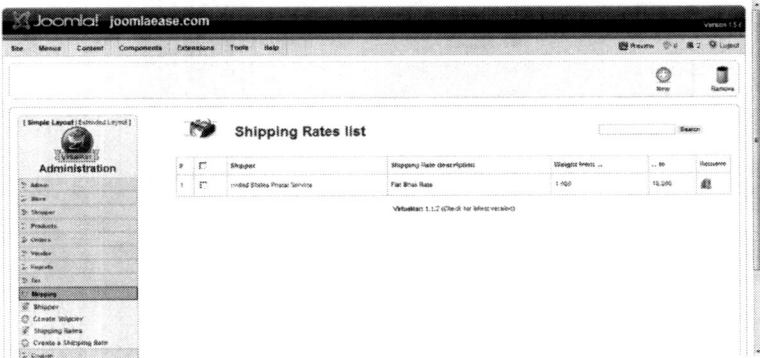

## Figure 269: Shipper Rate

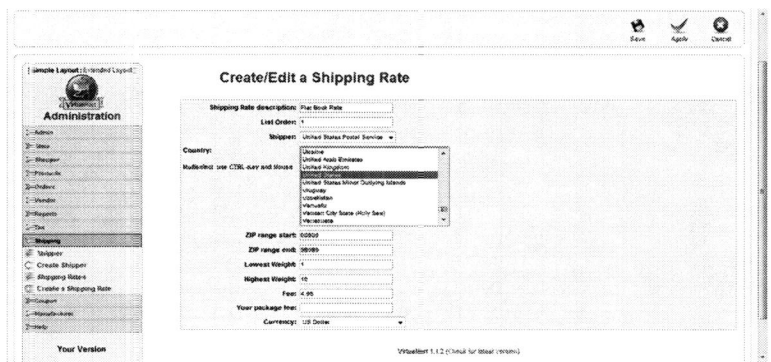

You are able to setup multiple shipping options. There is also a module called Flex Shipping which allows you to charge a flat rate and then a percentage of sales of a certain weight. The Flex Ship is found under Store/ Shipping Module List.

## Figure 270: Shipping Module List

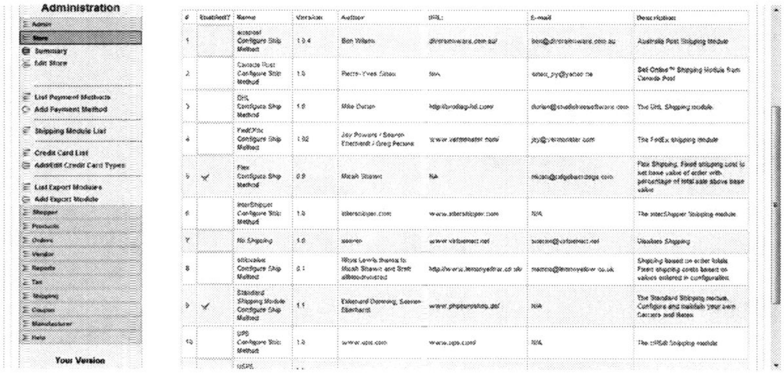

284  Virtuemart™

To Modify the Flex Ship, click on the little button configure ship method.

**Figure 271: Flex Shipping**

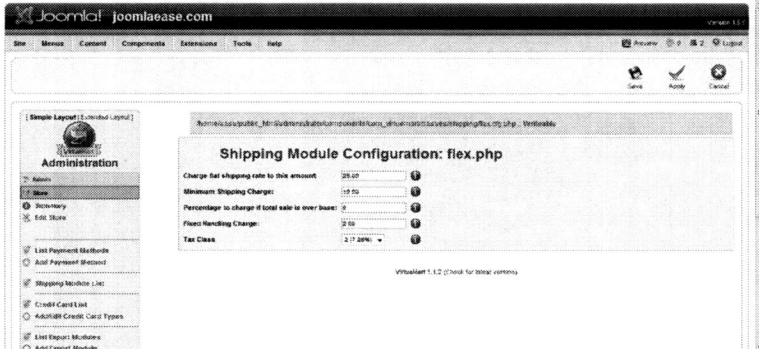

To deactive either Flex Shipping or Standard and reactive another methods is done in the Configuration file under Shipping.

**Figure 272: Configure Shipping**

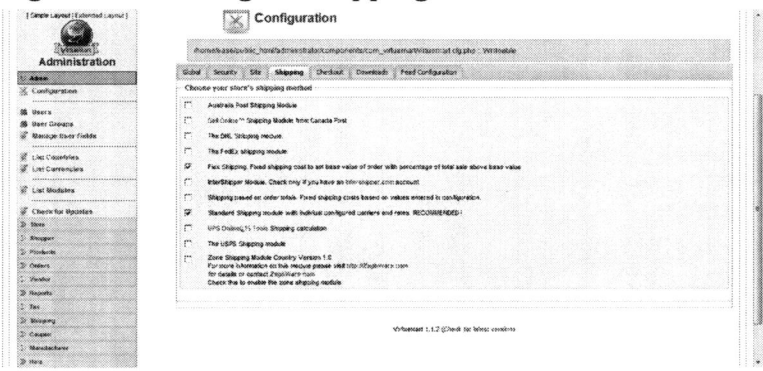

I have setup my shipping as $0 dollars for downloaded product. Given that I will also have items that physically ship, I do not want to disable shipping completely.

Order Process 285

### Figure 273: Step 2 - Select Shipper

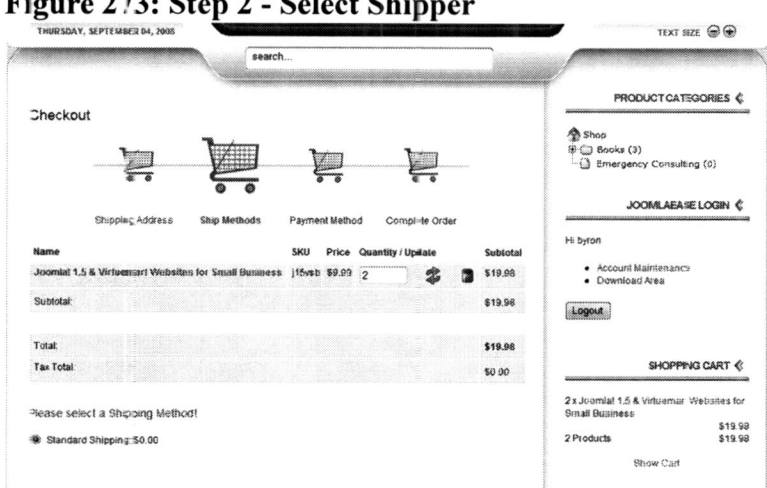

The order is ready to process, click next and select Payment method.

### Figure 274: Step 3

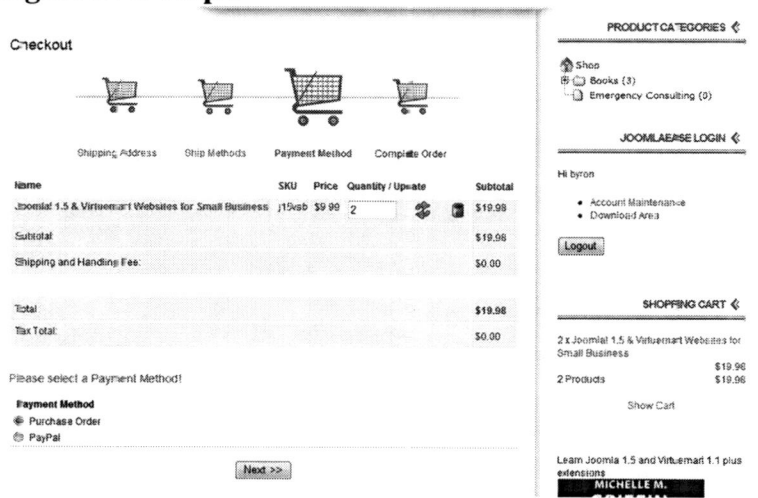

I recommend you write TEST in the "Please leave a Note box". Therefore you do not accidently try to process this order, go ahead and press confirm.

## 286 Virtuemart™

## Figure 275: Step 4

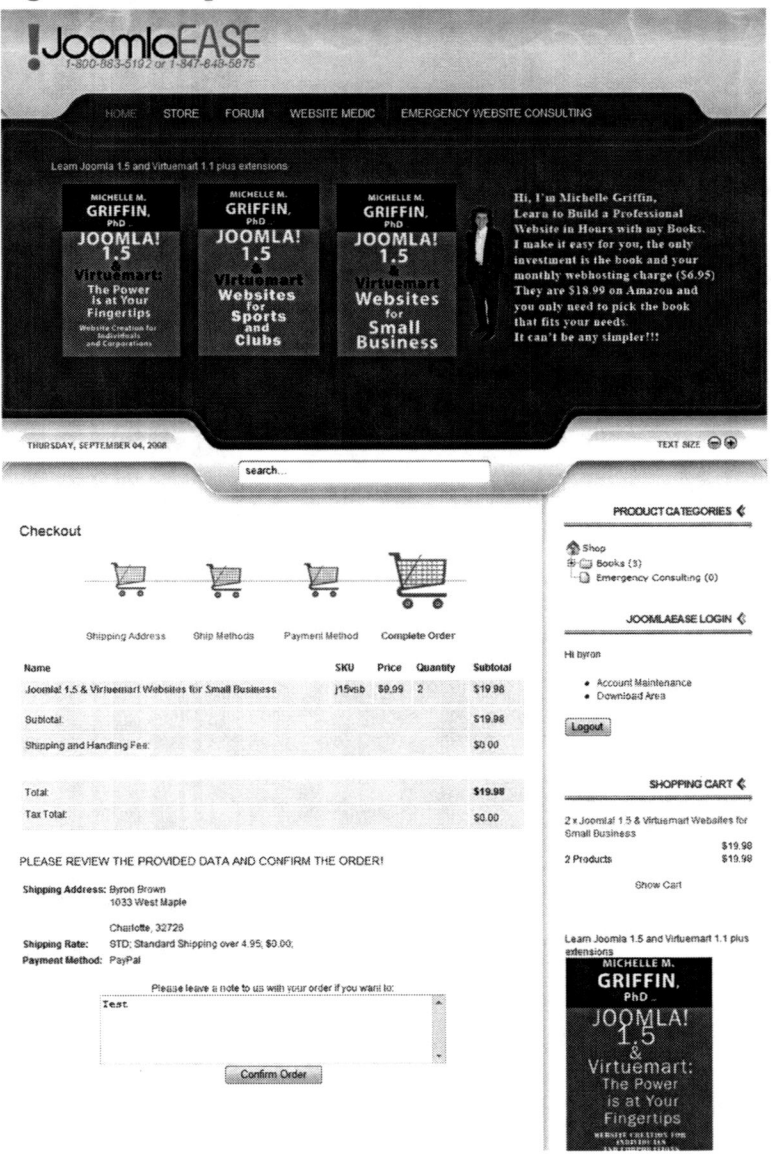

Order Process 287

### Figure 276: Pay by Purchase Order

If you are using Paypal your Paypal screen should come up. For this order, I will just click on the link to return to the website.

### Figure 277: Pay by Paypal

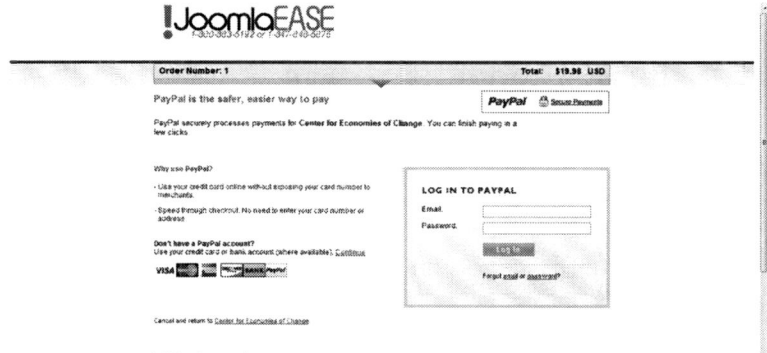

The customer receives the following invoice for placing their order as well as the administrator is notified there is a new order. The email for notification is driven off the email in the Joomla Global configuration file.

288   Virtuemart™

Therefore this email needs to be an email which has the ability to service the customer when orders come in. If you set this email up as a generic email, for instance registration@nusc.info then many people could receive copies of the email, just by adding it to their Outlook account.

**Figure 278: Customer Order Confirmation**

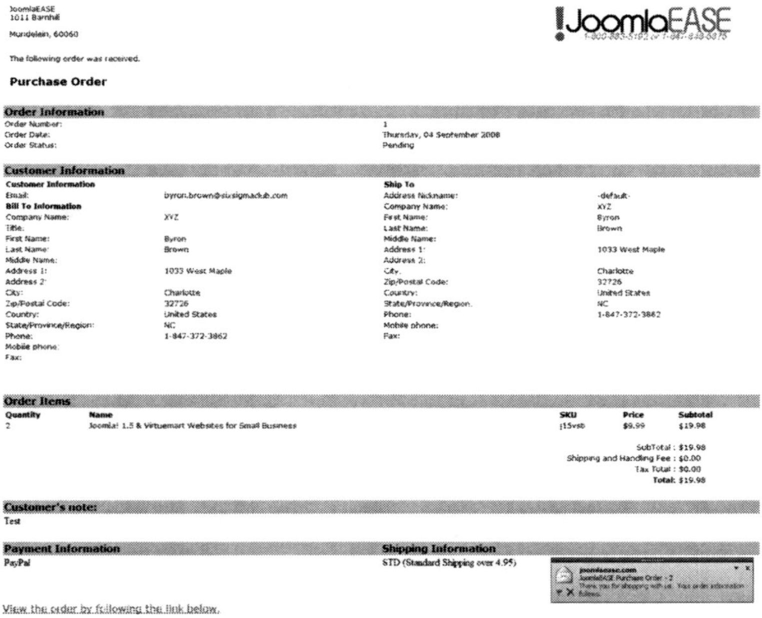

If you click on the link at the bottom of the purchase order which came through the email, it takes the customer their order online in their account. They need to login when the link redirects them.

Congratulations, if you made it here with no errors you did everything correctly.

Once your customer places an order they will be able to download the product purchased, if the product is setup for download.

**Figure 279: Website Download**

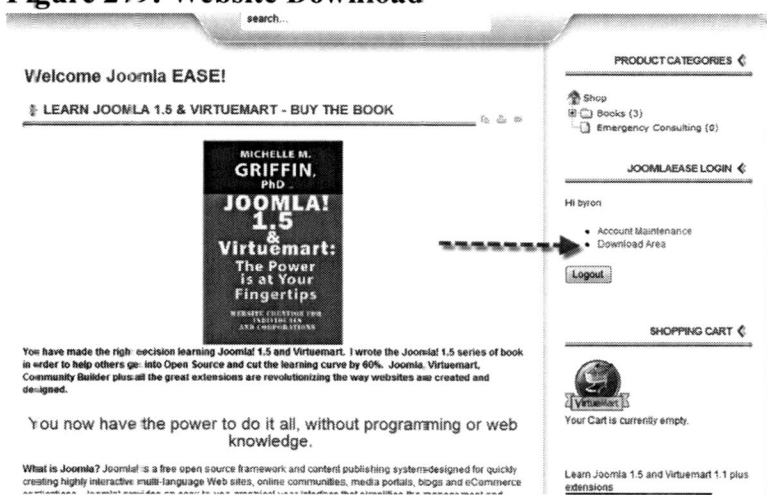

Your customer then clicks Download under the Login to be taken to the download area, where they enter their code they received in their email.

**Figure 280: Download Area**

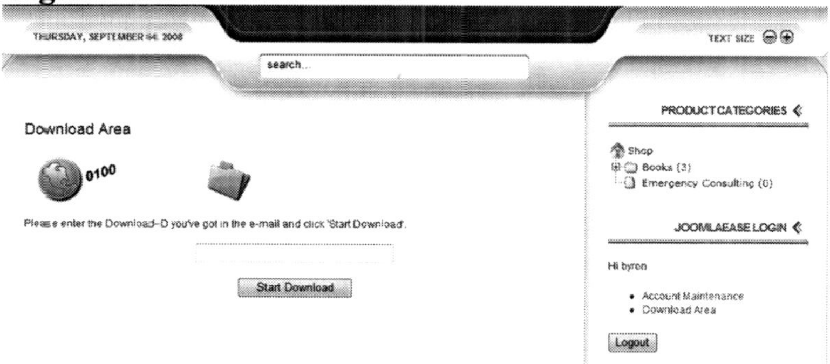

# Virtuemart Order Status

Before we process this order, let's review order status types, this is a very nice feature in Virtuemart.

Order status types are important because it allows your customer and your back office people to be able to track the stages of orders. Order Status types are found in the Virtuemart Control Panel under Orders.

**Figure 281: List Order Status Types**

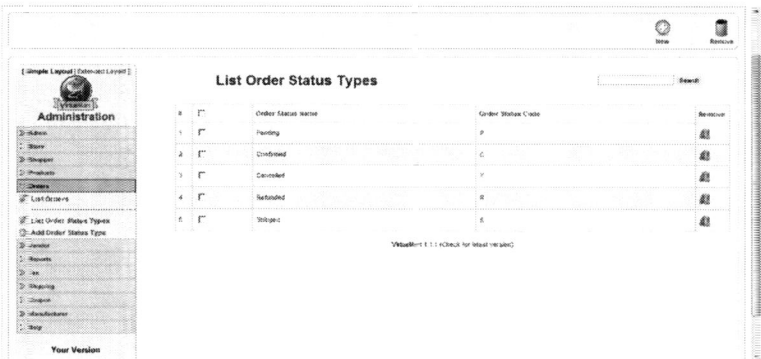

The Order Status types are customizable. But once orders are placed, it is not recommend you changed these. Therefore review these carefully to determine if they best suit your needs.

For instance, if you are running a Restaurant or a Customer pickups their product, instead of shipped you may want Delivered.

Based on the types of sites you are running, really dictates the types of steps which are required. For this example I am going to leave them as the default.

## 292  Virtuemart™

### Figure 282: Order Status Detail

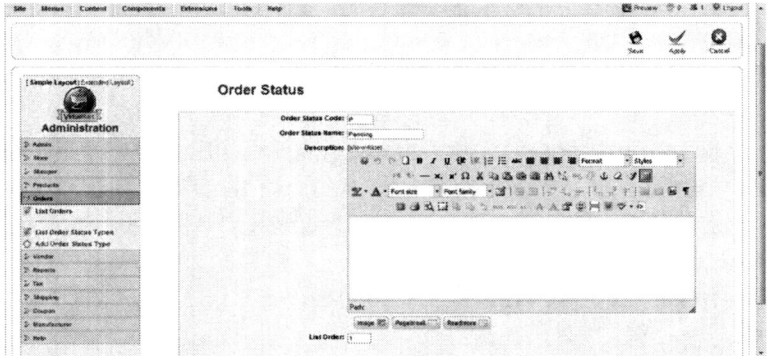

# Virtuemart Orders

To access the Order processing screen, go to the Virtuemart Control Panel and click on List Orders under the Orders heading.

**Figure 283: Order List**

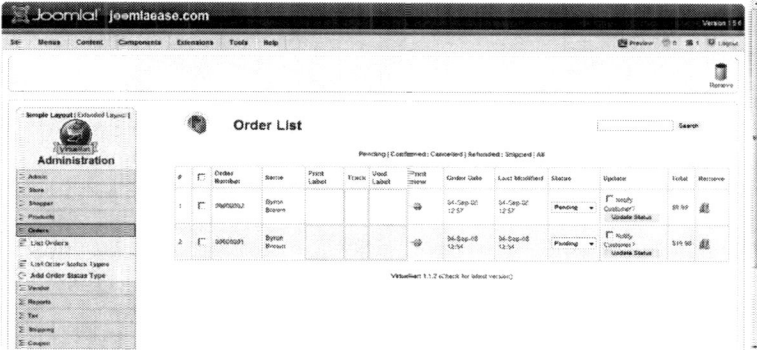

Click on the Order Number to access the order.

All the information you need on the order is on this screen. The payment information is at the bottom. Once you receive the order and begin processing it, you would want to confirm the order. Now, if you have different people the order process through, you may want to go back and add additional order status types at this time.

When you confirm the order the customer receives notification that the order has been accepted.

You can confirm the order from the Order listing or from the Order detail. If you do it at the order listing, then you need to check the box for Notify customer and click update status. This triggers the email to the customer. If you do it in the Order detail then you need to change the status and click update.

## Figure 284: Order Detail

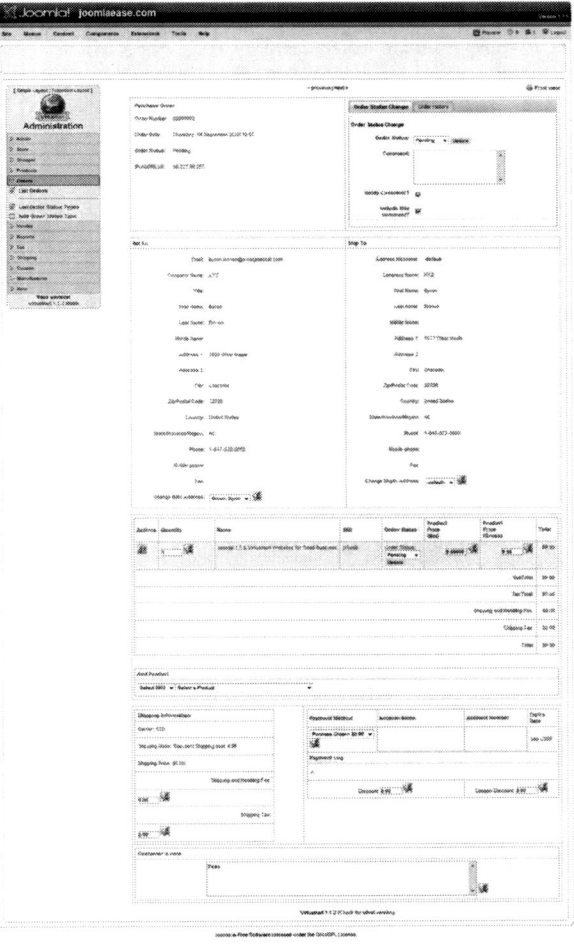

## Figure 285: Order History

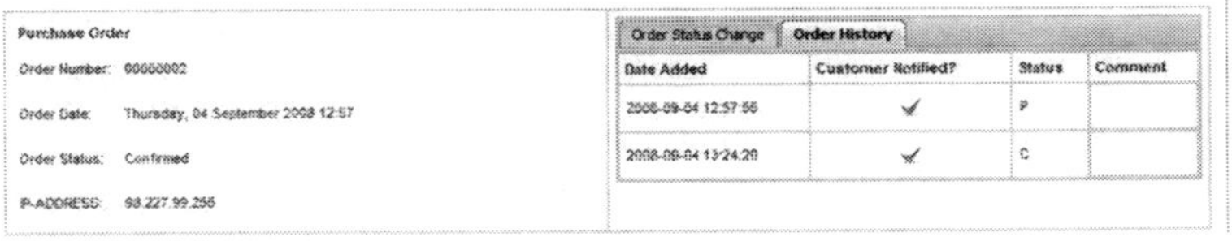

The Order History tab tracks the time any changes occur with the order. It does not tell you who made the change which would be a nice feature in the future. But it is nice to track what changes have occurred.

**Figure 286: Order Status Confirmed Email**

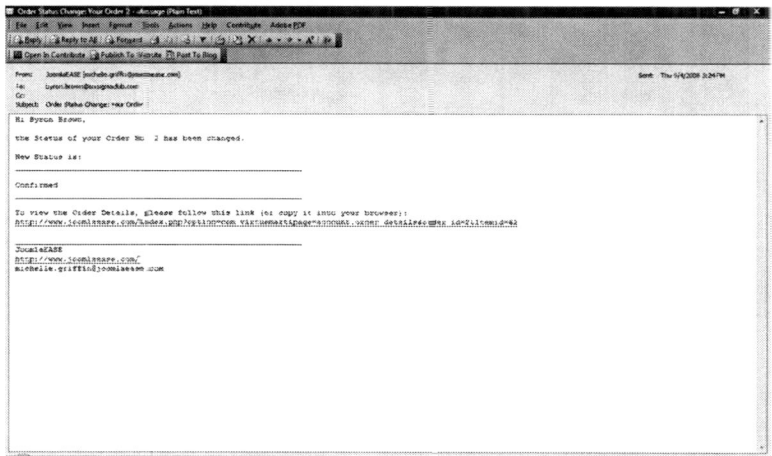

Once you ship the product then you will need to change this to shipped. There are nice little reports or you can extract your files at the end of the month, quarter or year in order to track your sales and to whom.

Within the email your customer can view their order by clicking on the link and logging into your website.

## 296 Virtuemart™

## Figure 287: Customer Views Order

# Virtuemart Inventory

Now that we have placed a sample order, we now need to go in and make sure the inventory is correct. Inventory was initially updated within the product detail. But it is easier to go to the inventory management screen. This is located in the Virtuemart Control Panel under Products/View Inventory.

**Figure 288: View Inventory**

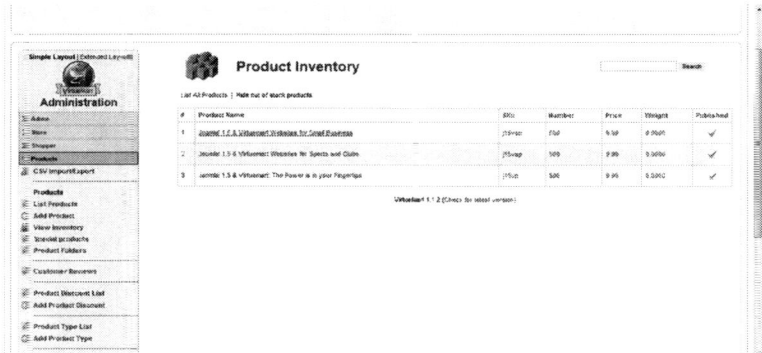

When you click on the product it brings you to the product detail screen, where you can adjust the inventory.

**Figure 289: Product Detail Screen**

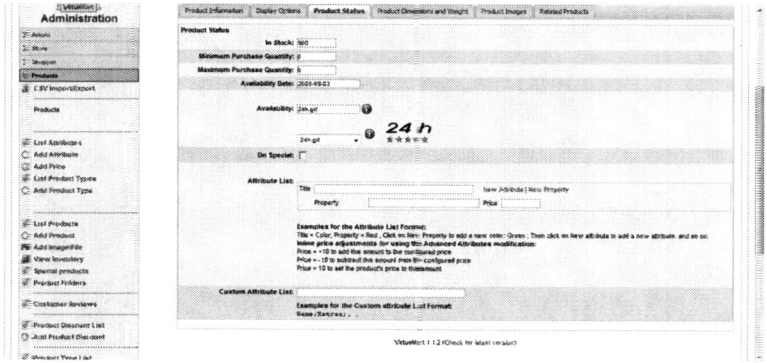

298   Virtuemart™

We do not have it setup to check inventory. If you run a business where you want the system to check available inventory prior to an order being placed, then you need to go back to the Admin/Configuration screen and under Inventory check the box for check inventory. This will not allow a user to add more inventory then what you have in stock to their cart.

**Figure 290: Configuration**

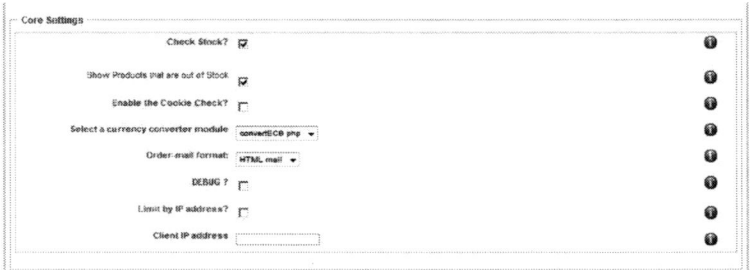

# Virtuemart Report

There are online reports, which cannot be extracted at this time but they are handy to view what transactions have occurred for your business. The report is access in the Virtuemart Control Panel / Reports

**Figure 291: Report Screen**

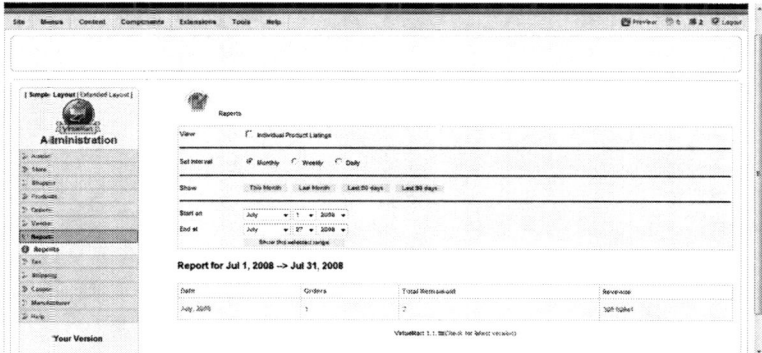

The reports can be ran daily, weekly or monthly. You can also check the box to view individual reports by product sold.

In order to run a report you need to select the time period, then either press one of the buttons in the Show row (this month, last month, last 60 days or last 90 days) or select a date range and press the button show this selected range.

300    Virtuemart™

**Figure 292: Report by Product**

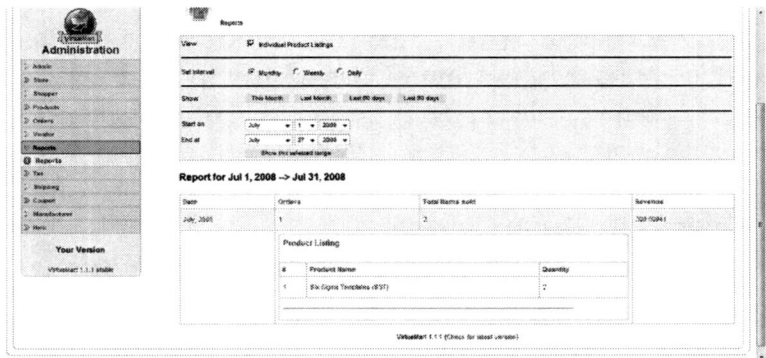

# Virtuemart Account Maintenance

Once your customer logs in they are able to track their orders and modify their profile. The account maintenance link is located in the login box once the customer login. Let's login to the account we used for the test order.

**Figure 293: Website login**

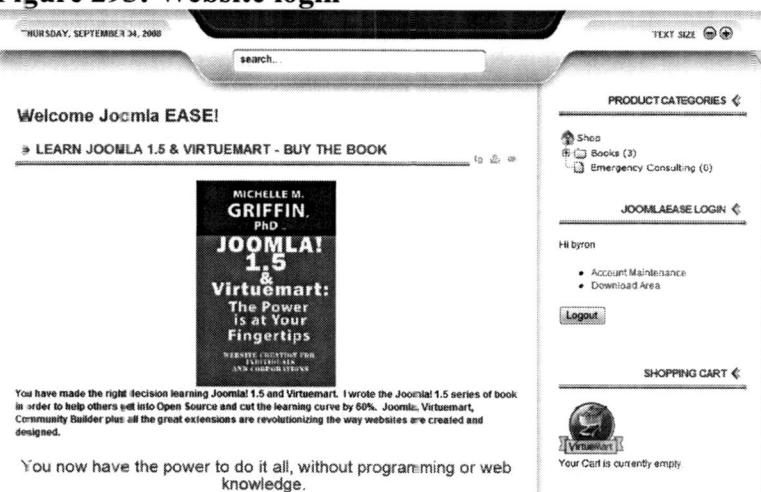

**Figure 294: Account Maintenance**

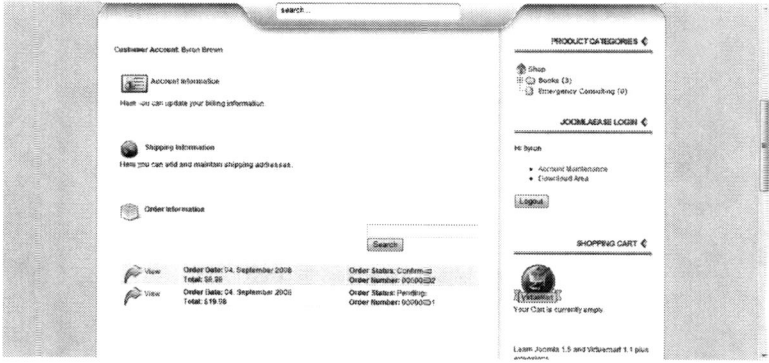

302  Virtuemart™

Once login then click on Account Maintenance. Your customer can view their account information and order history as well as their status.

Click on Account Information to view the detail.

**Figure 295: Account Information**

# Extensions Overview

In this section, I will walk you through how to install some extensions. There are well over 3000 extensions available on Joomla today.

**Figure 296: Joomla Website**

The words of caution, I give you are the following:

1. Only install Native 1.5 Joomla Extensions - this is for the security of your site and also for upgrade ability as Joomla 1.5 advances. If you wish to turn on Legacy to use old extensions, this is your decision but I recommend only advanced users do this. There is nothing in legacy which I can't live without and therefore on none of my sites have I ever customized or installed Legacy. This comes from my SAP experience as a consultant for 20 years. Customizing only leads to problems. It is best it is not done.

2. Only use extensions which have a lot of positive comments. I steer clear of extensions until others test them out. I have hit some extensions which have broke my sites. Therefore I would rather be safe then sorry especially with a customer facing website which is critical.

All the extensions are found on the Joomla website under extensions. Also remember many of the extensions are created by Freelance developers. If you use it on your site. Be sure to donate to them individually. Even $25 dollars goes a long way in saying thank you for your time.

Go to the Joomla website at www.joomla.com and click on extensions.

This brings you to the extensions page where you can navigate or search for the desired extension.

**Figure 297: Extension Page**

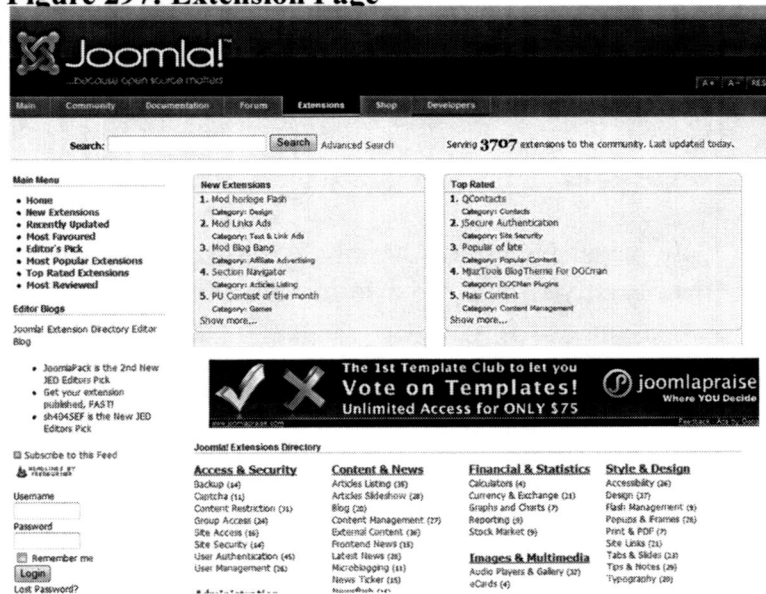

There are two types of extensions: Commercial and Non-Commercial. Commercial charges a fee to use their extensions and Non-Commercial accepts donations.

There are also a number of types of extensions:
- Native 1.0 - Made for Joomla 1.0 only
- Native 1.5 - Made for Joomla 1.5 only
- Legacy 1.5 - This means a 1.0 module which has been adapted to fit 1.5 with Legacy turned on.

The screen shot below shows a sample Legacy 1.5 and Native 1.5 module.

Now do you see the second extension in the screen shot it shows Native 1.0 and Native 1.5. You will need to test this module because many extensions say Native 1.5 but are not.

If they are true Native there will be separate downloads for Joomla 1.0 and Joomla 1.5

**Figure 298: Extensions Printout**

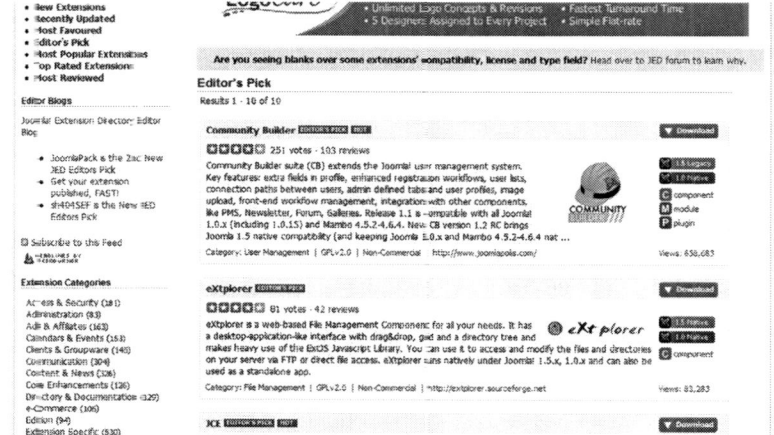

# Image Slide Show

This module worked the first time I tried it and it is cute. This extension is located under Images and Multimedia then under Image slideshow.

### Figure 299: Images Extensions

### Figure 300: Image Slideshow Extension

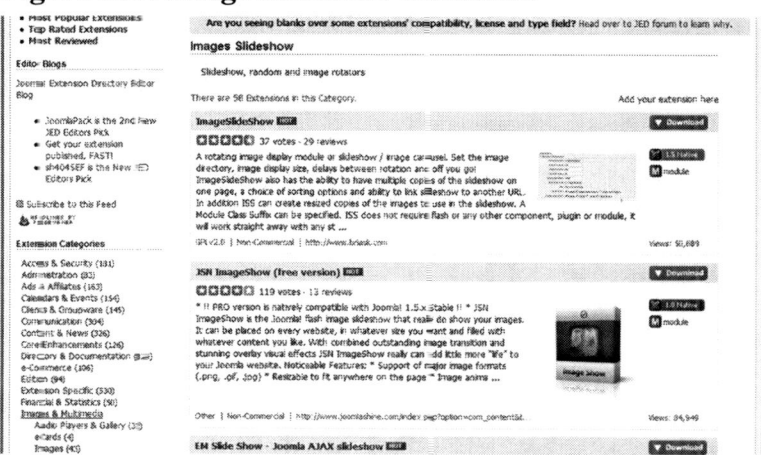

308   Extensions

Click the Extension title to go to the detail page.

### Figure 301: Image Slideshow detail page

Click download, it then takes you to the www.briask.com

### Figure 302: Download Image Slideshow

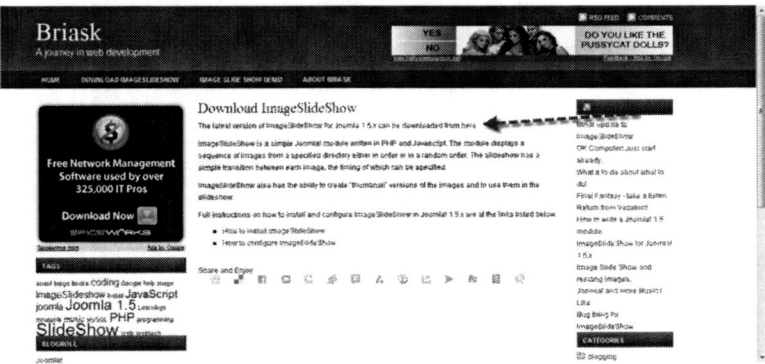

On the website it is hard to find the download button. I tried to highlight the download button, with the arrow.

Image Slideshow 309

Go to Extension Manager and upload the module.

**Figure 303: Extension Manager**

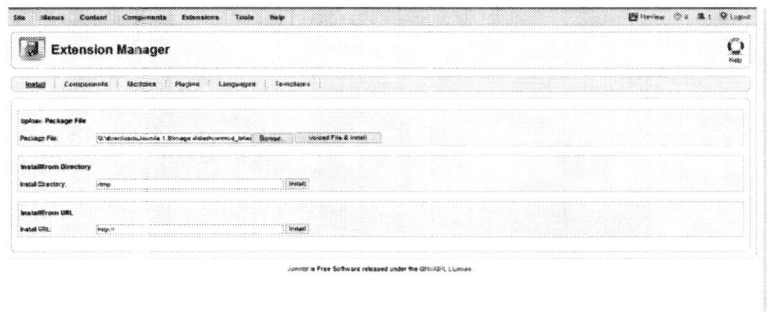

Go to Module Manager and find the Image Slideshow and click it to go to the detailed page.

**Figure 304: Module Manager**

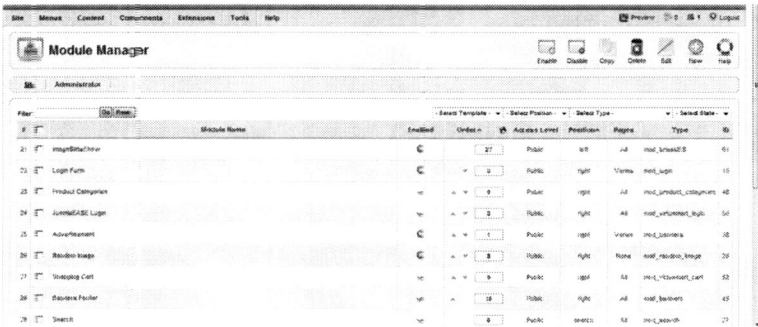

Once on the detail page, you need to enable the module and decide where to place it on your web-page. I am going to place it at the bottom of my website in User 4 position.

310   Extensions

**Figure 305: Image Slideshow Detail**

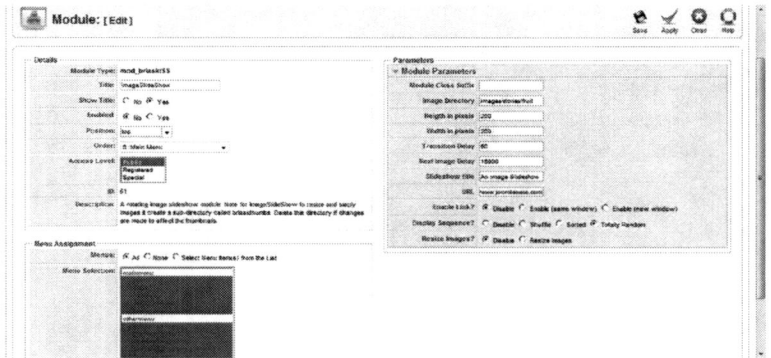

Now, let's refresh the website and see what it looks like.

**Figure 306: Website Slideshow**

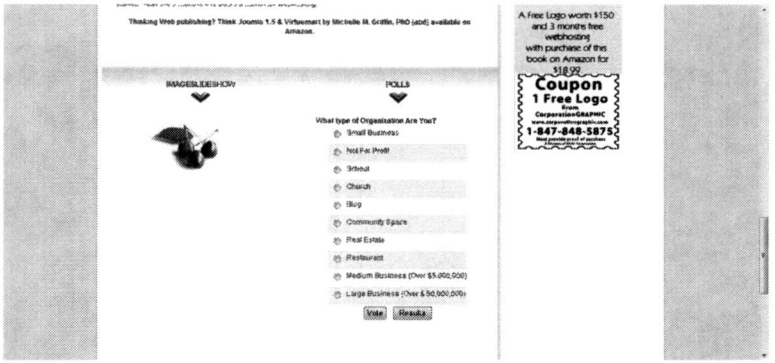

Now that we know it works. Let's add our own pictures in order to customize it.

In the Image Slideshow Detail in the Module Manager we saw the directory for the images is:

Images/slideshow/fruit

Image Slideshow 311

We can find this folder in the Media Manager. Media manager is located under Site. Click on the Stories folder. You can either create a new folder or use the fruit folder to store your images. I am going to create a new folder.

Type your new folder name in the Create Folder space and click create folder. I highlighted it in the figure below by the arrow. Your folder name cannot have any spaces.

**Figure 307: Media Manager in Stories Folder**

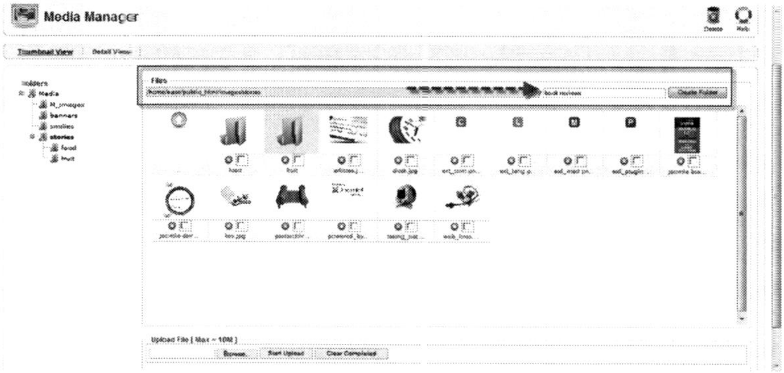

Double click and go into the folder that you will be storing the images. Now, I am going to upload some images into this folder.

**Figure 308: File Upload**

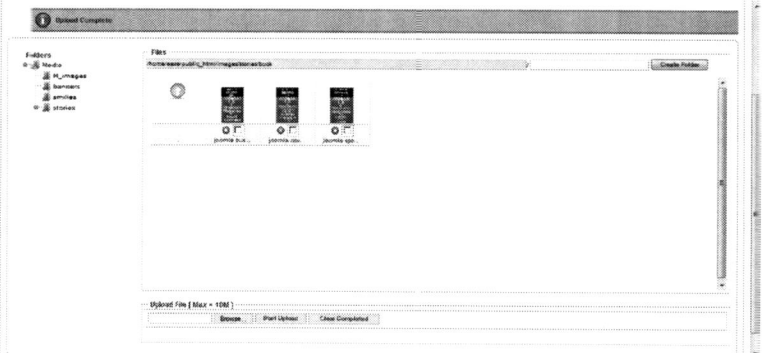

312   Extensions

Now that we have uploaded the images. Let's go to Module manager and modify the image slideshow module.

**Figure 309: Slideshow detail**

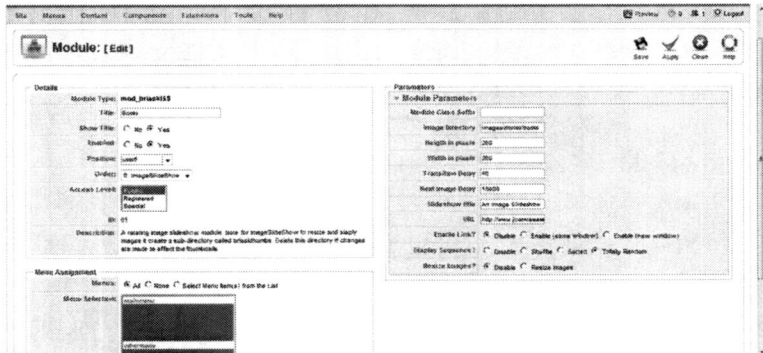

On the right hand side, I changed the image/directory to the new directory I created: Images/stories/books.

I then changed the slideshow title field to just Books. Tweak the settings until it appears like you would like. Remember to refresh your website and see what each change did.

This extension was created by Briask. Their website is www.briask.com. This is an amazing extension and if you use, please be sure to let them know through your donations.

# Attachments

This extension allows you to have attachments within articles. To install, let's go to the Joomla website and then click on extensions. Search for "attachments"

**Figure 310: Attachment Extension**

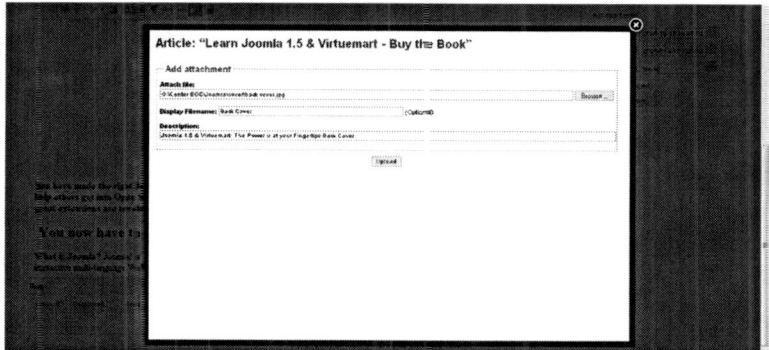

Then click on the name of the extension to go to the download page.

**Figure 311: Attachment Download**

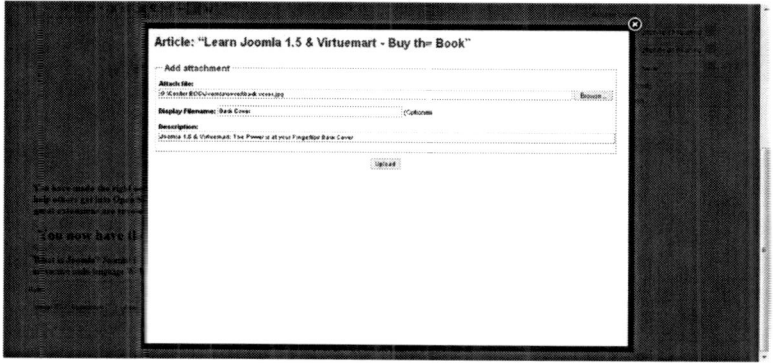

314    Extensions

### Figure 312: Download page

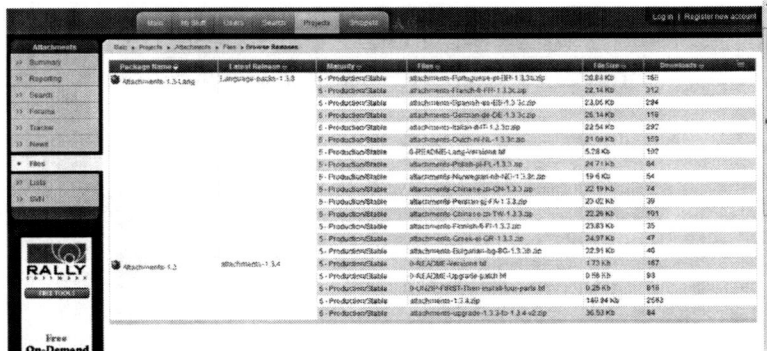

Download the file: attachments.1.3.4.zip. Once download and saved you need to go to Windows Explorer and unzip the files.

Then go to Extensions/Install and let's install the component. Once the component is installed then you need to install the three other plugins.

### Figure 313: Success install

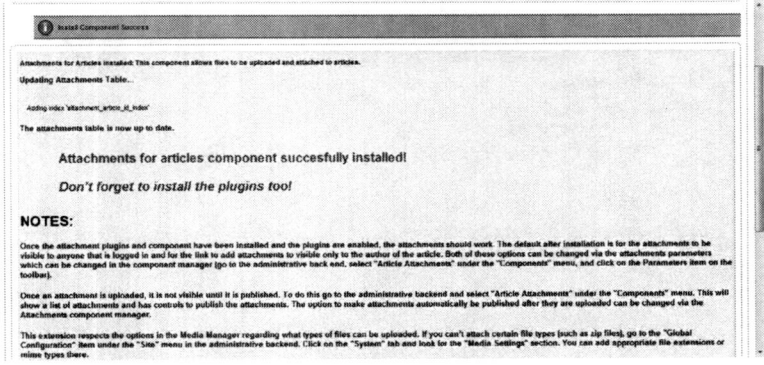

Attachments 315

Let's now activate the plugins. Before we configure the attachment components. Remember there were 3 plugins.

**Figure 314: Plugin Manager**

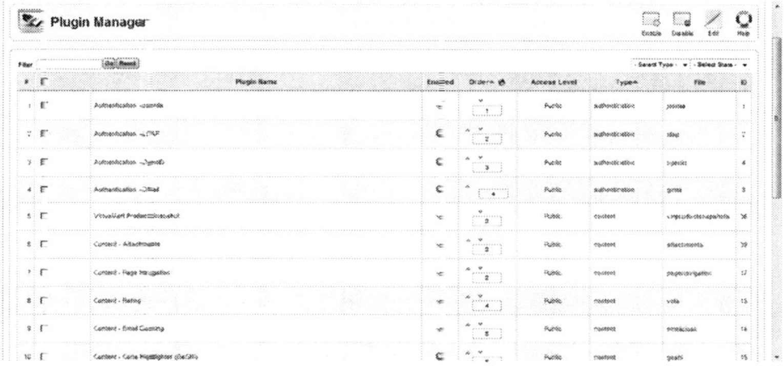

**Figure 315: Attachment Parameters**

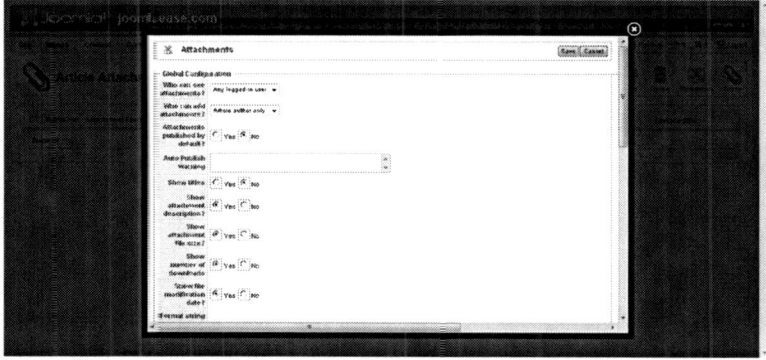

Now go to the Article manager and open an article that you would like to attach a file. At the bottom of the article page is a button for Attachment, click this.

316 Extensions

**Figure 316: Article**

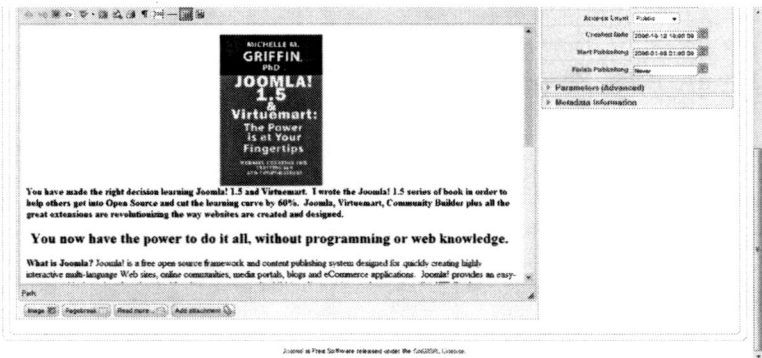

Enter your file information and click upload.

**Figure 317: Upload Attachment**

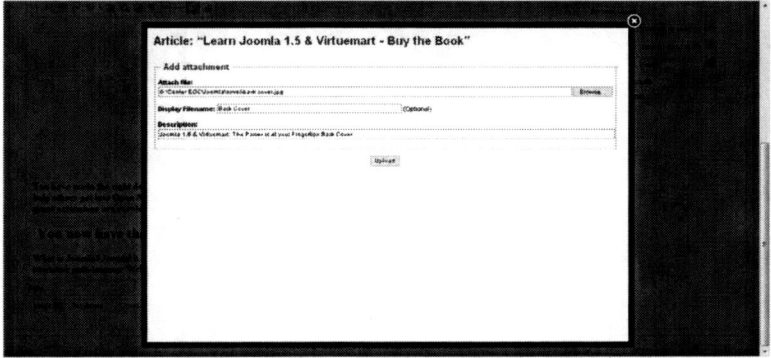

Once I pressed Upload, I received a 500 error, which tells me the folder was not created when I installed the Attachment extension. This is usually due to a security setting within the server.

Therefore we will add the folder manually through the CPanel/File Manager.

Attachments 317

### Figure 318: 500 Error

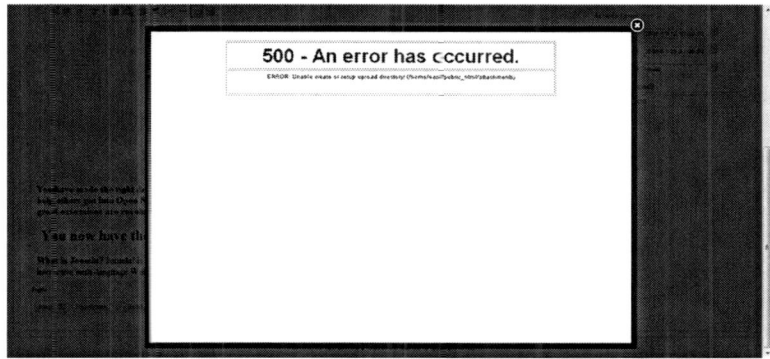

We have to create a new folder called attachments. The default permissions are 755, we need to change these for this folder to 777.

### Figure 319: File Manager

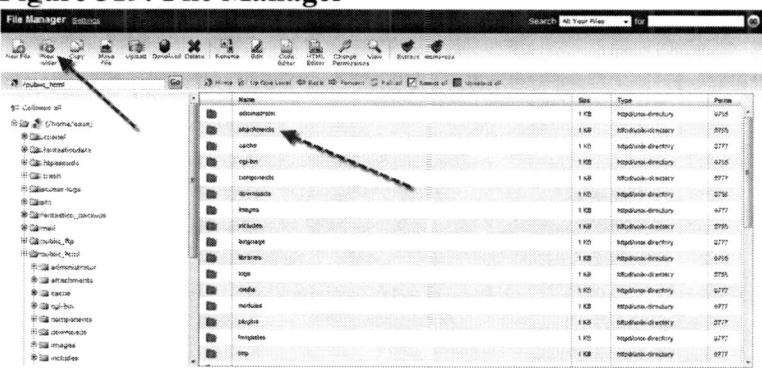

Let's go back to our article and try uploading again. See if it works.

318  Extensions

**Figure 320: 500 Error Index.html**

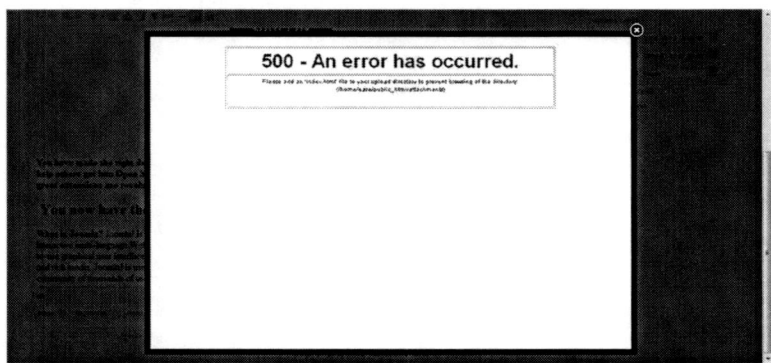

We received another error. This one is an index.html is missing from the attachment folders. This is a nice check. The reason to have an index.html file in there is to prevent someone from browsing your folder. Therefore all we will do is copy an index.html from another folder to this one.

Given we are storing documents and images. I am just going to copy the index.html file from the images folder. If you need a more robust index.html then please look on Google for more information.

**Figure 321: File Manager Copy index.html**

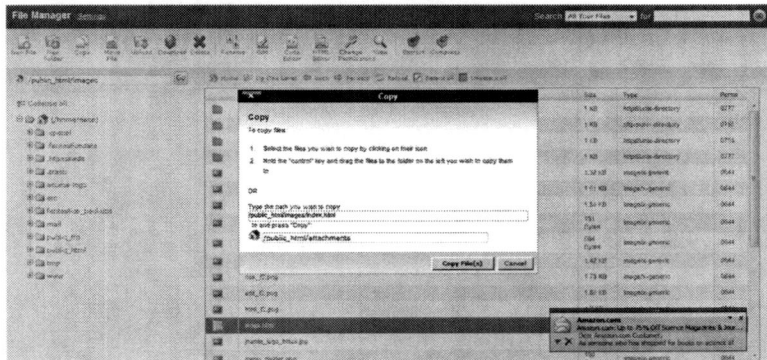

First highlight the index.html file and then press copy. Change the directory it will be copying to Attachments.

**Figure 322: Attachment folder with Index.html**

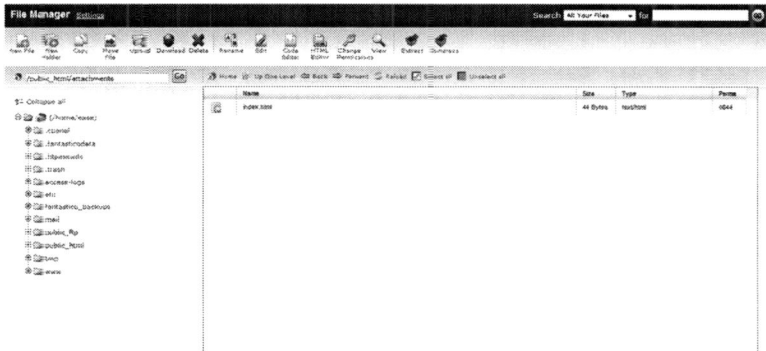

Let's go back to the article, go to the bottom and click attachments, fill in the information and press upload. This time it should work.

You won't be able to see anything in the article, because in the article parameters: Attachments published by default is set to NO. Therefore we have to activate the attachments. If you do not want to review attachments then you can change this parameter to YES.

**Figure 323: Attachment Manager**

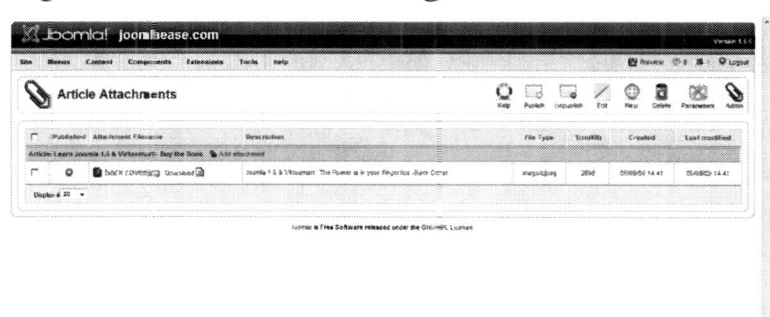

320   Extensions

If everything looks good then you need to publish this attachment, by either checking the box and click the publish icon or clicking the red x to turn it to a green checkmark.

Now to refresh your website. The attachment should be at the bottom of the article.

**Figure 324: Website Attachment**

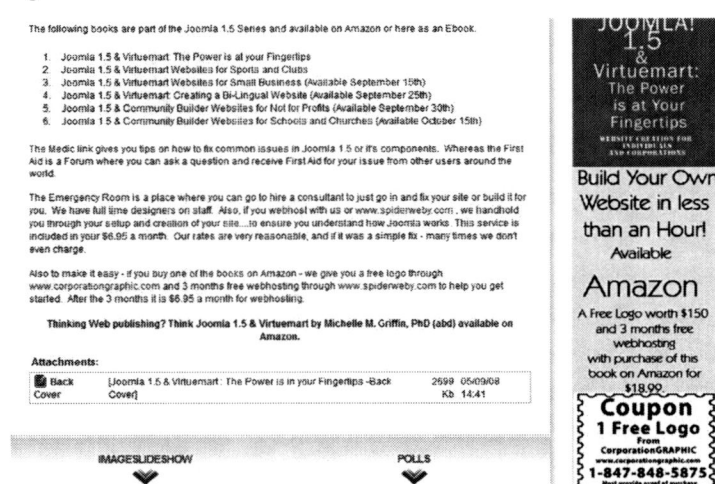

This extension was created by Jonathan Cameron and is a pretty fantastic extension. If you use this extension and like it make sure to let him know by leaving reviews and of course donating to allow him to make more extensions.

# View Source

If you are out browsing other sites and saw something cool that you would love to have on your site. First you would need to figure out if they have Joomla. If they have Joomla then you need to figure out what extension it is by reading the code.

In order to see if they are using Joomla, if it is not obvious from looking at the main page. You need to right click on their home page and click VIEW SOURCE.

**Figure 325: Sample Website**

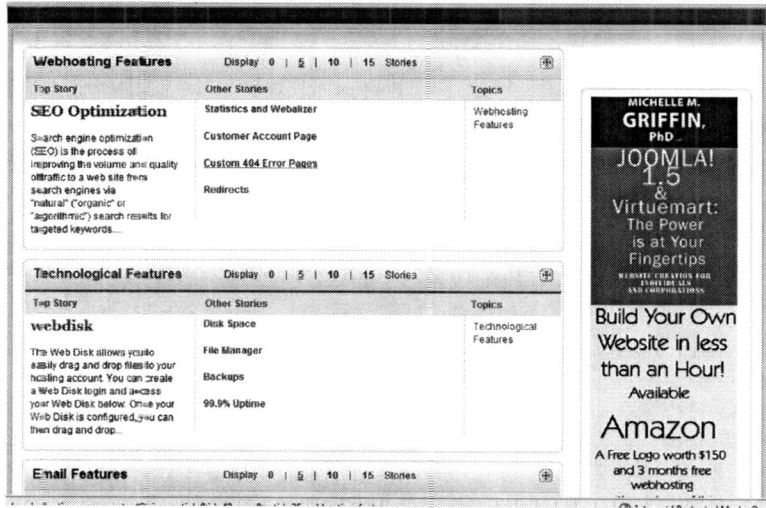

Let's say for example we like this layout of articles. I wonder how they did it. To find out I right click on the site and click VIEW SOURCE.

322  Extensions

### Figure 326: View Source

```
<!DOCTYPE html PUBLIC "-//W3C//DTD XHTML 1.0 Transitional//EN" "http://www.w3.org/TR/xhtml1/DTD/xhtml1-transitional.dtd">
<html xmlns="http://www.w3.org/1999/xhtml" xml:lang="en-gb" lang="en-gb">
<head>
    <meta http-equiv="Content-Type" content="text/html; charset=utf-8" />
    <meta name="robots" content="index, follow" />
    <meta name="keywords" content="Joomla, Joomla" />
    <meta name="description" content="Joomla! - the dynamic portal engine and content management system" />
    <meta name="generator" content="Joomla! 1.5 - Open Source Content Management" />
    <title>Welcome to SpiderWEBv</title>
    <link href="/index.php?format=feed&amp;type=rss" rel="alternate" type="application/rss+xml" title="RSS 2.0" />
    <link href="/index.php?format=feed&amp;type=atom" rel="alternate" type="application/atom+xml" title="Atom 1.0" />
    <script type="text/javascript" src="/media/system/js/mootools.js"></script>
    <script type="text/javascript" src="/media/system/js/caption.js"></script>

    <link rel="shortcut icon" href="/images/favicon.ico" />
    <link href="/templates/rt_terrantribune_j15/css/template_css.css" rel="stylesheet" type="text/css" />
    <link href="/templates/rt_terrantribune_j15/css/blue.css" rel="stylesheet" type="text/css" />
    <link href="/templates/rt_terrantribune_j15/css/rokmininews.css" rel="stylesheet" type="text/css" />
    <link href="/templates/system/css/system.css" rel="stylesheet" type="text/css" />
    <link href="/templates/system/css/general.css" rel="stylesheet" type="text/css" />
    <link href="/templates/rt_terrantribune_j15/css/typography.css" rel="stylesheet" type="text/css" />
    <style type="text/css">
        div.wrapper { margin: 0 auto; width: 962px;padding:0;}
        #left-column { width:0px;padding:0;}
        #right-column { width:230px;padding:0;}
        #center-column { margin-left:0px;margin-right:230px;padding:0;}
    </style>
    <!--[if IE 7]>
    <link href="/templates/rt_terrantribune_j15/css/template_ie7.css" rel="stylesheet" type="text/css" />
    <![endif]-->
    <script type="text/javascript" src="/templates/rt_terrantribune_j15/js/rokutils.js"></script>
    <script type="text/javascript" src="/templates/rt_terrantribune_j15/js/ie_suckerfish.js"></script>
</head>
<body id="ff-default" class="f-default bc-blue iehandle">
    <div id="page-bg">
    <!-- Begin Wrapper -->
    <div class="wrapper">
                <div class="shadow-left">
                 <div class="main-page">
                  <div class="main-page2">
                   <div class="main-page3">
                    <div class="main-page4">
                    <!-- Begin Header -->
                    <div id="header">

                        <div id="accessibility">
```

I see from looking quickly at the code that this is a Joomla 1.5 site. Exactly what I was hoping for. Now let's figure out the module name, so we can go to google and type in the name and find out if this is a commercial module (have to buy) or a non-commericial module and where to download it.

### Figure 327: Find Module

# Silent No Right Click

In the last chapter we looked at how to see what modules other people are using. Go to your website and right click to View your Source code that everyone can see.

Now having your source code visible is a security threat. Because if I know you have a Joomla site, all I have to do is type in your domain name with administrator and then either guess or run a program which will break your username and password. Therefore it is best, if you block access to people viewing your source code to protect your site, your design and your images.

Therefore here is a neat little extension found on the joomla website under Site Security.

### Figure 328: Silent No Right Click

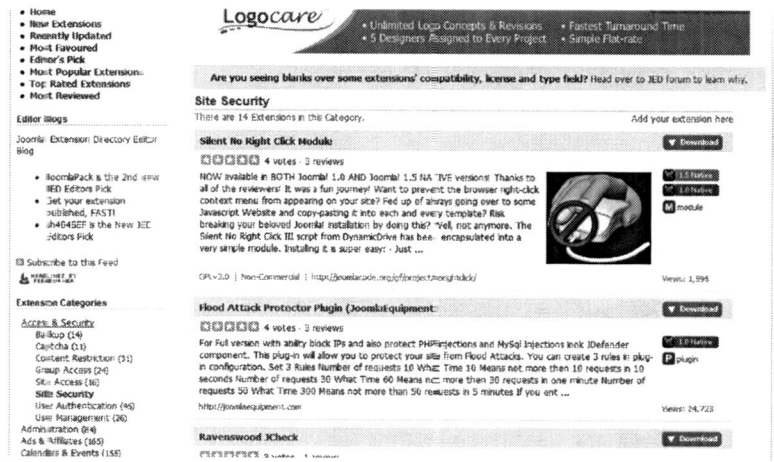

324    Extensions

Click the Download page and download the Version for Joomla 1.5 only zip file.

**Figure 329: Download**

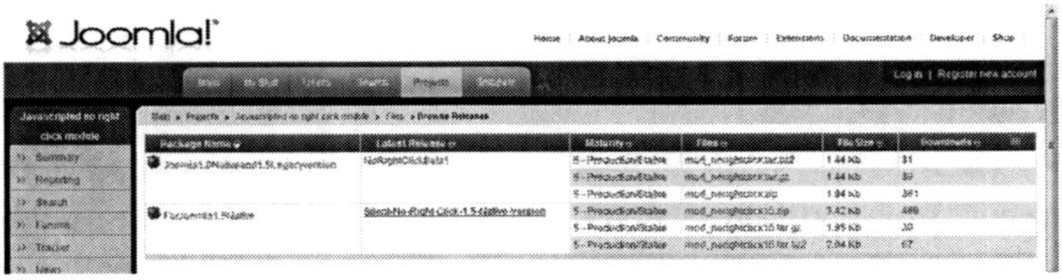

Once downloaded and saved to your folder. We now need to go back into Joomla Extensions/Install and install the module.

Once installed then we go to the Module Manager and find the No Right Click Module and go to the detail page.

**Figure 330: No Right Click Module**

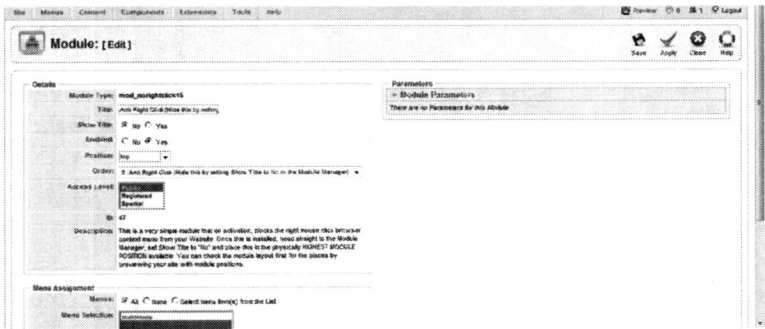

There are a few things you need to do to make this work:
1.  Enable the Module
2.  Change Show title to NO

Place in the highest position of your website. You will need to look at your template - in my instance the highest is TOP or Newsflash. I place it in Top.

Now go back and refresh your website. Right Click should no longer work.

This is a fantastically simple extension and the developer did a great job. This extension is developed by Salocin.TEN and their website is located at www.salocin.info. To leave a review or donate please go this his website.

# Editor Switch

This is a fantastic extension which is handy if you need to switch from JCE Editor to No Editor due to using HTML code or putting images manually in articles, for instance if you are using the RoKNewsRotator by www.rocketheme.com.

This extension was developed by NetDream and their websites is at joomla@netdream.it. Please donate to these guys and let them know what a fantastic extension this is.

Go to the Joomla Extensions website and look under Administration/ Admin Interface.

**Figure 331: ND Editor Switch**

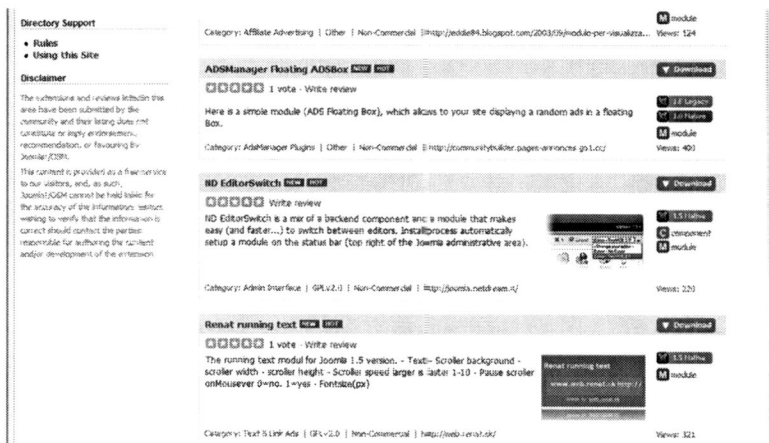

Let's download this to our folder and then go to our Joomla Extensions/ Install to install this module.

## Figure 332: Installed Editor Switch

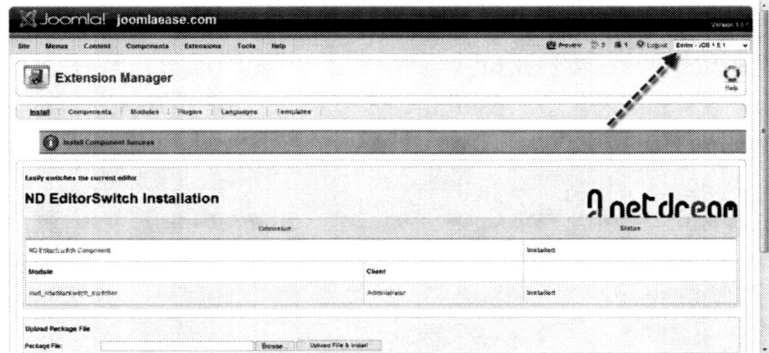

Your switcher is now in the upper right hand corner of your control panel.

No more going in to the User or Configuration to flip back and forth. This is a very cool extension.

# Employment Opportunities

This extension allows you to post employment opportunities with your company. It is simple to install and operate. The extension is called Employment Listing by Bob Steen. This extension is located on the Joomla Extension website under Ads & Affiliate/ Classified Ads.

**Figure 333: Employment Listing**

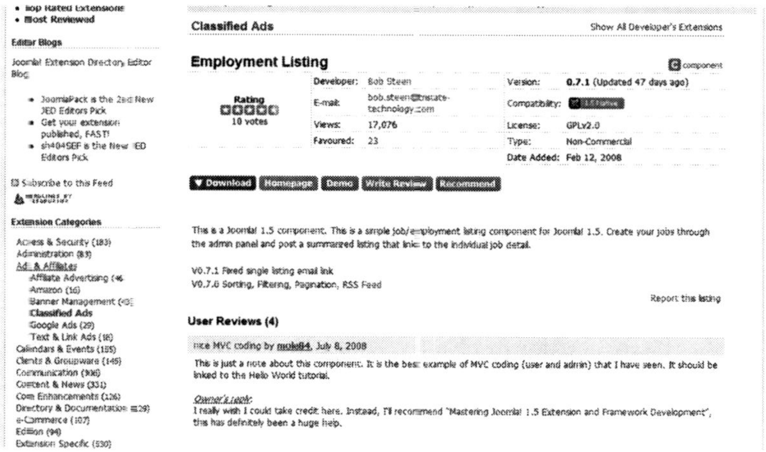

Click download and save to your computer, then install the employment listing extension. Go to your main menu and add a new menu item linking to Employment Listing and Select All Job Postings.

Once the detailed menu item comes up look on the right hand side at the variables. Modify the one's which fit your site.

330  Extensions

### Figure 334: Employment Menu

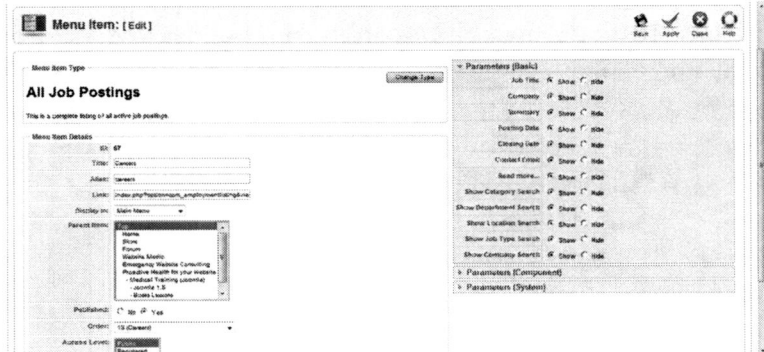

Once done save and refresh your website to be sure it works. Now even though, I stated place on your main menu you can actually place this module in any of your menus or create a new one. It is strictly up to you how you want it displayed on your site.

Now go to Component and let's configure it Companies first. Just change the default to your company name.

### Figure 335: Companies

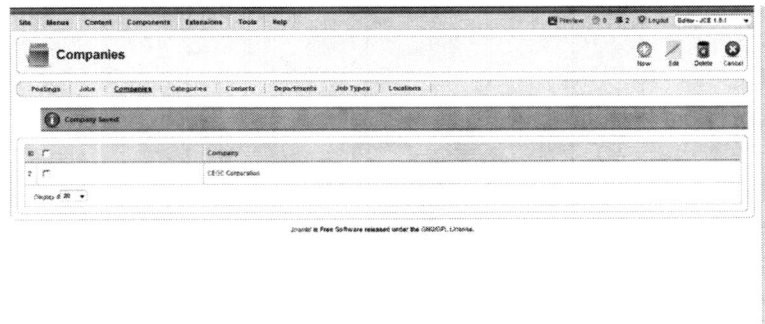

Once complete click on Categories and let's change this.

Employment Opportunities 331

**Figure 336: Categories**

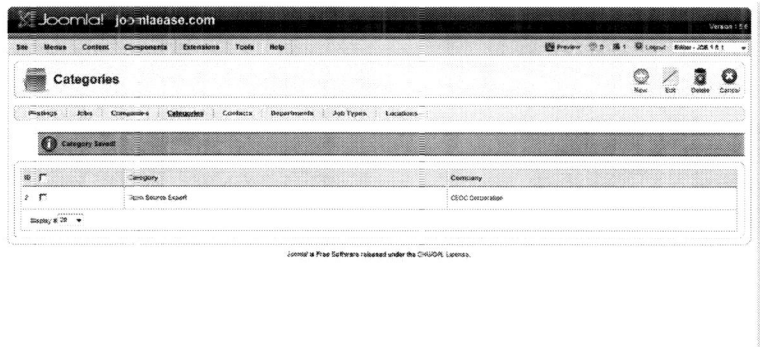

**Figure 337: Contacts**

Now go through and fill out Departments, Job Types and Location. Then click on Jobs to enter the actual job and make sure you go to Postings to put the time frame.

Refresh your website, how does it look?

332 Extensions

## Figure 338: Websites

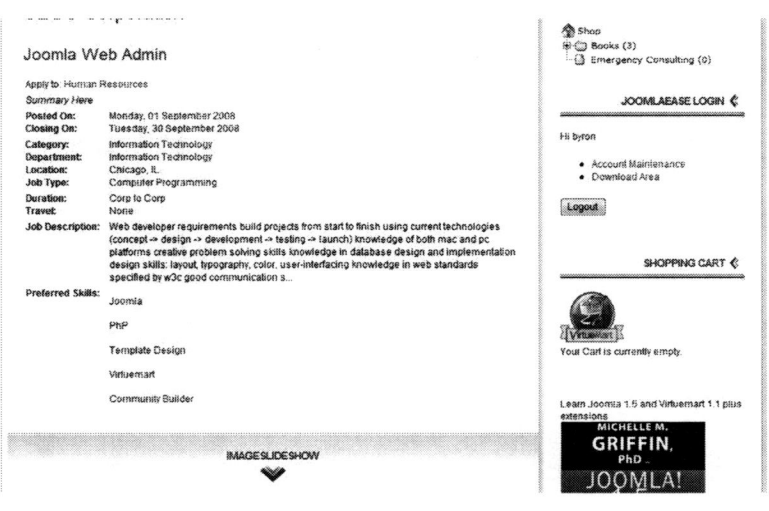

# Speeding up your Website

Your website is database driven and therefore every time a new user visits your web page it is accessing the database then presenting them the page. The more extensions and images you have loaded the slower your page goes. This can be avoided by caching your pages. This means setting your website up to offer static pages rather than newly created ones every time a user accesses your site.

You turn on cache after your website is complete and the majority of the changes are completed. Once cache is on any changes made in the backend may not be visible on the frontend for up to 15 minutes.

This is done fairly simply within the Joomla Configuration file. First you need to change your configuration file in the File Manager to 777 in order to write to it.

Once the permissions have been changed to to your Joomla Control panel and open the Configuration file.

**Figure 339: Configuration Cache**

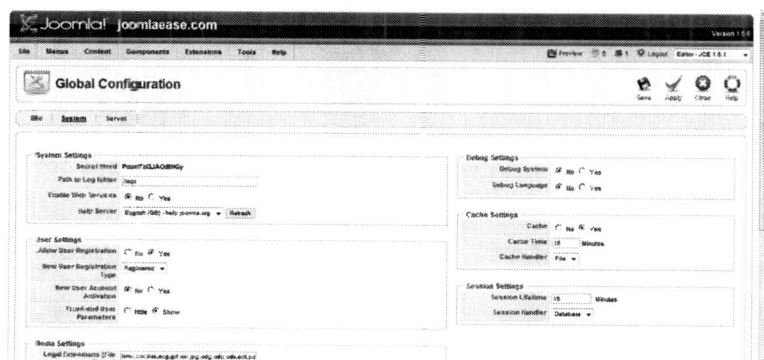

334   Optimizations

Next go to your Cache Manager under Tools labeled Clean Cache. If you have not accessed your website yet. This should be blank. Open another browser and refresh your website. Then go back to the Clean Cache session and refresh it. You should not see content in it.

**Figure 340: Cache Manager**

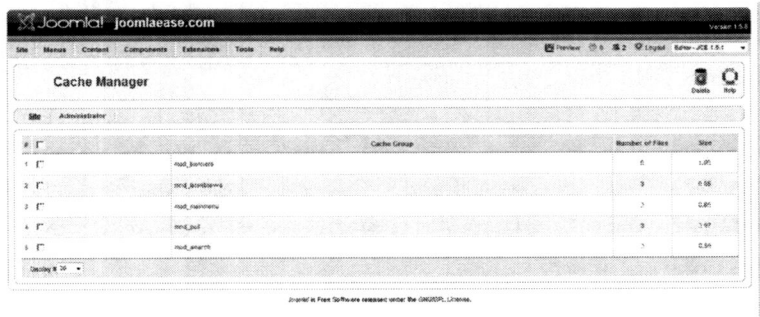

If you make changes to your website you need to delete these cache files to avoid conflicts and ensure the latest pages are presented to your visitors.

To optimize your site even more, you can go into each Module and enable caching.

**Figure 341: Module Manager**

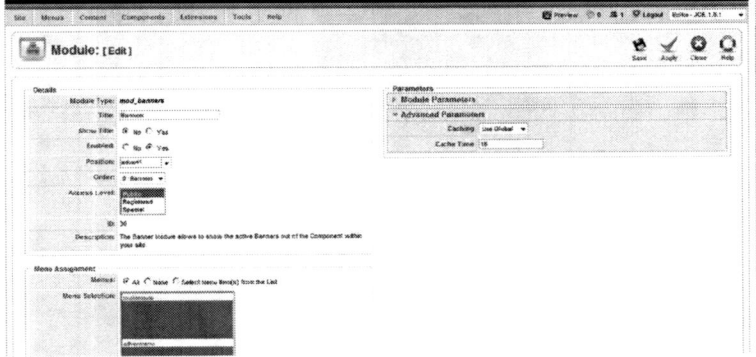

# Search Engine Optimization

There is no one way to do Search Engine Optimization. Whatever you do ultimately will take time for it to move up the search engine rankings. Below are things you can do to increase your findings in search engines.

1. Enable your .htaccess on your site. This was a chapter we covered in this book.

2. Ensure in Global Configuration the SEO settings are all turned to YES.

3. In Global Configuration that you have meta keywords entered.

4. In your articles you have added key words in the parameters section of each article.

Google is excellent at telling you how to increase your ranking. But you can't do this until the Google spider has found your site the first time. Also, if you did an upgrade, you must change the .htaccess file to the latest one and have the Google spider find your site again before it will verify without receiving an error.

Go to Google and type in Google Webmaster tools the google site will popup. You will need to register with Google.

Once registered, it asks you to enter in your site name.

Then a screen pops up telling you the last time Google found your site and you need to verify the site is yours in order to receive more information.

Optimizations

### Figure 342: Google Verify

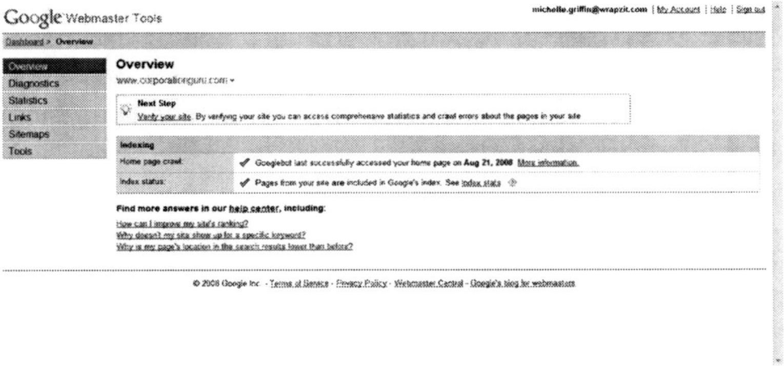

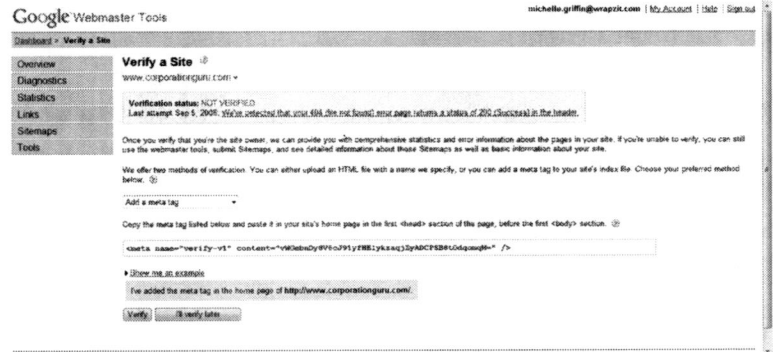

You need to select a method to verify the site. The simplest is to just place an html file with the name google specifies.
Let's click Verify my site.

### Figure 343: Verify Meta tag Selection

In order to verify with the Metatag method we need to download and install an extension from Joomla.

The Extension is located under Searching & Index / SEO & Meta Data extensions .

# Search Engine (SEO) 337

There is a handy extension called Google Verify. Written by Michael Bijland, if you use this extension make sure to write a review and if possible donate so he continues to make great extensions.

### Figure 344: Google Verify

Let's download it and install it in Joomla! Once complete then go to Plugin Manager and activate the plugin.

### Figure 345: Plugin Manager

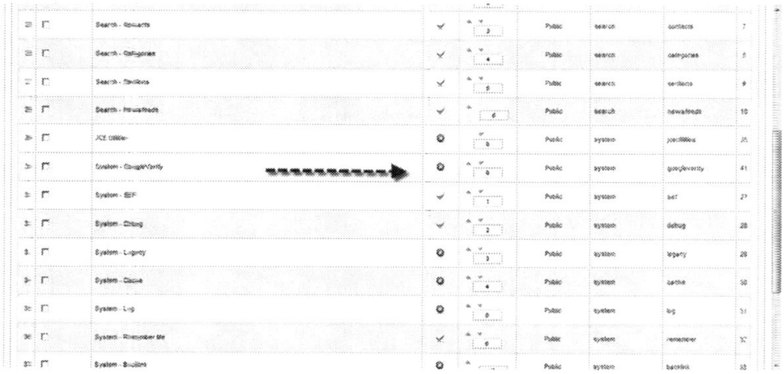

338   Optimizations

Open the Google Verify Plugin and paste in the key from google. You do not need the whole Meta Name just the key ending in = with no quotations.

Example:
vWGebnDy8V8cJ91yfHE1ykzaqjZyADCPSB8tOdqomqM=

**Figure 346: Plugin Key**

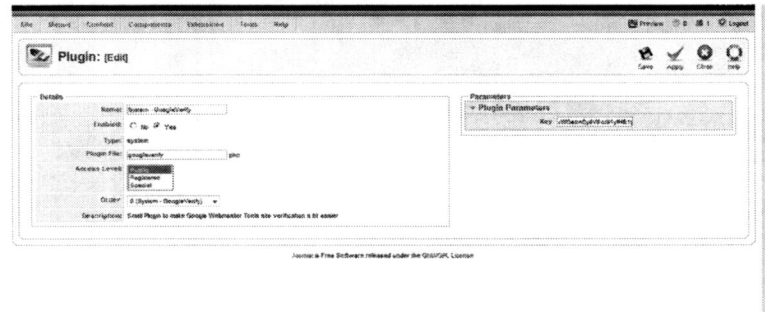

Now go back to Google and press verify.

**Figure 347: Verified**

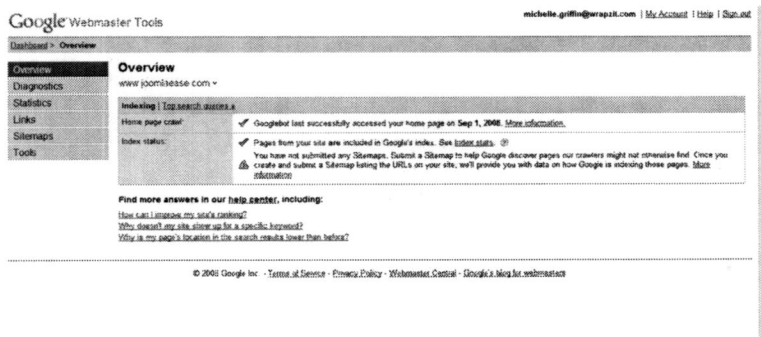

# Search Engine (SEO) 339

Now that you have been verified. You can check what information Google has found on your site. Click on the Home page crawl to see how many times the googlebot has accessed your site. Given this is a new site is has only been accessed a few times.

**Figure 348: Googlebot stats**

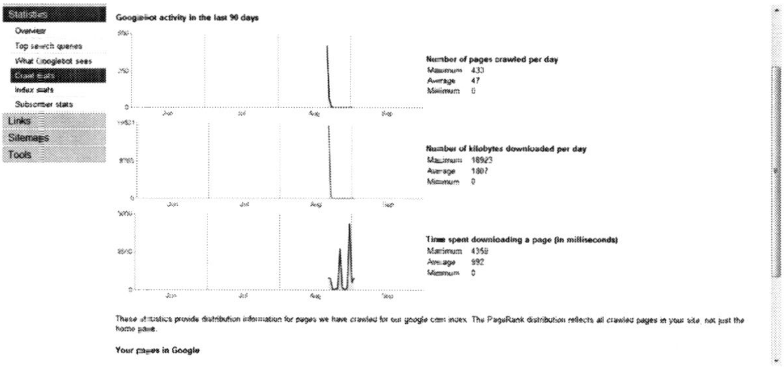

Then click back and let's look at the Index Status to ensure it is finding all your pages. Click Index Stats

**Figure 349: Index Stats**

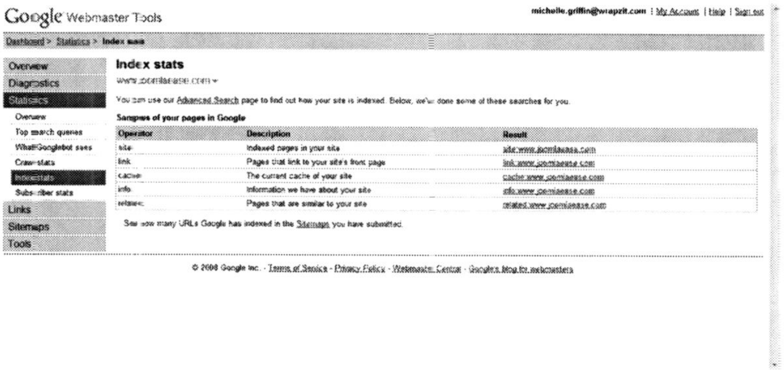

### 340  Optimizations

Click on each link to see that Google has found all your pages. Realize that the GoogleBot only goes around once a week to your site, therefore any new additions may not be appearing.

# Site Security

There are a few things you can do to ensure your site is protected from potential hacking threats.

1. Install No Right Click in order to stop visitors from seeing that you have Joomla installed and also what components you have as well as their directory paths.

2. Always keep your website current with the latest patches for Joomla, Virtuemart and your extensions. The more you hack your site, the more vulnerable it becomes since you are unable to upgrade easily. Try not to hack unless you are a developer and spend a lot of time maintaining your site.

3. Change your Administration password frequently. Most corporations have you change your network password every 6 to 9 weeks. Your website is your corporation. You need to have a process for how often your password is changed in order to prevent hackers from easily finding your site.

4. Your Administration password should be complicated. In order to stop hackers a password with small characters, large characters, numbers and special characters is much harder to crack and many hackers using automatic password crackers will give up trying after 24 hours. A hackers goal is to get in, if it is taking too long to break your password they move on, since there are millions of sites with easier passwords. Also your password should be a mininum of 8 characters.

5. Check to ensure your configuration.php file is set to 644. This you should check on a regular basis.

6. Backup your site regularly

7. Given that your Administrator password is your most important password, do not have it the same as all your other passwords on the internet (email). If one site gets hacked and they find your username and password then your website gets hacked next.

8. Ideally you have two websites, one for testing and one for production. I know this is not always the case, but it is nice to test extensions first before trying them on your site. Our website at www.joomlaease.com hosts a number of extensions which we test first to ensure they work. Check out this site to see if we have tried it. Also, if you host with www.spiderweby.com we have a development website for users to test extensions before uploading to their site.

9. Only use Joomla 1.5 Native extensions, do not turn on legacy.

10. Subscribe to the Joomla and Virtuemart security alerts.


There is additional information found on the Joomla and Virtuemart websites regarding Site Security.

# Joomla Pack Backup

In order to ensure you do not lose your site during a hack attempt. You should perform regular backups. There is a cool extension which has made it super easy for anyone to create backups. It is called Joomla Pack by the JoomlaPack Team at www.joomlapack.net. This extension is fantastic and a tremendous help therefore if you use the extension be sure to leave comments and of course donate, so this great extension continues to be improved.

Go to the Joomla Extensions website and under Access & Security/ Backup and look for Joomla Pack for Joomla! 1.5 Native.

**Figure 350: Joomla Pack**

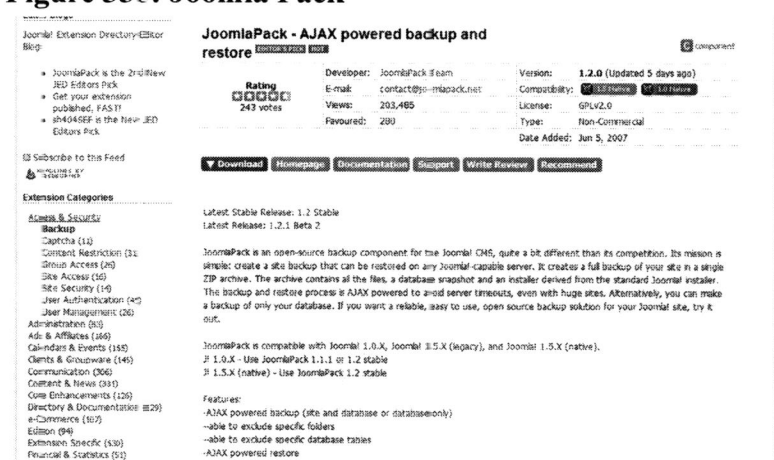

Click on Download, this takes you to the JoomlaPack website to download the file.

344  Optimizations

### Figure 351: JoomlaPack Website

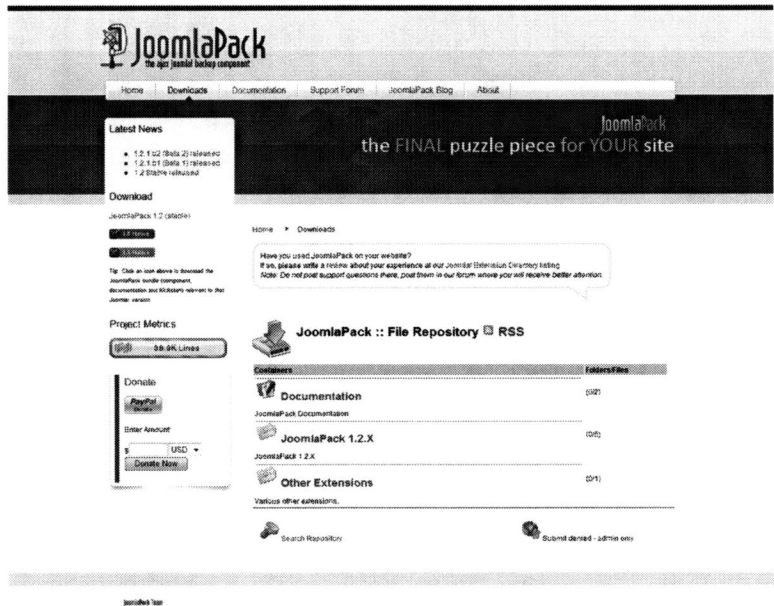

Click on the JoomlaPack extension download folder in this case it is called JoomlaPack 1.2.X

### Figure 352: Download JoomlaPack

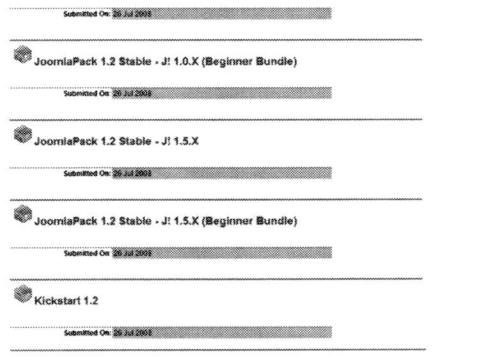

Backup 345

Download the JoomlaPack version for 1.5 Beginners addition. This includes the instruction manual on using this extension. Save to your computer and then unzip the files. Once the files are unzipped let's go back to your Joomla dashboard and install the JoomlaPack component in the Extensions Manager/Install.

Once you have it installed then go to Component/JoomlaPack and then Control Panel.

**Figure 353: JoomlaPack Control Panel**

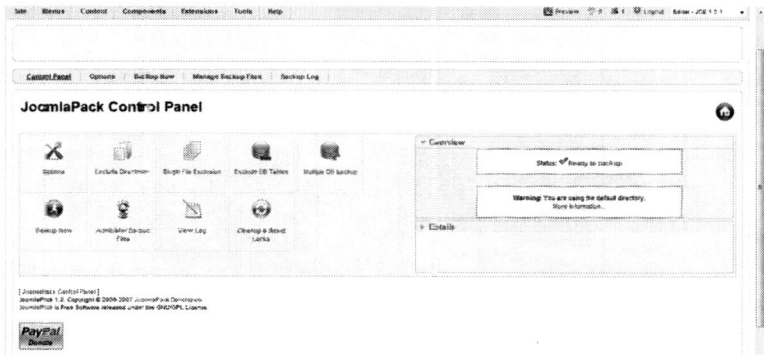

Let's click on Options, this shows you where your backup files will be stored. The directory path is:

/home/ease/public_html/administrator/components/com_joomlapack/temp

Given temp is the default - you do not want to leave as temp. You should go to CPanel File Manager and create a new directory outside of the Joompack component and then re-enter the file location here. If you do not change the directory you set yourself up to be hacked. Just go to the File Manager and create a new folder, just be sure the permissions are the same as the

346   Optimizations

temp folder. Once you change the folder you are ready to test a backup.

Go back to the JoomlaPack Control Panel and press Backup Now.

**Figure 354: Backup Now**

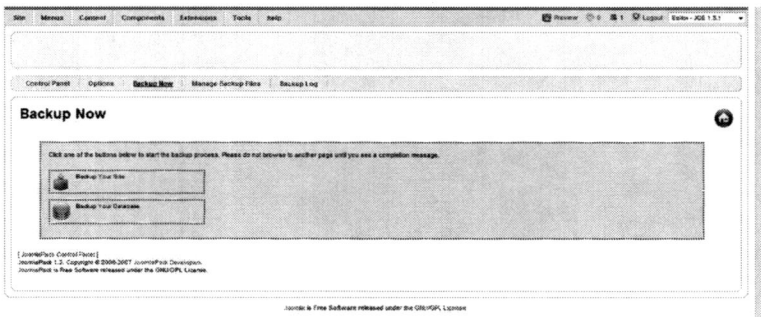

There are two separate backups which occur, one to backup your site and the other to backup your sql database.

Let's click Backup your site. The following screen appears as it backs up your site. Do not touch any buttons while this process is occurring.

**Figure 355: Backup Site**

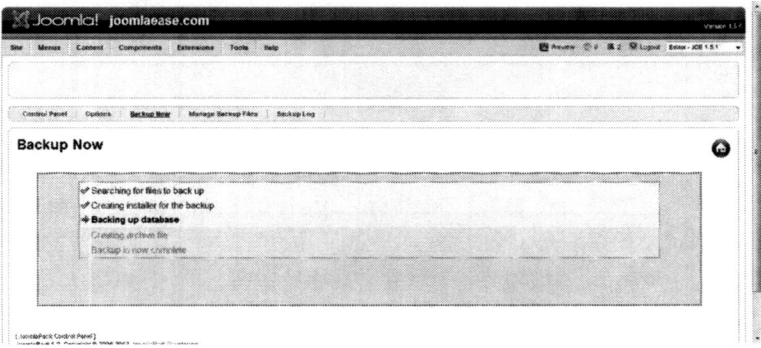

Backup 347

When the backup is complete the following appears.

Figure 356: Backup Complete

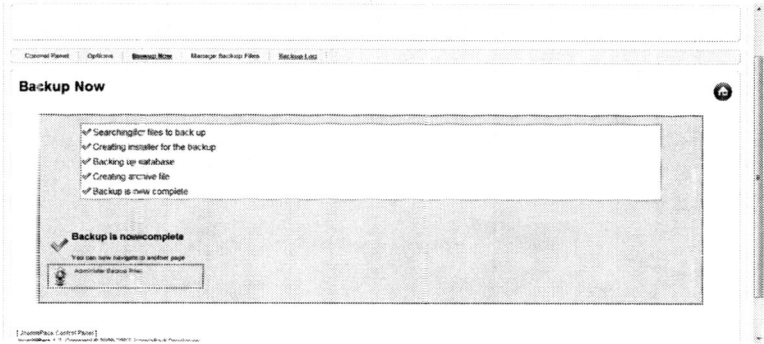

Click the Backup Now button again and backup your SQL database. Once complete click the button at the bottom of the screen to navigate to your Administrator files or click the button Manage Backup files.

Figure 357: Manage Backup Files

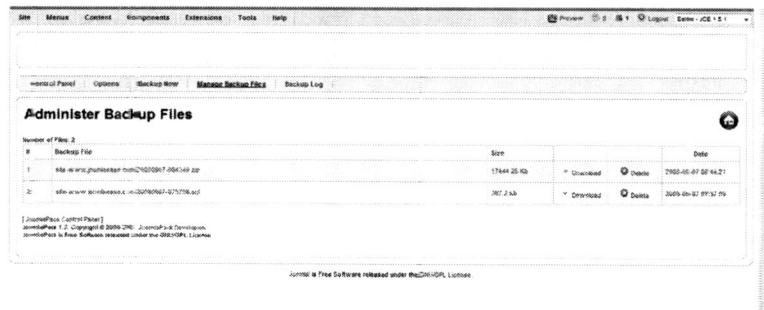

Now let's download the files to your computer for safe keeping.

348    Optimizations

### Figure 358: Download Files

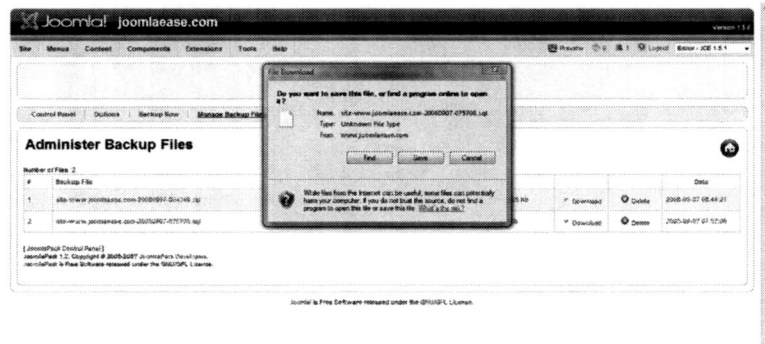

Once you are complete go back to the JoomlaPack Control Panel and click Cleanup and Release Locks. This releases any table locks which occurred during the backup process.

### Figure 359: Release Locks

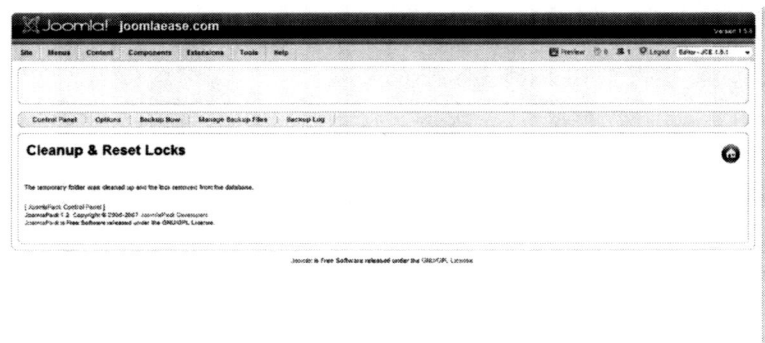

Please read the user manual for additional information and FAQ's.

# Index

## Symbols

500 error  308–312
.htaccess  76–78, 77–78, 323, 331

## A

Access Level  96–98
account maintenance  293–294
Account maintenance  204–210
Alias  101
Apache  31, 33
Apache Mod_rewrite  80–82
Archive  96–98
article  99–101, 100–101, 101
article manager  99–101
Article Manager  95–98, 113–114, 118
Article Parameters  101
articles  305
Articles:  130–134
attachment  307, 310, 312
Author  96–98, 98, 99–101

## B

Banners  149–152, 153–162
Beta  105–112
Briask  304

## C

cache  321, 322
cart  202–210, 268–282
Categories  113–114
Category  96–98, 101, 115–116, 117–118
Category Manager  118
component  104–112, 105–112, 106–112, 109–112
Components  130–134
Configuration  211–226, 254–256

configuration.php 77–78, 81–82, 329–330, 331–332
Contacts 130–134
content 95–98
Content Management 49–53
Copy 97–98
Cpanel 28–31, 30–31, 37–46, 43–46, 47–53, 48–53, 53, 73–78, 81–82, 144–148, 175, 253–256
CPANEL 27–31, 30–31

## D

DEDICATED SERVER 31
domain name 52–53
Domain names 35–36
Domain registrar 35–36
Dotster 35–36
Drupal 49–53

## E

edit 99–101, 100–101
Edit 97–98
editor 100–101, 101
email 38–46, 39–46, 43–46, 44–46, 45–46
extension 299, 304, 305, 308, 312, 315, 317, 319, 320

## F

Fantastico 48–53, 175
file manager 73–78, 76–78, 78
File Manager 81–82, 144–148
files 73–78, 75–78, 76–78
filter 99–101
front page 99–101
Front page 95–98
Front Page 119–122, 125–128
FTP 29–31

## G

Global Check-in 71
Global configuration 83–94

Index 351

Global Configuration 101
GLOBAL CONFIGURATION 79–82
global settings 101
Google 323, 324, 325, 326, 327, 328
Group permissions 75–78

# H

Heading 100–101
Hits 96–98
hosting 35–36

# I

image 100–101, 120–122, 151–152
images 315
Images 299, 302–303, 304
index.html 310, 311
Install/Uninstall 109–112
internet 48–53, 52–53, 55–59
inventory 289–290
IPOD 90–94

# J

JCE 168–174
JCE Admin 105–112, 109–112
JCE editor 100–101, 101
JCE Editor 103–112, 108–112, 109–112, 319, 333
Jonathan Cameron 312
Joomla 47, 49–53, 50–53, 51–52, 51–53, 51–53, 51–53, 51–53, 51–53,
       52–53, 55, 55–59, 56–59, 57–59, 58–59, 59
Joomla! 1.5 33, 50–53, 51–53, 83–94
Joomla 1.5 Native 330
Joomla administrator 55–59
Joomla dashboard 51–53, 55–59, 78, 83–94
Joomla Dashboard 113–114
Joomla Dashboard. 125–128
Joomla modules 89–94
Joomla website 103–112, 109–112

## K

keywords 323

## L

Login Form 67–70, 68–70, 70
logo 143–148

## M

main menu 129–134
Main Menu 129–134
Mambo 49–53
Mambot/Plugin 108–112
manufacturer 239–240
Media Manager 149–152
Menu Manager 125–128, 129–134
Meta data 80–82
Meta Description 80–82, 101
Meta Keywords 80–82, 101
Michael Bijland 325
module 61–63, 62–63, 63, 104–112, 105–112
module manager 65–70
Module Manager 57–59, 58–59, 59, 61, 61–63, 153–162
Move 96–98

## N

nameserver 35–36, 37–46
Name Servers 35–36, 36
NetDream 319
News Feed 131–134
No Right Click 329–330

## O

Open Source 49–53
Order 285–288
Order History 287–288
Order status 283–284
Outlook 39–46, 40–46, 43–46, 45–46
Owner permissions 75–78

Index 353

## P

Package Name 109–112
page layouts 261–266
Paragraph 100–101
parameters 99–101
Parameters 97–98
password 51–53, 55–59
Patch 193–198
patches 329–330
Payment 229–232
Paypal 279–282
PayPal 231–232
permissions 73–78, 74–78, 75–78, 76–78, 77–78, 78
PHP 31, 33, 49–53
Plesk 30–31
plug-in 107–112, 109–112
poll 123
Poll 131–134
PRODUCTION 105–112
products 241–252
product scroller 207–210
Published 95–98, 101

## R

registration 169–174, 270–282
report 291–292
Rocket Themes 83–94

## S

Saloccin.TEN 317
search 163
Search Engine Optimization 323
search engine robots 101
section 115–116
Section 96–98, 99–101, 101, 117–118
Section Manager 113–114
Sections 113–114
security 75–78, 77–78

Security 96–98
SEO 76–78, 79–82, 80–82, 323, 324–325, 335
Shared Web hosting 27–31
slideshow 299, 302–303, 304
SMTP 43–46, 44–46, 45–46
SQL 29–31, 31, 51–53

## T

Tax 233–234
template 83–94, 85–94, 86–94, 91–94, 92–94
Template Manager 83–94, 85–94, 87–94, 92–94
Tiny MCE 103–112
TinyMCE 100–101

## U

Unarchive 96–98
UNIX 75–78
Unpublish 96–98
URL 79–82, 80–82
User manager 167–174
username 51–53
Username 55–59

## V

VIEW SOURCE 313
Virtuemart 188–198
Virtuemart Control Panel 211–226, 229–232
Virtuemart Login 253–256
VPS 30–31

## W

webhoster 27–31, 28–31, 29–31, 31, 35–36
web hosting 27–31, 31
webhosting 27–31, 29–31
Weblinks 131–134, 135–138, 139–142
website 48–53, 52–53, 61–63, 62–63, 63, 95–98, 96–98
Windows Explorer 90–94, 190–198
Winzip 191–198

World permissions 75–78
Wrapper 131–134
Wrappers 139–142
WYSIWYG 103–112, 173–174

# X

XML 33

# Z

Zlib 33

# Biography

Currently, Michelle Griffin 44, is Chief Operating Officer of the C.E.O.C. Corporation. The mission is "creating innovation solutions to everyday global business issues."

Prior to this appointment, Griffin had served since August 2003 as Vice President of Customer Experience where she spent four years improving the service revenue and profitability, managing a $750 million dollar, service revenue stream for Océ North America, Inc. Her focus was on revenue, customer retention, and visual performance management dashboards.

Prior to this, she was Senior Vice President Group Operations at Bank of America. She served five years as Chief Information Officer for Instanet Manufacturing Corporation. Michelle consulted for over 15 years as a firefighter on Baan and SAP Implementations. Working as a Sub-contractor for Deloitte and Touche, Cooper and Lybrand and Arthur Anderson.

Michelle was called in when a Baan or SAP implementation was struggling due to special requirements of the software or the processes.

She received her Undergraduate degrees from Broome Community College and Binghamton Univerisity. Binghamton University is where she received her MBA in 1986. Michelle is currently finishing her Doctorate at Benedictine University, in Chicago. Her Doctorate is in Organization Development.

Michelle's expertise is in profitability of corporations and has a deep understanding of organizations, financially and operationally.

She is industry independent, because business is business. She has consulted and worked in many industries from Banking, Automative, Service to a variety of "Make to Order environments."

Michelle loves speaking at conferences and corporation meetings. If you wish to invite Michelle to your next conference please contact her at michelle.griffin@corporationguru.com or call at 1-800-883-5102 or 1-847-372-3862.

# Coupons

With the purchase of Joomla 1.5 & Virtuemart book, you are entitled to 1 free logo for your website. All you have to do is provide proof of purchase. A graphic design project manager will call you from Corporation GRAPHIC and will work with you in designing your logo.

## *This is a $150 dollar value!*

You will have all rights to your logo and it can be used for your website as well as printed materials.

With the purchase of Joomla 1.5 & Virtuemart book, you are entitled to 3 months free wehhosting for 1 website. Upon verification of proof of purchase your website will be available within 1 hour of contacting Spiderweby personnel. You will have to set your nameservers, through your domain registrar.

ns1.spiderweby.net

ns2.spiderweby.net

The Spiderweby staff will also provide phone support during your initial setup of your website, as you learn to build your website using the Joomla! 1.5 & Virtuemart book.

## *This is a $150 dollar value!*

You will have all rights to your logo and it can be used for your website as well as printed materials.

Free Webhosting is for non-commercial or commercial sites. Adult sites are prohibited, as well as sites focused on spamming.

At the end of 3 months, you may sign up for a month to month hosting at $6.95 a month or $70 dollars a year.

| Webhosting Features | |
|---|---|
| Setup | CPanel |
| Add On Domains | Parked Domains |
| Sub Domains | FTP Accounts |
| Online User Accounts | Customized Error Pages |
| Customer Account Page | 24/7/365 Support |
| FTP Session Control | Latest Visitor Log |
| Webalizer | Redirects |

| Email Features | |
|---|---|
| Unlimited Emails | Pop3- Your Website |
| SMTP - Your website | IMAP |
| Easy Email Account Setup | Default Address |
| User Level Filtering | Account Level Filtering |
| Email Delivery Route | Forwarders |
| MX Entry | Responders |
| Web Mail | Mailing List |
| Mass Mail | Spam Assassin |
| Catch-all Address | |

| Technological Features | |
|---|---|
| Storage | Bandwidth |
| MySQL | Front Page Extensions |
| Dreamweaver Compatible | CGI Bins |
| 99.9% Uptime | Offsite Disaster Recovery |
| Tape Backup | Power Generator |
| Redundancy | Backups |
| Backup Wizard | File Manager |
| Disk Space Usage Monitor | Web Disk |

| Extra Features | |
|---|---|
| Fantastico | PHP My Admin |
| Perl Support | PHP Pear |
| SSI - Server Side Includes | Ruby on Rails Support |
| Macromedia Support | Adobe Support |
| Midi Support | Real Media Support |
| Audio Support | Streaming Video |
| Flash Support | IP Deny Manager |
| Imaage Manager | Index Manager |

Made in the USA